Such a Great Salvation

Expositor's Guide to the Historical Books
Dale Ralph Davis

No Falling Words: Expositions of the Book of Joshua
Such a Great Salvation: Expositions of the Book of Judges

Such a Great Salvation

Expositions of the Book of Judges

Dale Ralph Davis

BAKER BOOK HOUSE
Grand Rapids, Michigan 49516

Printed in the United States of America

The exposition in chapter 20 draws heavily on "Comic Literature—Tragic Theology: A Study of Judges 17–18," *The Westminster Theological Journal* 46 (1984): 156–63. The author wishes to acknowledge the journal editors' permission to use much of that study in this book.

Library of Congress Cataloging-in-Publication Data

Davis, Dale Ralph.
   Such a great salvation : expositions of the Book of Judges / Dale Ralph Davis.
     p. cm. — (Expositor's guide to the historical books / Dale Ralph Davis)
   Includes bibliographical references.
   ISBN 0-8010-2996-1
   1. Bible. O.T. Judges—Criticism, interpretation, etc.
 2. Bible. O.T. Judges—Homiletical use. I. Title. II. Series:
Davis, Dale Ralph. Expositor's guide to the historical books.
BS1305.2D38 1990
222'.3207—dc20

                          89-77403
                             CIP

Contents

PART 3 The Confusion of a Depraved People *(Judges 17–21)*

Preface

I want to apologize publicly to Samson. I was going to credit the writer of Hebrews for loaning me the title for this book (see Heb. 2:3). Imagine my surprise to discover that—perhaps—even the writer of Hebrews had borrowed it from Samson (Judg. 15:18)! Hence, both my apologies and gratitude to Samson.

The church (in general) has a problem with the Book of Judges. It is so earthy, so puzzling, so primitive, so violent—in a word, so strange, that the church can scarcely stomach it. As with many Old Testament books, the sentiment seems to be, "If we just study the epistles long enough, maybe it will go away." The church has her way of dealing with embarrassing Scripture: ignore it. Yet that is difficult to do with Judges. It's so interesting. Only people who take tranquilizers before sitting down can doze off while they read it.

Yet there is danger in that. When a book and its human characters are so colorful and dramatic, we may miss the book's intention—to be a revelation from God about God. That's why I try to give a *theo-centric* exposition in this second volume of the Expositor's Guide to the Historical Books. We must see the beauty of Yahweh our God here; if we do, we can be sure we have begun to handle Scripture rightly.

I allude to a number of English translations, but otherwise the translations are my own.

Hearty thanks to Allan Fisher, Jim Weaver, Linda Triemstra, and others at Baker Book House, who can both support a writer with encouragement and serve the Lord with mirth; and to the saints at Aisquith Presbyterian Church, Baltimore, for allowing my teaching ministry to spill a little ink. Thank you to Jim Raun and Betty Baker, friends and colleagues, whose ministries immensely lighten my pastoral and administrative load. I want to dedicate this volume to Dad and Mom Herron whose quiet steadfastness through many troubles has shown that Yahweh does not let go of us.

Pentecost 1989

Abbreviations

IB	*Interpreter's Bible*
IBD	*Illustrated Bible Dictionary*
IDB	*Interpreter's Dictionary of the Bible*
IDB/S	*Interpreter's Dictionary of the Bible/Supplementary Volume*
ISBE	*International Standard Bible Encyclopedia*
JB	Jerusalem Bible
JSOT	*Journal for the Study of the Old Testament*
KJV	King James Version
Moffatt	The Bible: A New Translation (James Moffatt)
NASB	New American Standard Bible
NEB	New English Bible
NIV	New International Version
NJB	New Jerusalem Bible
RSV	Revised Standard Version
NJPS	Tanakh: A New Translation of the Holy Scriptures According to the Traditional Hebrew Text (1985)
TEV	Today's English Version
TWOT	*Theological Wordbook of the Old Testament*
ZPEB	*Zondervan Pictorial Encyclopedia of the Bible*

Non-Introduction

This introduction is an apology for omitting an introduction. Not that it couldn't be done. We could wade through it all: the question of the Deuteronomic History, the matters of *Überlieferungsgeschichte*, the definition of a *shō-phēt*, moral "problems" in the stories, chronology, archaeology, date, authorship—all those exciting things readers are just dying to know.

But the idea of omitting an introduction came to me in part from reading I. Howard Marshall's explanation for not writing an introduction to Luke in his magnum opus on the third Gospel: "in so far as an introduction to the Gospel can be written, an excellent piece of work has been done by E. E. Ellis in his important commentary, and I am not capable of writing a better one."[1] In a similar vein, I can only confess that as for an introduction to Judges, an excellent piece of work has already been done by the author of the book, and I am not capable of writing a better one. Indeed, I have a growing conviction that we would find far more fun and profit in Bible study if we gave more heed to the introductions the biblical writers themselves prefaced to their works than to the welter of opinions (helpful as they may sometimes be) about a biblical book, drearily culled from the last two hundred years of biblical scholarship.

1. I. Howard Marshall, *The Gospel of Luke: A Commentary on the Greek Text,* New International Greek Testament Commentary (Grand Rapids: Eerdmans, 1978), 29.

We do better, I think, to jump straight into the biblical text and get dirty with *its* ink.

One word of anticlimax. Does this mean we begin without any idea of the overall development or content of Judges? Perish the thought! The book can be summarized in this outline:

I. The Failure of a Second Generation, 1:1–3:6
II. The Salvation of a Long-suffering God, 3:7–16:31
III. The Confusion of a Depraved People, 17–21

Hope to meet you in the text.

PART 1

The Failure of a
Second Generation
(Judges 1:1–3:6)

1

Is This an Ancient Geography Book?
(1:1–2:5)

Let's admit it: geography has fallen on hard times. Our local paper recently carried a blurb about a convention of geography teachers and buffs. At the convention they bemoaned widespread geographical illiteracy and the minimal attention geography receives in the educational schema. Geography was in the pits. And the newspaper proved it, for whoever supplied the headline for the story had written "*Geology* Courses Get Low Grade." Geography is so low that when editors read the word—repeatedly—it just doesn't register!

A year or so ago I found in my father's study a scrapbook he had begun. It was an old elementary-school geography book in which he had taped and pasted family mementos. That's what old geography books are for—to keep you from having to invest in a proper scrapbook. Not that I can blame newspaper editors or my father. I myself can remember only one item about fourth-grade geography—we studied about Baghdad. And I can only remember one thing about that—I was not interested in Baghdad.

Now I should guess a reader's reaction to Judges 1 is much the same. Such a catalog of Palestinian places. Readers won-

der: "What have I hit upon? An ancient geography book? I'm
not interested in geography. I'd better meditate in the Gospel
of John today!" Don't turn that page. The living God has a
word for you from this conglomeration of locations and
squiggly trails. There is vital teaching here. We'll get right to
it as soon as we deal with several preliminaries.

Preliminary Matters

First, remember that Judges 1 deals with a second movement of the conquest of Canaan. The Book of Joshua, especially
in chapters 1–12, tells of "taking" the land, breaking the back
of Canaanite resistance in something of a blitzkrieg style.
Judges 1 emphasizes the process of "possessing" the land in
which separate tribes or tribal groups were to follow up the
previous conquest and nail down and settle their assigned territories. I am not going to substantiate this matter, because I
have already done so in *No Falling Words: Expositions of the
Book of Joshua* (pp. 88–90, 99–100, 110–11, 133–35, 142–43).

Second, for many readers Judges 1 raises once more the so-
called moral problem of the conquest. How horrid that Israel
butcher innocent Canaanites, wreak havoc and misery, grab
their land—and all, allegedly, at Yahweh's command! If only
the Canaanites could know how much emotional support they
receive from modern western readers. And the conquest *was*
frightful. But people who bemoan the fate of the poor Canaanites don't view the conquest from the Bible's own perspective.
They forget one vital fact: the Canaanites were not innocent.
Moses was emphatic about that; he humbled the Israelites by
insisting that Yahweh was not giving them Canaan because
they were such godly folks but because the Canaanites were
so grossly wicked (Deut. 9:4–6). If you want all the gory
details, see Leviticus 18:6–30 and Deuteronomy 18:9–14.[1]
These texts show that the conquest was an act of justice,
Yahweh's justice. Israel was the instrument of his just judgment upon a corrupt and perverted people. The Bible, of course,
does not claim the conquest will be palatable; but it does insist
it was just. Anyway, contemporary western church members

---

1. See also the apocryphal Wisdom of Solomon 12:3–11.

who vicariously and avidly gorge themselves on violence via
television and cinema have forfeited any right to throw the
first stone at the biblical conquest.

Third, let us set forth the structure of 1:1–2:5 so that we
can see at a glance how this material develops and holds
together, for, contrary to appearances, this section is not simply a pile of stuff but a carefully organized pile of stuff:

Yahweh's guidance and assurance, 1:1b–2
  Success of Judah, 1:3–21
    Joint tribal effort, 1:3–7
      (Bezek)
    Assault on Jerusalem, 1:8
    Against the Canaanites, 1:9–18
      Hill country, 1:10–15
      Negev, 1:16–17
      Coastal area, 1:18
    Summary, 1:19–21   (Yahweh's presence, 19a)
  Failure of the north, 1:22–36
    Initial success, 1:22–26
      Joint tribal effort
      (Bethel)   (Yahweh's presence, 22)
    Incomplete conquest:
      Canaanites among Israel, 1:27–30
      (Manasseh, Ephraim, Zebulun)
    Incomplete conquest:
      Israel among Canaanites, 1:31–33
      (Asher, Naphtali)
    Conquest in reverse, 1:34–36
      (Dan)
Yahweh's accusation and threat, 2:1–5
  Review of covenant grace, 2:1
    "I brought you up . . ."
    "I brought you in . . ."
    "I told you . . ."
  Statement of covenant stipulation, 2:2a
    "But *you* . . ."
  Accusation of covenant transgression, 2:2b
  Announcement of covenant judgment, 2:3
  Response of the people, 2:4–5

Several observations about this structure: (1) The opening
section of "Yahweh's guidance and assurance" (1:1b–2) forms
a contrast with "Yahweh's accusation and threat" (2:1–5) at
the close. (2) The two major sections of chapter 1 likewise stand
in sharp contrast: the "success of Judah" (vv. 3–21) finds its
antithesis in the "failure of the north" (vv. 22–36). (3) The
"failure of the north" (vv. 22–36) follows a step-by-step declen-
sion intended to depict the steadily downward direction of
northern tribal fortunes. (4) In the material about Judah,
verse 9 seems to hold the structural clue for verses 10–18, for
it specifies the three areas of combat (the hill country, the
Negev, and the Shephelah) to which the following record con-
forms (vv. 10–15, hill country; vv. 16–17, Negev; v. 18, Shephelah and beyond).[2]

An additional observation is not apparent from the preceding outline: the writer uses a form of the verb *'alah* (to go up)
to open each of the major divisions of 1:1–2:5 (see 1:4, 22; 2:1;
note also that *'alah* is used in 1:1, 2, 3 as well).

Theological Concerns

Let us now seek to hear the witness of these opening
sections.

A Picture of Divine Adequacy

First, observe how we meet a picture of divine adequacy in
1:1–21. Israel and/or Judah receives divine direction (vv. 1–
2a) and divine assurance (v. 2b) and experiences the divine
power (v. 4) and presence (v. 19a). It is in light of all this that
readers are to view the "success of Judah": their victories at

---

2. Debir (vv. 11–15) may belong to the Negev section if Achsah's statement
(v. 15) is taken strictly. Otherwise it belongs to the hill country and should
probably now be identified with Khirbet Rabud, seven and one-half miles
southwest of Hebron; cf. Moshe Kochavi, "Debir (City)," *IDB/S*, 222, and the
report "Where Is Biblical Debir?" *The Biblical Archaeology Review* 1 (March
1975): 5–7. For more detailed discussion on 1:9ff. (including "the valley,"
Hebrew, *ha'emeq*, in v. 19) see Bachmann's position as cited in Paulus Cassel,
The Book of Judges, Lange's Commentary on the Holy Scriptures, in vol. 2,
Numbers-Ruth (1865; reprint ed., Grand Rapids: Zondervan, 1960), 39.

Bezek (vv. 4–7), Jerusalem (v. 8),[3] Hebron (v. 10),[4] Debir (vv. 11–15), Zephath/Hormah (v. 17),[5] and the towns on the coastal plain (vv. 18–19).[6]

We must ask then in what circumstances this divine adequacy shows itself. It shows itself in historical crisis. Don't pass by the opening clause of the book, which may be translated, "Here's what happened after the death of Joshua" (1:1a). I take this as a general title for the book. Probably not everything reported in chapter 1 occurred after Joshua's death (cf. vv. 10–15 with Josh. 15:13–19). But, generally, 1:1a provides the backdrop against which we are to view chapter 1 and the whole book.

Have you ever noticed how new beginnings are punctuated by the earthly end of God's servants?

Exodus begins with the death of Joseph.

Joshua begins with the death of Moses.

3. There is no substantial conflict between verse 8 and verse 21. Judah and Simeon took (Hebrew, *lakad*) Jerusalem, decimating its population and setting the site on fire. Benjamin, on the other hand, did not dispossess (Hebrew, *yarash*) the city's residents and so possess and control the city. The verbs *lakad* and *yarash* carry different connotations, as I have argued in *No Falling Words: Expositions of the Book of Joshua* (Grand Rapids: Baker, 1988), 88–90. What has been taken may later need to be retaken in order to possess it completely. Unless a site was settled when it was taken, the remnant of the conquered town could filter back and control it again.

4. Again, some see a rub between Joshua 15:13–14, where Caleb dispossesses (*yarash*) the three sons of Anak, and this text (Judg. 1:10), where Judah attacks or smites (Hebrew, *nakah*) them. Even if we disregard the different verbs used, verse 20 is careful to point out that whatever part the tribe of Judah may have had in the overthrow of Hebron, it was Caleb in particular who effectively cleaned out the area.

5. Zephath or Hormah may be identified with Tel Masos, some twenty-two miles (for a crow) south/southwest of Hebron. Cf. Yohanan Aharoni, *The Land of the Bible: A Historical Geography,* rev. and enl. (Philadelphia: Westminster, 1979), 215–16, and John J. Bimson, *Redating the Exodus and Conquest,* JSOT Supplement Series 5 (Sheffield: JSOT, 1978), 203–4. Other biblical references to Hormah include Numbers 14:45; 21:1–3; Joshua 12:14.

6. There is no conflict between verses 18 and 19. The former only claims Judah took (see n. 3) Gaza, Ashkelon, Ekron, and their environs, not that he controlled them, as he did the hill country ("possessed," v. 19). Indeed, at that time Judah was not able to possess (i.e., permanently control) the valley areas to the west of the Shephelah (lowland hills).

Judges begins with the death of Joshua.

1 Kings begins with the death of David.[7]

And yet for all that, God's kingdom does not collapse, not even when Sheol takes God's most useful servants. The kingdom of God continues though the servants of God die. That is the witness of Judges 1. Joshua died, but "Yahweh said, 'I have given the land into Judah's hand'" (v. 2). Joshua died, but "Yahweh gave the Canaanites and the Perizzites into their hand" (v. 4). Joshua died, yet "Yahweh was with Judah so that he possessed the hill country" (v. 19). The point should not be lost on contemporary Christians. Your help is in the name of the Lord, not in the name of your favorite Christian hero. Even when the Lord himself "went away," it proved a boon for his church (John 16:7).

But the divine adequacy also appears as God's people operate in corporate unity. "Judah said to Simeon his brother, 'Go up with me into my portion and let us fight against the Canaanites, and I too shall go with you into your portion'; so Simeon went with him" (1:3). "Then Judah went with Simeon his brother and they attacked the Canaanites who live in Zephath" (1:17). When "the sons of Joseph"—presumably Ephraim and Manasseh acting in concert—accost Bethel, "Yahweh was with them" (1:22) and gave success. Each time Israel acted in some sort of tribal unity Yahweh granted victory.

We can easily think "so what?" about these observations. Probably, however, we shouldn't, for the unity of Israel seems to be one of the author's primary concerns. He makes his point by his fragmentation-of-Israel theme; throughout the book he depicts Israel's unity as progressively deteriorating—and with it Israel's fortunes. We need not trace this theme in detail

7. I suppose if one wanted to stretch the matter (especially in light of the division of books in the English Bible) one could add that 1 Samuel begins with the deaths of Eli and sons (1 Sam. 1–4), 2 Samuel begins with the deaths of Saul and Jonathan (in the report to David and his lament), and 2 Kings begins with the taking of Elijah (2 Kings 2).

here.[8] We simply note it in order to argue that the notes about tribal unity and cooperation in chapter 1 are not sentimental little ditties for our author. He regards them as significant— as Yahweh's people assist one another they receive Yahweh's help.

One does not torture this text by applying it to the body of Christ at large or to any group of worshiping believers. The Lord's people thrive on mutual assistance; God has given us one another as channels of his help and strength. Indeed, the apostle prayed "that you, having your roots and foundation in love, might have the strength to grasp *together with all the saints* how wide and long and high and deep Christ's love is" (Eph. 3:17–18, italics added). Getting a grip on the staggering limitlessness of Christ's love for us is not something the believer does in blissful isolation. It can only be done/ attempted "together with all the saints"! The unity and fellowship of God's people is not a wimpy idea weaker Christians dote on. It is an essential condition for experiencing the strength of our God.[9]

One of the unique marks of this chapter is the inclusion of interesting little episodes related to the tribal conflicts and settlement. This leads me to suggest that when Yahweh shows how adequate he is, he does so in fascinating detail.

Could we interview Adoni-bezek he likely would testify that

8. See, for example, 5:15b–17, 23; 8:1–4, 5–9; 12:1–6; 15:11–13. But for more textual data and argumentation see J. P. U. Lilley, "A Literary Appreciation of the Book of Judges," *Tyndale Bulletin* 18 (1967): 98–99; also my "Proposed Life-Setting for the Book of Judges" (Ann Arbor: University Microfilms, 1978), 66–78.

9. On Ephesians 3:18 see F. F. Bruce, *The Epistle to the Ephesians* (London: Pickering and Inglis, 1961), 68. As for Judges 1:3, A. R. Fausset aptly comments: "The lot of Simeon fell within that of Judah, and was assigned out of it. Simeon was one of the least important of the tribes, and Judah one of the most important; yet Judah does not hesitate to solicit Simeon's alliance and help against the common foe. We Christians cannot afford to despise the aid and sympathy of even weaker brethren, in our spiritual conflict for the goodly land, against the prince of darkness. God can bring forth strength out of even the most humble (Rom. xiv.3, 4; 1 Cor. i.27); so that he that is high as the head, cannot say to those who are low as the feet, I have no need of you, seeing that all believers are members of one another (1 Cor. xii.21; Acts xi.17, xv.8, 9, 11)" (*A Critical and Expository Commentary on the Book of Judges* [London: James Nisbet, 1885], 15).

Israel's God acts in justice (1:4–7). Yahweh granted Judah victory at Bezek.[10] Adoni-bezek fled but was captured and mutilated. Judah's troops cut off his thumbs and big toes, which, at the very least, would force his early retirement from military service,[11] not to mention life (v. 7b). What can Adoni-bezek be but philosophical? "Seventy kings," so he claims, "with their thumbs and big toes cut off have been picking up food under my table; as I have done, so God has paid me back" (v. 7).

A second vignette contains a touch of romance. Othniel thought attacking Bookville (Kiryath Sepher/Debir) worth the risk if it meant winning Achsah, Caleb's daughter.[12] Achsah urged Othniel to ask for some additional cultivatable land from Caleb. Who knows whether Othniel did so? But at least Achsah was sharp enough to know they would need guaranteed water rights for such land, and she pressed her father to grant that (v. 15).[13]

10. Aharoni (*The Land of the Bible*, 214) and J. Simons (*The Geographical and Topographical Texts of the Old Testament* [Leiden: Brill, 1959], 281) identify the site as Khirbet Ibziq, thirteen miles northeast of Shechem. See 1 Samuel 11:8.

11. See Theodor H. Gaster, *Myth, Legend, and Custom in the Old Testament,* 2 vols. (New York: Harper Torchbooks, 1969), 2:416–18.

12. Othniel could have been either Caleb's nephew or younger brother (v. 13; cf. Leon J. Wood, "Othniel," *ZPEB*, 4:552–53, and C. F. Keil, *The Books of the Chronicles,* Biblical Commentary on the Old Testament [1872; reprint ed., Grand Rapids: Eerdmans, 1966], 89–90, on 1 Chron. 4:13). "Brother" could be used as "military confederate" (Robert G. Boling, *Judges,* The Anchor Bible [Garden City, N.Y.: Doubleday, 1975], 56). The text of verse 14 is also difficult but not so gaseous as the New English Bible suggests.

13. It is always useful to wonder why an episode like verses 11–15 is included in Scripture. One cannot always answer this "why," but one should keep asking it nevertheless. And, of course, one must always so question the text in light of its larger context. However, we need to beware of deriving a useful application from a text merely to "justify" its existence as Scripture. I think it is illegitimate to use Achsah's request as a paradigm for Christian prayer (as does Fausset, *Judges,* 32–34). I do not know, ultimately, why this apparently inconsequential episode was included in Scripture. But any Israelite would know that in that land water was no inconsequential matter. And Achsah had the sense to know that access to water could spell the difference between life and disaster. She was prudently concerned over a necessity of life. Any Israelite would be as concerned about that as a midwestern farmer about weather in wheat harvest. What is a minor incident to us is no trivial matter at all. Perhaps we must ride Achsah's donkey to fully understand her request.

The third little incident (1:22–26) breathes intrigue. The Joseph tribes persuade a resident of Bethel/Luz to show them the entrance to the city, which was obviously not the city gate but likely a secret, hidden entrance to the fortified area.[14] It proved a splendid way to surprise and conquer a town.

Granted, you may not get excited over what happened at Bezek, Bookville, and Bethel. You may not be greatly interested in Adoni-bezek's toes or Achsah's springs or Bethel's camouflaged entrance. But I think such anecdotes of justice, romance, and intrigue are fascinating. And the testimony of the text is that "Yahweh gave" Israel's enemies into their hands (v. 4) and that "Yahweh was with them" (v. 22). And that is typical of the God of the Bible. When he shows how adequate he is, he usually gives us some stories to tell. God seldom gives his people up to monotony but leaves them vivid episodes to remember.

A Lesson in Theological Geography

Secondly, we are taught a lesson in theological geography in 1:22–36. Please look back at the outline of the structure set out earlier in this chapter and note again the section called "the failure of the north" (1:22–36). These verses show a progressive failure of the northern tribes to possess their territories. After an initial success by the Joseph tribes, tribal efforts wane until, with the Danites, the conquest hits a reverse flow. The section has been put together very carefully.

Naturally, western readers are apt to regard this incessant listing of places with impatience. Some will wonder if the pen of inspiration wasn't picked up by a frustrated cartographer. No—by a preacher. And the preacher keeps pounding home his message: such-and-such a tribe "did not drive out" (or: dispossess, a form of the verb *yarash*). Seven times he accuses in

---

14. Anson F. Rainey, "Ramat Rahel," *The Biblical World: A Dictionary of Biblical Archaeology*, ed. Charles F. Pfeiffer (Grand Rapids: Baker, 1966), 473: "There was an underground postern gate leading into the citadel through its northern wall. The outer opening is just wide enough for one person to enter at a time." This gate at Ramat Rahel belonged to Level V/A, about 600 B.C.

this way (vv. 27, 28, 29, 30, 31, 32, 33).[15] What we have here is not geographical tedium but theological accusation, that is, theological geography.

Without doubt there were pragmatic reasons why Israel needed absolute control over many of these sites. Somewhere along the time line they would likely see the strategic folly of failing to possess Beth-shan (v. 27), a massive site guarding the juncture of the Jordan and Jezreel valleys, through which "passed the main arteries of the ancient world."[16] They would live to regret the failure to dominate Taanach, Ibleam, and Megiddo (v. 27), crucial fortresses along the Plain of Esdraelon.[17] Maybe they could have prevented cocky Sisera (chaps. 4–5) from strutting all over Israel. We could also point out how strategic Gezer (v. 29) was; but no more of this, for we are getting away from our author's concern.

The motivation for driving out Canaanites was not pragmatic but spiritual. Yahweh had warned through Moses: "Do not let those people live in your country; if you do, they will make you sin against me. If you worship their gods, it will be a fatal trap for you" (Exod. 23:33 TEV). Remaining Canaanites would not be so much a military threat as a spiritual cancer (see Exod. 23:23–33; 34:11–16; Deut. 7:1–5). That's why Israel was to eliminate the Canaanites and other "-ites." That's why Israel was to wreck and demolish all their worship centers (every Saint-Baal-on-the-Hill Shrine and Our Lady of Harvest Chapel). To be sure, Yahweh would make them able to do this in a somewhat gradual manner (Exod. 23:29–30). But it *was* to be done. If Canaan's native populations are tolerated, it will lead Israel willy-nilly to intermarriage with them—and you can kiss covenant faith good-bye (Exod. 34:15–16; Deut. 7:3–4). Grandkids will know Yahweh as an also-ran fertility god. So our writer's "[they] did not dispossess" rings with spiritual emergency. It is the preacher's accusation of God's people for

15. If one adds the note about Judah (v. 19) and Benjamin (v. 21) the tally is nine.

16. Anson F. Rainey, "Beth-shean/Beth-shan," *ISBE* (rev. ed.), 1:475. See also George Adam Smith, *The Historical Geography of the Holy Land,* 22d ed. (London: Hodder and Stoughton, n.d.), 357–59.

17. See Smith's description, *Historical Geography,* 379–91; also John Garstang, *Joshua-Judges* (1931; reprint ed., Grand Rapids: Kregel, 1978), 94.

covenant failure.[18] They are like a surgeon who removes only part of the cancer because even cancer has a right to grow and find fulfillment. Tolerance and suicide are congenial bedfellows.

Though our writer repeatedly accuses Israel of covenant failure (she "did not dispossess"), he nevertheless describes her military success. This point is frequently missed. Four times he tells us that the Canaanites or Amorites became subject to "forced labor" (vv. 28, 30, 33, 35). What does this mean? It means that if once Israel's tribes were not strong enough to expel the local residents (cf. vv. 19, 27), the time came "when Israel grew strong" (v. 28) and could dominate the Canaanite population. But instead of expelling, instead of driving out these enclaves—which, according to the biblical text, Israel was now perfectly able to do—she put them to forced labor, in violation of Yahweh's commands. The picture Judges 1 gives us is of an Israel in substantial control of Canaan,[19] a people clearly successful though certainly disobedient. Pragmatic success and spiritual failure—a strange but possible combination. So Israel is dominant if not obedient; she enjoys superiority even if she does not maintain fidelity.

This text carries its admonition for God's people in any age. For one thing, it tells us that it is possible for the believer's life to display the marks of success and yet be a failure in the eyes of God. Christian success (whether personal or in the form of a glossy evangelical enterprise) is not necessarily the same as pleasing God.

The text also underscores the importance of "small" faith-

18. I have since discovered that Brevard S. Childs has taken the same view of Judges 1: "The function of the introduction [= chap. 1] is to mark the beginning of a period of disobedience which stands in sharp contrast to the period which preceded. A theological judgment is made by its characterization of the period. No leader after Joshua has arisen. The unity of the nation has been fractured. The successes from the divine blessing have given way to a failure to repel the enemy. That the introduction performs this negative role is made explicit in 2.1–5 which confirms the judgment of God on the nation's disobedience" (*Introduction to the Old Testament as Scripture* [Philadelphia: Fortress, 1979], 259).

19. Yohanan Aharoni and Michael Avi-Yonah, *The Macmillan Bible Atlas,* rev. ed. (New York: Macmillan, 1977), 50–51. See also *No Falling Words,* 110–11.

fulness. Certainly nothing is too tragic by the end of chapter 1. Israel has not dispossessed the Canaanites, but does hold them under forced labor. Israel is—to a large degree—in control. Hence her lethargy seems to have been "minor" disobedience. Precisely here, however, we need to see a larger picture. Hence the following general structure for 1:1–3:6:

> Title, 1:1a
> The conditions for apostasy develop, 1:1b–36
> Sorrow over Yahweh's word, 2:1–5
> Transition: The new generation, 2:6–10
> The course of apostasy described, 2:11–3:4
> Summary and digest, 3:5–6
>> 3:5 summarizes 1:1b–2:5
>> 3:6 summarizes 2:11–3:4

By looking at the two largest blocks of material (1:1b–36 and 2:11–3:4) in this structure, one can readily see how crucial Israel's failure in chapter 1 was. In chapter 1 Israel permitted conditions which brought no instant disaster. The impact of her failure became visible later (2:11–13, 19; 3:5–6).[20] What began as toleration became apostasy. What seemed so reasonable proved lethal. Living with Canaanites led to worshiping with Canaanites. Tolerate Baal's people and sooner or later you bow at Baal's altar. But it seemed like a rather small matter at the time. After all, Sinai didn't smoke when Israel "did not dispossess" the Canaanites. "Faithful in little" (cf. Luke 16:10) hardly describes our idea of a glamorous career, but nothing else much matters in the kingdom of God. Let each man examine himself.

A Question of Genuine Repentance

Third, the Bokim (or Bochim) episode poses for us a question of genuine repentance (2:1–5). Uncertainties about the text in verse 1b do not obscure the message. In the Angel of Yahweh's speech Yahweh himself addresses Israel, as the repeated "I"

---

20. Childs, *Old Testament as Scripture*, 259: "The introduction of ch. 1 offers a theological judgment on the nature of disobedient Israel. The Deuteronomic introduction [= 2:6–23 for Childs] which follows assumes this breakdown."

shows. Yahweh accuses Israel of breach of covenant (v. 2b)[21] and announces the discipline and judgment they would endure (v. 3).[22] They have now forfeited the promised help in 1:2, 4. The primary peril, however, will be spiritual (v. 3c).

Note the response. There are tears all over the place. "The people lifted up their voice and wept" (Hebrew, *bakah*, v. 4b). The place was even named for their tears—Bokim ("Weepers," vv. 1, 5). And the tears led to sacrifice (v. 5b). So far so good. It is usually a good sign when God's people can still weep, when we can be moved to tears. Would that it would happen more often! We are either too sophisticated, too refined, too hard-hearted, or, what's worse, all of these, to cry over our sins.[23]

Yet the text keeps us hanging. There is no neat closing, no answer to "What happened then?" So they wept and sacrificed. What did all that produce? The Angel of Yahweh's sermon induces weeping, tears, and profound impressions. Does anything go beyond Israel's tear ducts? Is anything more lasting than water produced here?[24]

21. The implication of 2:2 is that Israel did enter into covenant agreements with remaining residents of the land, evidently promising them life in exchange for servitude, much as Joshua and Company mistakenly did with Gibeon in Joshua 9.

22. For the structure of 2:1–5 see the outline at the beginning of this chapter. Matthew Henry has a most useful observation on the intrusion of the Angel of Yahweh here: "It was the privilege of Israel that they had not only a law in general sent them from heaven, once for all, to direct them into and keep them in the way of happiness, but that they had particular messages sent them from heaven, as there was occasion, for reproof, for correction, and for instruction in righteousness, when at any time they turned aside out of that way" (*Commentary on the Whole Bible*, 6 vols. [New York: Revell, n.d.], 2:126).

23. As John R. W. Stott has written of preachers: "I constantly find myself wishing that we twentieth-century preachers could learn to weep again. But either our tear-springs have dried up, or our tear-ducts have become blocked. Everything seems to conspire together to make it impossible for us to cry over lost sinners who throng the broad road which leads to destruction" (*Between Two Worlds: The Art of Preaching in the Twentieth Century* [Grand Rapids: Eerdmans, 1982], 276).

24. "This was good, and a sign that the word they heard made an impression upon them: it is a wonder sinners can ever read their Bibles with dry eyes. But this was not enough; they wept, but we do not find that they reformed, that they went home and destroyed all the remains of idolatry and idolaters among them. Many are melted under the word that harden again before they are cast into a new mould" (Henry, *Commentary*, 2:128).

While a pastor in Wales, Martyn Lloyd-Jones was accused of encouraging emotionalism. Lloyd-Jones's retort was that "it is very easy to make a Welshman cry, but it needs an earthquake to make him change his mind!"[25]

Our response to Yahweh's accusing word should be more than wet eyes. It is good to be moved to tears but better to be brought to repentance. God wants to produce "good grief" in us (cf. 2 Cor. 7:8–11). Yahweh's demand via Joel keeps the perfect balance and needs no hermeneutical doctoring for the church: "Return to me with all your heart, with fasting and weeping and mourning, and tear open your heart, not your garments" (Joel 2:12–13).

25. Iain H. Murray, *David Martyn Lloyd-Jones: The First Forty Years 1899–1939* (Edinburgh: Banner of Truth, 1982), 315–16.

2

Generation Degeneration
(2:6–3:6)

If you wanted to visit the Civil War battlefield at Vicksburg, Mississippi, you could simply drive in and begin working your way through the battlefield park, for however many miles, looking at monuments, and so on. However, unless you are already well-versed in the particulars of the Vicksburg siege, you would do well to stop at the Visitors' Center and see the film which provides the background and framework for appreciating and understanding what you will see as you peruse the battlefield. Otherwise you may see only a maze of monuments to that Alabama regiment or that Pennsylvania company. The film helps bring order to and make sense of all the details.

Judges 2:6–3:6 functions as a sort of visitors'-center film for the Book of Judges. It provides the necessary preview for understanding what is happening in the rest of the book, particularly chapters 3–16. This section is a summary which interprets for the reader the significance of the judges' stories. If you want to understand Judges you must stop here for perspective, to get a handle on what to look for in the upcoming stories and how to understand the various episodes you read. In particular, 2:6–3:6 will show you what *God* is doing in the period of the judges—and, for understanding the Bible, nothing could be more crucial than that.

Now you may as well know that many biblical critics (a neutral term in itself; I too am a biblical critic in the sense of seeking to weigh and assess the biblical text) would say that

what I have just told you is all wrong. They would say (1) that
we must understand that Judges came into being through a
very long and complicated process,[1] (2) that you must realize
that 2:6–3:6 is one of the latest additions to the Book of Judges,
(3) that this section comes from the hands of the Deuteronomistic (or, Deuteronomic) editors, (4) that these editors
worked just before, in, and after the exile (587 B.C.), some six
to seven hundred years after the time of the judges, (5) that
2:6–3:6 constitutes "their interpretation" of that historical
period, and (6) that this Deuteronomistic interpretation does
not—even at best—do full justice to the facts (whatever they
were).

Many scholars, therefore, would say that 2:6–3:6 comes
from later Deuteronomic editors; they would set this Deuter-
onomic/-istic interpretation over against "how it really was."
Such interpreted, schematized history must of necessity over-
simplify, distort, and twist the actual state of affairs.[2] (But
where do we find meaningful history that is not interpreted
history?) In this view, the bottom line usually is: 2:6–3:6 can
tell you how the Deuteronomists viewed the judges' period, but
their view was not historically accurate (to a greater or lesser
degree)—that is, it was not, to whatever degree, true. If this
view is correct, it is difficult to understand what possible
authority such a passage could have for the church.

Knowing how interesting this is to my reader (I speak as a
fool), I will carry on a bit more. The only problem I have with

1. So complicated in fact that it's almost a miracle we received the Book
of Judges as we now have it. See the complex compositional history posited
by M. G. Rogers, "Judges, Book of," *IDB/S*, 514, or that by Georg Fohrer,
Introduction to the Old Testament (Nashville: Abingdon, 1968), 208–14.

2. I am sure that what Georg Fohrer says of Deuteronomic editing in 1–2
Kings he would also apply to the same in Judges: "Of course history was often
distorted in the process by gross oversimplification and schematic
reinterpretation. . . . The pedagogical intent of the Deuteronomic school, in
which it made historical tradition serve its own purposes, markedly impaired
the worth of its literary activity. But this activity pursued ends that were not
historical, but religious and pedagogical" (*History of Israelite Religion* [Nash-
ville: Abingdon, 1972], 306). For very readable presentations of the Deuteronomic history/school/editors, see John H. Hayes, *An Introduction to Old
Testament Study* (Nashville: Abingdon, 1979), 206–18, and Bernhard W.
Anderson, *Understanding the Old Testament*, 3d ed. (Englewood Cliffs, N.J.:
Prentice-Hall, 1975), 138–39.

this common critical position on Judges 2:6–3:6 is that there is hardly any linguistic evidence that the section is Deuteronomic. Dentures may fall out over that one. But the fact is that two and a half verses at most can be claimed as Deuteronomic. My guess is that when many Old Testament introductions and handbooks blithely dub 2:6–3:6 Deuteronomic, they may simply be repeating what has become an orthodox critical truism (biblical criticism, like most religions, holds its share of yawn-producing shibboleths) without weighing the actual evidence of the text. I have elsewhere analyzed the vocabulary and terminology of 2:6–3:6 line upon line, in tedious and laborious detail, and found what could be *provable* Deuteronomic influence quite limited (= 2:11–12, middle of v. 19).[3] Hence I make no apology for dismissing the usual view that 2:6–3:6 is a bit of later, history-distorting theologizing or for therefore accepting the section as an overview that provides the proper perspective for the judges' stories.[4] Now—to the teaching and to the testimony (Isa. 8:20)!

The Continuing Emergency of Our Faith

First, our passage underscores the continuing emergency of our faith (2:6–13). In order to understand this emergency we must try to understand a bit about Baal worship.

Many readers of Genesis 1 are unaware that they hold in their hands a piece of revolutionary propaganda. It propounds the novel idea that sex is a *human* activity. This God of Israel is strange. Yahweh has no wife, no consort. Biblical religion holds that you will find Yahweh acting in history (creation, flood, call and preservation of the patriarchs, deliverance from Egypt, cutting off of the Jordan), not pulsating in nature

3. In "A Proposed Life-Setting for the Book of Judges," (Ann Arbor: University Microfilms, 1978), chap. 4, pp. 137–88. See also Kenneth A. Kitchen, "Ancient Orient, 'Deuteronism,' and the Old Testament," in *New Perspectives on the Old Testament*, ed. J. Barton Payne (Waco: Word, 1970), 1–24.

4. I should say I have nothing *against* finding touches of Deuteronomy in Judges; indeed, such discovery wouldn't surprise me since I hold that Deuteronomy stems from the Mosaic period. But many biblical critics hold that Deuteronomy was published much later in the Old Testament period, about 622 B.C. Hence other passages having a Deuteronomic tinge must date as late or later.

(though nature, too, is under his sway). Yahweh sits on a throne, high and lifted up, from which he rules, creates, preserves, and redeems; he does not lounge in some celestial bedroom, copulating with his feminine divine counterpart. It has become so difficult for us to grasp how different, how holy, the God of the Bible is!

But the Canaanites were not so—neither was Baal their god. Baal was the god of storm and fertility, and, for the Canaanites, of course, fertility was the name of the game—fertility of crops and livestock and family. Baal, nature god that he was, naturally had his female consort, Ashtoreth or Ashtart.[5]

In Canaanite theology (and agriculture) the fertility of the land depended upon the sexual relationship between Baal and his consort. The revival of nature was due to sexual intercourse between Baal and his partner. But the Canaanite faithful didn't simply sit back and say, "Let Baal do it." There was no "let-go-and-let-Baal" thinking among them. Instead their watchword was: Serve Baal with gladness, all ye glands. Hence the Canaanites practiced "sacred" prostitution as a part of their worship. A Canaanite man, for instance, would go to a Baal shrine and have intercourse with one of the sacred prostitutes serving there. The man would fulfill Baal's role and the woman Ashtart's. The idea was that the copulating of the worshiper and of the holy whore would encourage the divine couple (Mr. and Mrs./Ms. Baal) to do their thing and thus the rain, grain, wine, and oil would flow again. Through sacred prositution it was possible to assist, encourage, and bring on the great orgasm of Baal in the sky; thus Baal would make "all things new."[6] However, nothing would happen unless the fertility powers were properly worshiped. (Here, incidentally,

---

5. See A. H. Sayce and K. G. Jung, "Ashtoreth," *ISBE* (rev. ed.), 1:319–20. In the Ras Shamra texts Baal's sister-consort is Anat; cf. "Asherah," *ISBE* (rev. ed.), 1:317–18.

6. Alec Motyer has somewhere compared the Baal process to teaching one's child to blow his nose. You take a handkerchief or tissue, put it up to your own nose, and make sounds of blowing *out* (why do kids always sniff in instead?), hoping that your child will imitate your procedure and catch on. So the fertility act in Canaanite worship was meant as a cue for Baal to catch on.

is the great divide between paganism and biblical faith; in paganism the gods must be coerced rather than trusted; see Matt. 6:7–8.)

If we turn on our imagination lights we can readily understand how Israelites would be lured toward Baal worship by the Canaanites they had allowed to remain in the land. One can almost hear a helpful Canaanite trying to talk a little religion—and sense—to his Israelite neighbor: "O yes, having Yahweh who brings you out of Egypt, who makes Pharaoh cry 'Uncle,' who divides the Jordan—all that is fine; and I've got nothing against this Yahweh, mind you; but here in Canaan it's not always the big bang that matters but getting into the rhythms of nature, I mean trying to manage the day-to-day situation with crops and flocks and so forth. Naturally, I might be able to help you know some of our secrets. Maybe you and your son would like to come with me to the high place for our midweek service?"[7]

Certainly there are holes in this witness. The God who works spectacular deliverances also makes daily provisions (see Rom. 8:32). Israel already knew Yahweh was the real "fertility God" (Deut. 28). Nevertheless Israel fell for it:

> They did not destroy the pagans
> as Yahweh had told them to do,
> but, intermarrying with them,
> adopted their practices instead.
>
> Serving the pagans' idols,
> they found themselves trapped
> into sacrificing their own sons
> and daughters to demons.
>
> They shed innocent blood,
> the blood of their sons and daughters,
> offering them to the idols of Canaan,
> they polluted the country with blood.
>
> They defiled themselves by such actions,
> their behaviour was that of a whore.
> Yahweh's anger blazed out at his people,
> he came to loathe his heirs. [Ps. 106:34–40 JB]

7. See Anderson, *Understanding the Old Testament,* 139–47, for a very readable description of the essence and attraction of Canaanite religion.

We should ask why Israel caved in to Canaanite faith and practice. Can we see any clues that may explain why Israel "forsook Yahweh" (vv. 12, 13)? The reader should remember that I have called this section "the *continuing* emergency of our faith," for the conditions that fostered Israel's faithlessness prove as lethal to God's people in any age.

For one thing, the Israelites maintained no distinctive separation from the paganism surrounding them. Here we hark back to 1:27, 29, 30, 31, 32, 33 (see Ps. 106:34–35). They did not drive out the Canaanites who remained after Joshua's conquest. (See the discussion in the previous chapter.) In Israel's case, God required the most radical separation—the peoples in Canaan must be eradicated, so polluted was their life and culture (Lev. 18; Deut. 9:4ff.). Israel did not do this and so lived with and chummied up to the Canaanites, to Israel's destruction. Israel failed to properly combat a godless culture.[8]

God's people in our day have no revealed mandate to swing the actual sword of God's justice at contemporary pagans. But the principle remains—we must retain a distinct separation from our culture while mounting an active opposition to it, else we will blend with it. We are still called to this separation from and combat with our own godless culture.

Time was when we used to smile a bit at the fundies who denounced television and the cinema (I mention these because they are very "Canaanite" in their sexual preoccupation), but the more recent pornographic explosion has sobered us. Celluloid is a powerful cultural medium, fully as dangerous to the Christian mind for what it suggests as for what it preaches, as perilous in what it finds laughable as in what it seriously propounds. But that is simply one aspect of our secularized culture.

The church needs not only saints who live godly lives but also saints who develop godly minds and thereby critique and

---

8. A. R. Fausset (*A Critical and Expository Commentary on the Book of Judges* [London: James Nisbet, 1885], 53) aptly wrote: "Our high calling is to be in the world, not of the world. It is not our being in the world that ruins us, but our suffering the world to be in us: just as ships sink, not by being in the water, but by the water getting into them."

expose the whole gamut of the godless culture in which we live, minds that can not only recognize false doctrine (whether it comes via advertising, education, or government pronouncements) but also unmask the assumptions behind Antichrist's propaganda. Is this not our mandate? "Instead of being moulded to this world, have your mind renewed, and so be transformed in nature, able to make out what the will of God is, namely, what is good and acceptable to him and perfect" (Rom. 12:2 *Moffatt*).

One word more. If the church is going to do this we must cease thinking that God calls only missionaries and pastors. We must ask God to call believers to be artists, journalists, politicians, and historians. That is, if we are to produce an effective counterculture we must begin by holding that all of life belongs to Yahweh (Baal has no royal rights at all in any compartment of Yahweh's universe). Our congregation has produced a brochure which we give to people we visit, part of which summarizes our beliefs. Among our essential convictions we include that "God rules over all of life: nothing is outside his dominion—whether business and politics, economics and education, science and sex, history and harvests, art and affliction, music and marriage. All of life is holy and must be submitted to his reign." That will not solve our cultural problem. But if we make any progress it must begin with that conviction. If we assume Baal has a corner on farming and sex, then we have already given the crown rights of Jesus to Antichrist.

Another cause of Israel's apostasy was the lack of experiential religion in the succeeding generation. As 2:10 says: "All that generation was gathered to its fathers as well; then another generation arose after them who did not know Yahweh nor even the work he had done for Israel." When we contrast this description with that of the previous generation "who had seen all the great work of Yahweh" (v. 7), we might surmise that the problem was ignorance, that the next generation did not know *about* Yahweh and his works. But that is surely incorrect (or incomplete). It was not that they did not know about Yahweh but that they did not know Yahweh. The "they did not know Yahweh" of verse 10 is parallel to the same clause in 1 Samuel 2:12, where it describes the two raunchy

sons of Eli, who were, unfortunately, priests at Yahweh's sanctuary. And "they did not know Yahweh." That does not mean
they did not know *about* Yahweh (obviously they did) or that
they were ignorant of his mighty acts according to Israel's
creed (surely they were not). Rather it means that they "had
no regard for" (RSV) or that "they cared nothing for Yahweh"
(JB). So in Judges 2:10, this next generation "did not know
Yahweh" or his works, that is, they did not acknowledge
Yahweh; Yahweh and his works didn't matter to them, had no
influence over them.[9]

That is a perennial peril. One generation can rejoice in a
living faith, enjoy intimate communion with God, revel in the
kingship of Jesus over daily life, even delight to teach their
faith to those closest them; yet the next generation may come
along and care nothing for all that. Not that they will formally
repudiate everything. It's just that they will know about the
Lord rather than know the Lord. They may remain within the
church in their own cold, dead, formal way. But there is no
fire in their "faith," no warmth in love, no joy from hope. What
Paul calls "the surpassing worth of knowing Christ Jesus my
Lord" (Phil. 3:8 RSV) sounds utterly foreign to them. They cannot fathom it. Our children must not merely ape our faith—
they need to be converted.[10]

Israel's loss of historical memory also helps to explain her
apostasy. It is a poignant report we read: "So they abandoned
Yahweh, the God of their fathers, who brought them out of the
land of Egypt, and they went after other gods . . ." (2:12). The
very description unmasks Israel's ingratitude. Yahweh is
called the "God of their fathers." There is no reason to limit
"their fathers" to the exodus generation; the term may well be

9. See Robert G. Boling, *Judges,* The Anchor Bible (Garden City, N.Y.:
Doubleday, 1975), 72; H. W. Hertzberg, *Die Bücher Josua, Richter, Ruth,* 2d
ed., Das Alte Testament Deutsch (Göttingen: Vandenhoeck und Ruprecht,
1959), 158.

10. Anderson has summed up Judges 2:10 well: "Faith in Yahweh was not
belief in a body of knowledge that could be transferred, like a bank account,
from father to son. To *know* Yahweh was to acknowledge him personally, to
be in covenant relation with him. The faith of parents does not necessarily
become the faith of their children, as we well know" (*Understanding the Old
Testament,* 138).

intended to include the patriarchs. All the pre-exodus stories
(beginning with Gen. 12) highlight Yahweh's faithful preservation of his fragile people (see Ps. 105:12–15). Otherwise
there would have been no Israel. Moreover, Yahweh is the one
"who brought them out of the land of Egypt." What but the
death and resurrection of the Messiah could compare with
that? That was Yahweh's mighty act in behalf of a hopeless
people. Israel abandoned this God! What gross ingratitude! Yet
the writer does not make his point by hurling an exasperated
prophetic invective at Israel but by simply describing in cold
but accusing print the God they had forsaken.

The Bible is clear: amnesia produces apostasy. That is why
Scripture is so frantic about the church not forgetting what
Yahweh has done for us (see Deut. 4 and 6). So Jeremiah diag-
nosed faithless Israel:

> They did not say, "Where is the LORD
>   who brought us up from the land of Egypt,
> who led us in the wilderness,
>   in a land of deserts and pits,
> in a land of drought and deep darkness,
>   in a land that none passes through,
>   where no man dwells?" [Jer. 2:6 RSV]

When we allow either his quiet keeping or his dramatic rescue
to slip into oblivion we are on our way toward Baal. Nor is it
merely some ancient Israelite problem. The apostle warns us
of false teachers who will be "denying the Master *who bought
them*" (2 Pet. 2:1 RSV, italics added). Which is good reason for
us to partake gratefully and frequently of the Lord's Supper.
Lest we forget.

The Astonishing Character of Our God

Secondly, verses 14–18 display to us the astonishing character of our God. A richly complex character it is. We see, for
example, the faithfulness of his anger in verses 14–15:

> So the anger of Yahweh became hot against Israel and he gave
> them into the hand of plunderers who plundered them; he sold

them into the hand of their enemies around them, and they
were no longer able to stand before their enemies. Whenever
they went out the hand of Yahweh was against them to bring
them disaster, as Yahweh had promised and as Yahweh had
sworn to them. . . .

Notice especially those words *as Yahweh had promised* and *as
Yahweh had sworn*. When the Lord gave Israel over to her
enemies, he was only executing what he had already threatened to do should she prove faithless (see Lev. 26:17 and Deut.
28:25 in context). Yahweh's hot anger shows his faithfulness
to his word. It is a *faithful* anger.

Such anger should not surprise us. It is the price we pay for
being loved. Yahweh had told Israel he would brook no rivals,
"for Yahweh's name is Jealous; he is the jealous God" (Exod.
34:14). Jealousy is the flip side of love; it is required where
exclusive love is called for.

Suppose a husband has sad but true evidence that his wife
is having an affair with another man. It is not a matter of
gossip or innuendo, but the matter has been established. Suppose too, for the sake of argument, that the husband, sinner
that he is, nevertheless has been—on the whole—attentive,
devoted, and tender toward his wife. And now she is having
this affair. What if the husband's reaction were: "Well, ya win
some an' ya lose some; that's the way the cookie crumbles"?
What would you think? Why, simply that he does not love his
wife, for if he truly loved his wife there could be no such non-
chalance. If lively love was there, he should be upset, he should
be jealous, he should be angry. Jealousy is love burst into its
proper flame.

Now that is the problem with having the God of the Bible
as our God. To have a God who loves his people is to have a
jealous God, and to have a jealous God is to have an intolerant
God. "Love divine" is not soft laxity but blazing intolerance,
an absolute claim (cf. Matt. 10:37–38). Such is the God of Israel
whose jealous love makes him faithful in his anger toward you.
Who ever heard of love and fidelity like that? You forsake him
and he will pursue you—in his anger.

Again, our God is astonishing when we consider the incred-
ibility of his salvation (v. 16). Put verse 14a and verse 16a

together and note the amazing sequence: "the anger of Yahweh burned against Israel," "and Yahweh raised up judges who saved them." If we were writing this, we would not have allowed those two statements to stand together. Time for an editor! We would have inserted after verse 15, "Israel turned from their evil way, forsook Baal, and sought the Lord." But there is none of that.

It seems that verse 16 was intended to stand out. Observe how it sits in the structure of verses 11–23 as a whole:

Apostasy, 2:11–13
  (from the God of historical grace)
    Wrath, 2:14–15
      ("and the anger of Yahweh burned against Israel")
        Grace, 2:16
Apostasy, 2:17–19
  (from the God of contemporary grace)
    Wrath, 2:20–23
      ("and the anger of Yahweh burned against Israel")

The section follows what some would call an *A B C A' B'* pattern, with the grace note in verse 16 being the hinge on which the unit turns. What a glad wallop it packs: the One who "gave them into the hand of plunderers" (v. 14) "saved them from the hand of their plunderers" (v. 16); the hand that is against them (v. 15) is nevertheless mysteriously for them (v. 16). Here is the fundamental miracle of the Bible: that the God who rightly casts us down to the ground should—without reason—stoop to lift us up.

I said "without reason." If there is one, it can only be the depth of his compassion, another surprise. Even in the face of Israel's persisting apostasy, Yahweh would raise up judges and use them to save Israel from their enemies. Why? "For Yahweh was sorry on account of their groaning because of those afflicting and oppressing them" (v. 18). This "groaning" connotes misery rather than repentance. (Even when Israel "cried out" [*za'aq*] to Yahweh, as in 3:9, repentance was not necessarily involved; but more on that in the next chapter.) God's heart is

stirred by the sheer misery of his people.[11] How it moves God
(can we say it?) emotionally to see his people—even his sinful
people—crushed. Once you see God's heart in Judges 2:18 you
are not shocked when you meet God's Priest in Hebrews 4:15.
If you but tumble into this abyss of divine mercy, you will be
convinced of one irrefutable fact: the God of the Bible is abso-
lutely uninventible.

One thing more. The "groaning" of verse 18 is a noun
(Hebrew, *ne'aqah*) used only three other times in the Old Testament, two of which are in Exodus (2:24; 6:5). There the
"groaning" is that of Israel under Egyptian slavery, a groaning
that God hears—and he remembers his covenant and delivers
them. The very word in Judges 2:18 should carry our minds
back to Exodus. So when we read that "Yahweh was sorry on
account of their groaning" it is as if the text is saying: "See!
Yahweh is still the same in 1100 B.C. as in 1400 B.C." (dates
approximate!). *His* mercies never come to an end! Hundreds of
years do not cool the warmth of his compassions. That makes
reading the ancient word of God an exciting matter for me in
my day.

Yahweh continues to amaze us, for we see the length of his
patience in 2:20–23 and 3:1–4. If Israel would not listen to the
judges who delivered them (2:16–17); if, after a judge's death,
Israel persisted in her passion for other gods (2:19); and if, in
light of all this, Yahweh's anger flashed out against such cove-
nant-breakers (2:20), we would expect the end for Israel.
Instead, Yahweh places them under disciplinary judgment to
"test" them (note the use of *nasah*, to test, three times; 2:22;
3:1, 4). Even within the limited judgment imposed (no longer
driving out the nations Joshua left), there is opportunity
extended, opportunity to show that "the way of Yahweh" (2:22)
still matters to them. Where we would think Yahweh's anger
would rain judgment, it, as it were, bridles itself and imposes
discipline. Here is Yahweh, the God who is "slow to anger,"
which gave Jonah fits (Jon. 4:1–2) but should create wonder

---

11. As Fausset (*Judges,* 54) has stated: "[T]heir groanings, by reason of
them that oppressed them, moved His compassion. It was not their repentance
of sin, but His repentance because of their cry in distress, that brought Him
to their help."

in us, for even Christians—if they've any sense of their sinfulness at all—can only say, "It is of the LORD'S mercies that we are not consumed" (Lam. 3:22 KJV).[12]

Packed into five verses (vv. 14–18) is a bracing description of an unguessable God. There is only one proper response for believing people to make to such a text, to such a God: fall down with the prophet Micah, exclaiming, "Who is a God like you?" (Mic. 7:18ff.).

The Increasing Slavery of Our Sin

Lastly, the text warns us of the increasing slavery of our sin. Yahweh may raise up judges to save Israel in her distress (2:16). However, Israel did not listen to her judges but "played prostitute after other gods" (2:17). Yahweh would raise up a judge and save Israel from her enemies through that judge (2:18). But "when the judge died, they turned back and acted more corruptly than their fathers, going after other gods to serve and bow down to them; they did not leave off their deeds or their stubborn ways"(2:19).

You discover the true nature of people by observing them when they are not bound by external constraints. Take a classful of second graders. Let the teacher leave the room and all Cain gets raised. They, like Israel, are showing their true

12. I think I have captured the point of 2:20–3:4, a rather difficult passage. John Gray thinks that the purposes of testing (2:22) and teaching war (3:2) reflect a theological embarrassment which feels compelled to explain why Israel did not occupy the land as their faith had proclaimed (*Joshua, Judges and Ruth,* The Century Bible—New Edition [Greenwood, S.C.: Attic, 1967], 258). Others are bothered by the (at least) double divine purpose in leaving the remaining nations (2:22 and 3:2). C. J. Goslinga, however, holds that 3:2 merely spells out the manner in which Yahweh would test Israel (2:22); see *Joshua, Judges, Ruth,* Bible Student's Commentary (Grand Rapids: Zondervan, 1986), 271–74. Arthur E. Cundall (*Judges,* Tyndale Old Testament Commentaries [London: Tyndale, 1968], 70–71) is not bothered by the multiplicity of reasons—and rightly so. Please note in passing that all the remaining nations listed in 3:3, apart perhaps from the Canaanites, stand on the fringes of Israel's land and not within her land—another hint that Joshua's conquest did give Israel basic control of the bulk of Canaan. On the coherence of 2:23–3:6, see Barry G. Webb, *The Book of the Judges: An Integrated Reading,* JSOT Supplement Series 46 (Sheffield: JSOT, 1987), 114–15.

nature. During a judge's lifetime Israel tolerates an external righteousness. But let the judge die, let the "restraining one" be taken out of the way, and there is continual slopping back into idolatry. Even the kindness of God (2:16, 18) does not move the Israelites to faithfulness or repentance. They do not and apparently cannot keep themselves from the slavery of sin (v. 19); they are held in sin's grip; they have Baal in their blood.

Sometimes we have difficulty understanding the slavery of sin (a key theme of Judges, by the way), understanding sin as power. There is a mystery about it.

I remember when I was about ten years old. We lived in a small western Pennsylvania town where my father was the United Presbyterian pastor. A new Methodist pastor named Reverend Galbraith moved to town. He and his wife were a cordial couple and became good friends with my parents. However, bashful as I was, I failed to speak to Mrs. Galbraith on one or two occasions. Hence she teasingly threatened that if I didn't speak to her when she saw me next, she would kiss me. Sheer, unmitigated terror! No problem, you say. All you have to do is henceforth to speak to her. Oh? You don't understand that such jesting threats bring on a kind of social paralysis. Mysterious it is. But for some inexplicable reason one simply "can't" speak to a woman who threatens to smooch you if you don't speak to her. It was so bad that when three of our local churches had our weekly Sunday evening services together, I would dash out of church immediately after the service to avoid having to face Mrs. Galbraith. Once when (after evening church) I was sitting in our family car, Mrs. G. and her husband were walking home. She came toward the car to speak to me—I jumped out of the car on the street-traffic side, almost into the path of an oncoming auto, obviously preferring a tragic rather than a romantic end to my life!

Now I cannot explain that. I cannot state why I didn't just speak to her and "be free." All I know is that, ludicrous as it sounds, I *could not* speak to her! I was enslaved. I was in bondage. I was helpless in the grip of that threat.

That was Israel's condition. "When the judge died, they turned back and acted more corruptly than their fathers" (2:19). Why did they always do that? Why could they not break that pattern? It *is* mysterious; but Judges does teach us that that is the tragic tyranny of sin. Sin is not simply an action you do or fail to do, that you can choose to do or not to do. Sin is a power that holds you in its grip. That is precisely what the apostle meant when he averred that all—both Jew and Gentile, both religious man and pagan man—are "under sin" (Rom. 3:9), by which he means "under the power of sin" (RSV). And until the church gets a proper view of sin, we will never see salvation as much more than a moving religious charade rather than as an act of holy, vicious violence by which Christ wrenches his people out of the clammy clutches of the prince of darkness (cf. 1 John 3:8).

So Israel in Judges is Sin's captive. Hence Yahweh can dub Israel "this nation" (2:20, Heb.) rather than "my people." This may be a subtle hint that Israel is more like the pagan nations than like the people of Yahweh. The summary section in 3:5–6 conveys the total helplessness of Israel: Israel lives among the pagans, intermarries with the pagans, and apes the worship of the pagans. Generation degeneration is complete. From "the people served Yahweh" (2:7) we have come to "they served their gods" (3:6). Maybe now we can understand Christmas, can understand the angel's command: "You shall call his name Jesus, for he shall save his people from their sins" (Matt. 1:21). We may be called the people of God and yet be the prisoners of sin. Religious as we are, we may be "children of wrath" as the rest are (Eph. 2:3), just as hopeless as they (Eph. 2:12), unless God really is *rich* in mercy (Eph. 2:4ff.).

PART 2

The Salvation of a Long-suffering God
(Judges 3:7–16:31)

3

A Paradigm of Salvation
(3:7–11)

Here we enter the second major division of the Book of Judges, covering 3:7–16:31, a division I have called "The Salvation of a Long-suffering God." Since the exposition breaks up the text into a number of smaller units, this overarching theme may be obscured. For that reason you might prefer a brief scheme by which you can carry the theme and contents of chapters 3–16 in your mental back pocket:

The salvation of a long-suffering God, 3:7–16:31
    The paradigm of Yahweh's salvation, 3:7–11
      (Othniel)
    The excitement of Yahweh's salvation, 3:12–5:31
      (Ehud and Deborah)
    The weakness of Yahweh's salvation, 6:1–8:32
      (Gideon)
    The antithesis of Yahweh's salvation, 8:33–9:57
      (Abimelech)
    The strangeness of Yahweh's salvation, 10:1–16:31
      (Jephthah and Samson)

This outline will enable the reader to keep together in short compass a massive amount of detail. Now, what about this fellow Othniel?

Recently a friend wanted me to play backgammon with him. I had not played the game in ages (and very little then) and

had no idea how to play. In such a situation the usual procedure is to explain the main principles of a game and then to
go ahead and actually play a first game as a sample game, a
kind of pioneering effort in which the ignorant one(s) can get
a handle on how the game goes. Judges 3:7–11 seems to be
like that: an initial example of the process described in 2:11–
23, a sort of paradigm of "how it went" in the judges' period.[1]
With a minimum of detail 3:7–11 places a little historical flesh
on the theological bones of 2:11–23 (or 2:11–3:6). Let us walk
our way through this pattern passage.

Israel's Infidelity and Yahweh's Wrath

First, we meet Israel's infidelity and Yahweh's wrath (vv.
7–8). Israel forgets Yahweh, serves the Baals and Asherahs:
"So Yahweh's anger burned against Israel so that he sold them
into the hand of Cushan-rishathaim, king of Aram-naharaim;
and the sons of Israel served Cushan-rishathaim eight years"
(v. 8). We expected as much in light of 2:13–14. "They served
the Baals" (v. 7) and so "they served Cushan-rishathaim"
(v. 8).[2] This sequence is not a natural episode of cause and

1. W. Richter (*Die Bearbeitungen des "Retterbuches" in der Deuteronom-
ischen Epoche,* Bonner Biblische Beiträge 21 [Bonn: Peter Hanstein, 1964],
90–91) calls the Othniel section an "example-piece." One can accept the terminology and concept without buying Richter's whole critical reconstruction.
2. The text (vv. 8, 10) says Cushan-rishathaim hails from Aram-naharaim
in eastern Syria/northern Mesopotamia to the northeast of Canaan. Aram-
naharaim (= Paddan-aram) was primarily the area between the River Habur
on the east and the section of the Euphrates flowing past Carchemish on the
west (see Kenneth A. Kitchen, "Aram, Aramaeans," *IBD,* 1:89–91). Some
scholars think an oppressor close at hand is more likely and so emend the text
to read "Edom" instead of "Aram" (see JB, and John Gray, *Joshua, Judges and
Ruth,* The Century Bible—New Edition [Greenwood, S.C.: Attic, 1967], 214,
261). The emendation is plausible in itself since the difference between "Aram"
and "Edom" in Hebrew is really only one letter each (equivalent to "r" and
"d" in English), and those two letters are easily confused (see 2 Sam. 8:13; cf.
1 Chron. 18:12). But the fact that "-naharaim" is attached to "Aram" in
verse 8 makes it less likely that "Edom" and "Aram" were simply confused
here. Those who emend the text to "Edom" must also explain "-naharaim"
(e.g., as a later explanatory gloss). That is not impossible, but, in my book,
when explanations increase in complexity their unlikelihood also increases.
Moreover, there is not a scrap of objective evidence for any textual variant
here.

effect but flows from the searing heat of Yahweh's wrath. We are so accustomed to our secularized, nonrevelatory view of history that depicts events as resulting from various observable causes, conditions, and factors, and, paradoxically, we are so familiar with biblical historiography that we fail to recognize how strange biblical (prophetic) history is. Not a tame natural process but blazing supernatural wrath explains Israel's servitude. Yahweh is the God who makes and orders history. And "who considers the power of thy anger, / and thy wrath according to the fear of thee?" (Ps. 90:11 RSV).

Yet even here, in Yahweh's anger, is hope for Israel, for his anger shows that he will not allow Israel to serve Baal unmolested. Yahweh's wrath is the heat of his jealous love by which he refuses to let go of his people; he refuses to allow his people to remain comfortable in sin. Serving Cushan-rishathaim may not sound like salvation to us—and it isn't, but, if it forces us to lose our grip on Baal, it may be the beginning of salvation. We must confess that Yahweh's anger is not good news nor is it bad news but good bad news. It shows that the covenant God who has bound himself to his people will not allow them to become cozy in their infidelity. "Steadfast love" pursues them in their iniquity and is not above inflicting misery in order to awaken them. The burning anger of Yahweh is certainly no picnic, but it may be the only sign of hope for God's people, even though they may be yet unaware of that fact.

Israel's Cry and Yahweh's Savior

Secondly, we hear of Israel's cry and Yahweh's savior in verse 9: "Then the sons of Israel cried out to Yahweh, and Yahweh raised up a savior for the sons of Israel, who saved them, that is, Othniel, son of Kenaz."

What does "the sons of Israel *cried out* to Yahweh" mean (the verb is *za'aq*)? Handbooks and commentaries of all stripes frequently assume that Israel's crying out implies repentance or conversion. Hence the much-touted cycle of Judges: apostasy-oppression-repentance-deliverance. But does *za'aq* necessarily connote repentance? I doubt it. In a previous study I reached this conclusion:

A study of its usage reveals that it denotes crying for help (frequently directed to Yahweh) out of deep distress or because of some unbearable circumstance; occasionally it simply signifies a cry of anguish directed to no one in particular.

And I appended this explanation:

This generalization is based on a study of the [over] 60 uses of [za'aq] . . . in their contexts. Possible exceptions to [this] conclusion . . . are few and, upon examination, prove to be apparent rather than real. Whenever [za'aq] appears associated with repentance or confession of sins (Judg. 10:10, 1 Sam. 12:10, Neh. 9:28) that repentance or confession is explicitly expressed by some additional clause or second verb, a factor which implies that [za'aq] by itself cannot and does not carry any idea of repentance. There are several passages (Isa. 30:19, Hos. 7:14, Psalm 107:13, 19) where [za'aq] may seem to approach a hint of repentance; yet in each case the emphasis remains on the condition of distress rather than on any expression of repentance.[3]

This is an important conclusion, for it shows that when "Yahweh raised up a savior" for Israel he was not reacting to any repentance on Israel's part.[4] If anything, he was responding to their misery rather than to their sorrow, to their pain rather than to their penitence. Who then can ever plumb the

3. "A Proposed Life-Setting for the Book of Judges" (Ann Arbor: University Microfilms, 1978), 146–47. For a similar view of za'aq as appeal for help rather than cry of repentance, see Frederick E. Greenspahn, "The Theology of the Framework of Judges," *Vetus Testamentum* 36 (1986): 391–95, and M. Weinfeld, "The Period of the Conquest and of the Judges as Seen by the Earlier and the Later Sources," *Vetus Testamentum* 17 (1967): 106–7. The very first occurrence of za'aq in Exodus 2:23 provides a good sample of its import; the cry arises from the experience of distress, not from the realization of sin. Nehemiah 9:4 may seem an exception, but it is as likely a cry of praise as of repentance; that is, it is more natural to view verse 4 in light of verse 5 than of verses 1–3.

4. The situation is the same as in the overview of 2:11–23, where Yahweh apart from any repentance on Israel's part raises up judges who save Israel (v. 16). Some allege that in 2:11–23 Yahweh delivers Israel apart from Israel's repentance whereas in the judges' stories (e.g., 3:9) he delivers in response to their repentance and that, therefore, the overview and the framework of the stories must come from different writers (see, e.g., M. G. Rogers, "Judges, Book of," *IDB/S*, 509). But a proper view of the verb za'aq tumbles that position.

abyss of Yahweh's pity for his people, even his sinful people, who are moved more by their distress than by their depravity? Yahweh is indeed the one "who could bear Israel's suffering no longer" (Judg. 10:16 NJB). What sheer grace then when Yahweh delivers!

Our primary problem is that verse 9 moves us only to yawn. After all, we already know the theological truth of verse 9— we've read that sort of thing often before. So we respond with a pleasant, nodding ho-hum. Isn't God nice? What's for supper? If we fail to see, to feel, to delight in the miracle of God's own nature, are we not strangers to rather than partakers of such unbelievable grace?

Israel's Oppressor and Yahweh's Power

Thirdly, verse 10 places Israel's oppressor and Yahweh's power side by side. The primary stress is on Yahweh's power via his Spirit coming upon Othniel; but since we did not pay much attention to Cushan-rishathaim in verse 8, let us now give him his due.

No one knows exactly what to make of Cushan-rishathaim's name. Its spelling in the Hebrew text means "Cushan of double wickedness." We might leave the mystery there. But let us press on with a suggestion, one that has been made before. It may well be that the writer (or a later scribe) intended a dig at Cushan-whomever and so adapted the spelling of the oppressor's name to "Cushan-double wickedness." Maybe he was trying to pun—because in verse 8 he calls him "Cushan-rishathaim king of Aram-naharaim." One can hear the assonance and/or rhyme between "-rishathaim" and "-naharaim." Cushan-double wickedness from Aram-double rivers! That kind of barb is the sort of thing oppressed and suffering people *can* inflict. Maybe they cannot throw off the oppressor's yoke at some time, but they can coin their own derogatory names for him. "Double evil from double river" isn't bad! And this may tell us something about Holy Scripture: when writing up redemptive history, the Holy Spirit and the biblical writers conspire to do it with spice! There is no reason for it to be humdrum. If "Cushan-double wickedness" was an Israelite slam on Cushan-whatever-his-name-was—well then, why not call him that in the sacred record? Surely you can see that God doesn't take away your humor when you belong to his people.

As I said, verse 10 places stress on Yahweh's power. It is "the Spirit of Yahweh" who empowers and equips Othniel;[5] it is Yahweh who "gave Cushan-rishathaim king of Aram into [Othniel's] hand." Indeed, it was Yahweh who "raised up a savior for the sons of Israel" (v. 9). There can be no missing it: "salvation is from the LORD" (Jon. 2:9 NASB).

Something to note in this connection: verse 8 says that Yahweh "sold them into the hand of Cushan-rishathaim" while verse 10 affirms "Yahweh gave Cushan-rishathaim . . . into his [Othniel's] hand." Here we have a glimpse of Yahweh as Lord of history, a picture of Yahweh's way in history in miniature. When Yahweh's own people are unfaithful, he raises up an instrument of his wrath to bring them low; but then the time comes when that instrument becomes too big for his international britches, when the instrument deludes himself into thinking *he* is lord rather than the feeble vassal of the Great King. Then Yahweh must bring down his instrument-that-refuses-to-be-an-instrument.

There is an excellent example of this pattern in Jeremiah 27. There were brass from Edom, Moab, Ammon, Tyre, and Sidon in Jerusalem, holding a conference with Zedekiah, king of Judah. Naturally, it would be billed as a purely economic summit. But many could smell that the primary economic question was: Will Judah join in the revolt against Nebuchadnezzar of Babylon? Now after one of the warm afternoon sessions filled with mint juleps, pleasantries, cajolery, and plotting, the various dignitaries emerge on the palace steps with a smiling Zedekiah, all of them furrow-browed, ready to speak with the gathered reporters and to answer evasively, innocuously, solemnly any questions directed to them by the major networks. When—alas and alack!—Jeremiah plods up, wearing these ridiculous yoke-bars on his neck. What a touch of class! But into the electric silence this strange creature announces Yahweh's word:

5. For a very helpful treatment of the Old Testament teaching about the Spirit of God, see B. B. Warfield, "The Spirit of God in the Old Testament," *Biblical and Theological Studies,* ed. Samuel G. Craig (Philadelphia: Presbyterian and Reformed, 1952), 127–56.

It is I who by my great power and my outstretched arm have
made the earth, with the men and animals that are on the earth,
and I give it to whomever it seems right to me. Now I have
given all these lands into the hand of Nebuchadnezzar, the king
of Babylon, my servant, and I have given him also the beasts
of the field to serve him. All the nations shall serve him and
his son and his grandson, until the time of his own land comes;
then many nations and great kings shall make him their slave.
[Jer. 27:5–7 RSV]

There it is: "until the time of his own land comes." Yahweh
may raise up one king or kingdom to chastise his people and/
or others; but then the "time of his own land comes," when
that kingdom must be brought down for its arrogance and
oppression (cf. Jer. 50:29–38).

It matters not whether it is Cushan-rishathaim or Assyria
(Isa. 10:5–34) or Babylon (Jer. 27, 50, 51; Hab. 2). They, as
much as the church, are under Yahweh's sovereign control. No
one wears the political pants of history unless Yahweh issues
them to him. And if he begins to strut (or goose-step) in those
pants, ere long "the time of his own land" will come. Now
Cushan-rishathaim may not have been a big-time operator
like Nebuchadnezzar. But he is witness to the same truth:
Yahweh, little Israel's God, is Lord of history. Not only "my
times" (Ps. 31:15) but history's times are in Yahweh's hands.
And the church is comforted by that.[6]

6. Verse 10 states that Othniel "judged Israel." I have retained the traditional rendering of the verb *shaphat* (to judge), even though there is uncer-
tainty about its exact meaning. If (in this text) the next clause ("he went out
to war") fleshes out the meaning of *shaphat,* then Othniel's judging consists
of securing justice for Israel and restoring her rights by delivering her from
her oppressor. The introduction (2:16–19) suggests that the judges (*shōphetim*)
not only delivered from oppressors but also exercised some spiritual leadership
or influence in holding Israel to Yahweh, much as Samuel did later (1 Sam.
7:6; 12:7, *shaphat* used in both texts; the latter may be translated "enter into
judgment with"; RSV has "plead with you"), though it is difficult to see how
someone like Samson (15:20; 16:31) fulfilled this function. In any case, "judge"
may convey too narrow a connotation to our minds whereas biblical usage and
background from Mari, Ugarit, and Ebla indicate a more general idea, to rule,
govern, or lead (R. D. Culver, "Shaphat," *TWOT,* 2:947–48; D. J. Wiseman,
"Abraham in History and Tradition–Part II: Abraham the Prince," *Biblio-
theca Sacra* 134 [1977]: 233–35; F. C. Fensham, "Judges, Book of," ISBE [rev.
ed.], 2:1156–57).

Israel's Opportunity and Yahweh's Gift

Lastly, verse 11 shows us Israel's opportunity and Yahweh's gift. "The land enjoyed rest forty years; then Othniel son of Kenaz died." The rest is doubtless rest from war (Josh. 11:23) and, therefore, from attack, oppression, and affliction.[7] Here is what is available to Israel; here is what she can enjoy; here is what Yahweh prefers to give his own. And this places responsibility on Israel. For is this not the kindness of God leading them to repentance (Rom. 2:4)? Does not our God seek to awaken us as much by his goodness as by his severity? Whether Yahweh sells his people to the Aramaeans or grants them a generation of security—both should draw them to repentance and faithfulness.

This rest is an opportunity that can be enjoyed only in ongoing fidelity to Yahweh. Israel cannot merely piddle with it, for it will not always be extended. As Carl Armerding has observed:

> The first five judges, all of whom, including the mysterious Shamgar, were deliverer-figures, represent a time when the land periodically enjoyed rest from conflict. . . . (See 3:11, 30; 5:31; 8:28.) In contrast, the latter period is characterized by minor judges . . . together with the rather unorthodox deliverers Jephthah and Samson. The land is never said to "have rest" and the picture is one of increasing moral, political and military decline leading to the shameful climax of events in the Epilogue (chs. 17–21). The lesson is clear: a people which fails to give wholehearted obedience to the LORD can only sink lower and lower.[8]

The rest that God gives must be met by the constancy of his people.

A footnote. Let us not as Christians be too hasty to spiritualize this rest into heavenly rest. It was *the land* that enjoyed rest. Even Christians, I would hold, should keep to the earthiness of the text here. There is no need to fly off to heaven

7. See further H. J. Austel, "Shaqat," *TWOT,* 2:953.
8. Carl Armerding, "Judges," *The New Layman's Bible Commentary* (Grand Rapids: Zondervan, 1979), 345.

at this point. Does not the apostle command us to pray "for kings and all those in authority, *that we may live peaceful and quiet lives* in all godliness and holiness" (1 Tim. 2:2, italics added)? To have rulers in one's country who can maintain social and civil order is one of God's wonderful gifts to his flock. And if your land has relative rest, you should thank the kind King who has granted it to you.

Some have problems with this episode. George F. Moore complained of its "emptiness."[9] Granted, 3:7–11 is basically a fill-in-the-blank section, as if 2:11–23 gave us the basic story and in 3:7–11 the writer simply inserts names, places, and numbers in the blanks. There are nothing but bare essentials here—and those are about what *Yahweh* had done. The problem with Othniel is that he is so colorless. There is no flash and dash about Othniel—nothing about being left-handed and making a dagger (so Ehud), no snazzy motto like Jael's "Step softly but carry a big hammer." Probably with good reason. It is likely that we have this first episode in such stripped-down style precisely so that we will see clearly what is most essential—the activity of Yahweh. Sometimes interesting people can obscure that, and we end up watching these fascinating folks but never see what our God is doing.

9. *A Critical and Exegetical Commentary on Judges,* The International Critical Commentary (Edinburgh: T. and T. Clark, 1895), 84.

4

What Shall We Do with a Left-handed Savior?
(3:12–30)

Now what are we going to do with this section of Scripture? (It is not only this passage but much of the Old Testament that poses this problem for some.) One expositor has apologized for the narrative: "By even the most elementary standard of ethics [Ehud's] deception and murder of Eglon stand condemned. Passages like this, when encountered by the untutored reader of the Scriptures, cause consternation and questioning."[1]

I cannot join in his lament. But you do sense the problem, don't you? Here we are in one of those apparently R-rated sections of the Old Testament and slightly embarrassed by it. But before you become a judge beware of hypocrisy—you who allow your children to glut their appetites on those violence-filled Saturday morning television cartoons (I speak partly in jest). Many of you permit far worse fare and think nothing of it, but you doubtless expect God to have higher standards . . . than to have all this blood and gore oozing out of his holy, inspired, infallible, inerrant book. Oh, to be sure, we allow David and Goliath into our elementary Sunday school materials—but Ehud? The lefty from Benjamin? Never!

Of course some folks have a way of dealing with an embar-

1. Phillips P. Elliott, "The Book of Judges: Exposition," *IB*, 2:708, 711.

rassing Old Testament. Their solution is that such Old Testament narratives don't mean what they say. For example,
Ehud's dagger is the "sword of the Spirit" (a la Eph. 6), the
word of God that is "sharper than any two-edged sword" (a la
Heb. 4). But I doubt if King Eglon got the point that way—in
fact he probably wished Ehud's dagger had been "only" the
word of God! Or, if we don't allegorize the text, we try to mor-
alize it, especially by looking for what lessons it may teach us.
Result? Ehud seems to be vengeful and hateful—don't be like
him. Or, how about a sermon on "The Peril of Being Alone"
with verse 19b as the text? Couldn't you wax eloquent over
how crucial the mutual support and presence of the Christian
fellowship is for each believer (Eglon a believer?!)? Looking for
lessons dredges up some strange candidates; why not "How to
Make and Use Daggers" or "Lefties Make More Successful
Assassins"?

However, this is not some light matter, for most of us (those
commonly dubbed evangelical Christians) are quite emphatic
that *all* Scripture is God-breathed and profitable (2 Tim. 3:16);
we get very upset if anyone even insinuates that the Bible is
not all true or if someone denies the authority of part of the
Bible. No sir! The Bible is our authority, the whole Bible. But
it is strange, isn't it, that we who pride ourselves on holding
to the full authority of Scripture have our own way of negating
its authority? That is, we simply ignore a good bit of it, especially those sticky parts of the Old Testament that embarrass
our enlightened sensibilities. Give us Jesus in the Gospel of
Mark or Paul in Galatians (and don't think *they* don't have
their rough spots) but Ehud in Judges? Must we take the
authority of the Bible that seriously? Well now, what shall we
do with this left-handed savior? And what shall we do with
this story about him?

The Theme of the Story

First of all, we must be clear about the theme of the story
(what it's about). You will find that in verse 15: "Then the sons
of Israel cried for help to Yahweh, and Yahweh raised up for
them a savior, Ehud the son of Gera the Benjaminite; he was
a left-handed man" (see also v. 28). There you have it, like a

big E on the optometrist's eye chart. What is the theme of this racy little episode in the history of God's people? It is a story about the way God saves his people in their afflictions (well-deserved afflictions to boot). And it says that Yahweh is responsible for this lefty Ehud—"Yahweh raised up for them a savior." Did you hear that? He did not say a murderer, or an assassin, or a liar, or a deceiver—but a *savior*. This is a story of *salvation*! The focus of the story is not "Why does God get himself all mixed up with a character like Ehud?" but "See how God delights to save his people in their afflictions!" We are not to see the problems God creates but the salvation he brings.

It is difficult to keep the proper focus. In one of Charles Schulz's "Peanuts" cartoons Linus is chomping on a peanut-butter-and-jelly sandwich. He notices his hands and exclaims, "Hands are fascinating things! I like my hands . . . I think I have nice hands . . . My hands seem to have a lot of character." Lucy now comes on the scene as Linus continues: "These are hands which may some day do marvelous works! They may build mighty bridges, or heal the sick, or hit home runs, or write soul-stirring novels!" In his crescendo Linus exclaims in Lucy's face, "These are hands which may some day change the course of destiny!" Lucy looks down at them and matter-of-factly observes: "They've got jelly on them."

I am not claiming that you will not have some problems with this story; I am saying that you'll miss the whole point if you go around whimpering about how here the Bible has jelly on it, when our Lord is trying to boom into your ears with all sorts of exclamation marks, "See how I delight to save you in all your troubles!" Aren't some of you who read this in such circumstances at the moment, so that this is precisely the good news you need to hear? That in your troubles—whether a result of your sins or not—you have a compassionate God who actually hears your cries for help and comes to save you in your distress.

The Telling of the Story

We turn from the theme to the telling of the story (i.e., how it's told), with primary attention on verses 15b–26. For a few minutes you must reach down and pull off your twentieth-century Florsheims, Naturalizers, Reeboks, or Nikes and slip on some Israelite sandals. Try to hear this story as an Israelite would have heard it (or told it), an Israelite, remember, who for eighteen years (v. 14) had been oppressed and taxed to the bone under blubbery King Eglon, an Israelite therefore living in persisting poverty, eking out some sort of borderline existence in the hill country of Ephraim—then you won't be surprised but rather will understand the pure enjoyment, the devastating humor, the biting satire, the sheer hilarity of this narrative. That is one trouble with the commentaries—most all of them are so serious. Of the eight or nine I consulted not one of them seemed to get the joke. Fortunately, Israel found this story entertaining.

Look at the details. Ehud is the head of the delegation that brings Israel's tribute (probably largely produce) to Eglon at Jericho (v. 15b). Ehud makes a dagger, perhaps fifteen to eighteen inches long, and straps it to his right thigh under his garments (v. 16), as a lefty (v. 15a) would. Probably Eglon's bodyguard looked for strange bulges on left sides since most folks were (alas, even then) right-handed.[2] Now the writer prepares you for what is to come by indicating parenthetically that Eglon was a "very fat man" (v. 17b). On that one fateful occasion after Israel had presented its tribute, Ehud returned, alleging he had a secret message for the king (v. 19a). Eglon stupidly dismissed all his attendants (can you hear some Israelite snickers?) and sat alone before Ehud (vv. 19b–20a). Ehud again announced he carried a "word of God" for Eglon. Hence in proper and superstitious reverence Eglon struggles and staggers to his feet (v. 20b; what an effort!). Then notice how in verses 21ff. the narrative camera slips into slow motion,

---

2. John Hercus, in his racy retelling of Judges, comments on the detail of Ehud's being left-handed: "Even the right- and left-handedness of life is important to God" (*God Is God* [London: Hodder and Stoughton, 1971], 31). As for Ehud's dagger, Arthur E. Cundall observes: "The ease with which the dagger penetrated the king's body, hilt and all (22), suggests that it had no crosspiece and thus would be the more readily concealable under the long, flowing outergarment" (*Judges*, Tyndale Old Testament Commentaries [London: Tyndale, 1968], 76).

highlighting every move, including every possible graphic detail:

> Then Ehud stretched out his left hand, took the dagger from his right thigh, and plunged it into his belly. And even the handle went in after the blade, and the fat closed around the blade for he did not pull the dagger out of his belly; so it came out the groin area; and Ehud went out to the porch area. . . .[3]

One can almost see the sarcasm in the Israelite ink in verses 24–25. Ehud has made his escape; Eglon's servants return from coffee break

> and they looked—*why,* the doors of the upper chamber were locked! So they said, "He's surely covering his feet[4] in the bathroom." So they waited to the point of shame and *still* he was not opening the doors of the upper chamber. Then they took the key and opened them and—*there he was!*—their master was fallen to the ground—dead!

The Hebrew particle *hinnēh* appears three times in these verses. Traditional English versions frequently render it "behold," which drains the life out of it. It is a particle that usually indicates something at least a bit unexpected. I have tried to capture the effect above with different renderings. The italicized words reflect *hinnēh.*

Any red-blooded Israelite would surely find this series of surprises amusing. Eglon's lackeys think he's using the facilities, so they dally and dally, pace around wondering why on earth he's taking so long—and all the time Ehud is making a splendid escape. Then, when they finally get the nerve to unlock the doors—there is the massive bulk on the floor. Surely if you read Israel's stories with Israelite goggles you can't help but see the satire and humor.

3. The translation of the end of verse 22 and first of verse 23 is very difficult because of two very rare words. Both of the Hebrew words, however, have endings denoting a place. I see a kind of deliberate play by the writer: the dagger comes out the groin area; Ehud comes out the porch area! But we cannot be certain.

4. A euphemism for using the restroom (just as "restroom" is also a euphemism).

The way the Israelites told or heard this episode shows they weren't the least bit embarrassed about it. Instead Israel enjoyed telling about it—so much so that when the writer relates it to us, he writes it in the form of humor (or with flashes of it). And what is this meant to teach us? This— (1) that it is a very perilous matter to oppress and crush God's people (even if you're a big man like Eglon), for you may well become the butt of one of God's "jokes"; (2) that God makes his people able to laugh again after their sorrow and to smile over the funny ways he has of delivering them from their troubles; (3) that there is no reason why God's way must be dull and boring. The people who know Yahweh as their God will never lack for excitement. (In fact, the humorous way the story is told is Israel's way of rejoicing in the undeserved grace of Yahweh; the narrative itself is a form of praise to Yahweh.)

But—let us return to our imaginary objector over here, who still feels this humor is gross and that this narrative sullies the pretty white paper of his Bible, who sees no practical use in this and is especially upset that God should have some role in it. Yet that is precisely why Israel relishes and rejoices in it: because her God and our God is not a God who stands off by himself in the chaos of our times. Isn't it true that for some readers life right now is like those wild, uncontrollable, rampaging days of the judges? Don't some of God's people today have to confess that life seems to have gone haywire, perhaps due to their own folly and sin and stupidity? Is Yahweh in touch with times like that? Does he bring his help near his people then?

Every father probably fears it—being left alone with his baby son or daughter for the first time. I had watched my wife—even helped—change our baby boy's dirty diapers. What would happen when some day I was keeping him by myself and he dirtied his diaper? We used paper, throwaway diapers only on special occasions like trips; for home, cloth diapers. The soiled diaper would be thrown into the bathroom stool, repeatedly dunked, rinsed, wrung out, and thrown into the diaper pail to await definitive cleansing. It was the dipping and rinsing that I feared. Could I bring myself to do that? Could I stoop to that level? (Strangely enough, necessity overcomes hesitancy.)

And that is the glory of this passage: it tells us that Yahweh deals with the dirty, mixed-up affairs of life in which his people find themselves. Here we are—some in family situations we have messed up; some in emotional trauma; some in grief and sorrow or in the clutches of temptation. Life seems to be a mass of twisted coathangers and disconnected doorknobs. And the glory of this text is that it tells us that Yahweh is not a white-gloved, standoffish God out somewhere in the remote left field of the universe who hesitates to get his strong right arm dirty in the yuck of our lives. The God of the Bible does not hold back in the wild blue yonder somewhere waiting for you to pour Clorox and spray Lysol over the affairs of your life before he will touch it. Whether you can comfortably put it together or not, he is the God who delights to deliver his people even in their messes and likes to make them laugh again; he is the God who allows weeping to endure for a night but sees that joy comes in the morning.

The Tragedy of the Story

For all this, we must nevertheless observe the tragedy of the story, why it's sad. To be sure, Ehud escaped, called out his troops, controlled the crossing-places on the Jordan (and so shut off a homeward escape for Moabite troops), and defeated Moab's finest troops (vv. 26–30a). But the story is sad in the long run, since "the sons of Israel again did evil in the eyes of Yahweh when Ehud had died" (4:1; a sort of refrain throughout Judges; see 3:12, 10:6, 13:1; whether, strictly speaking, the Hebrew means "to do evil again" or "continued to do evil" makes no difference here).

Ehud, sorry to say, is not a totally adequate savior, for though Yahweh brings a certain kind of salvation and help through Ehud, nothing Ehud did could change the hearts of Israel. He may have exerted some beneficial influence on them while he lived (4:1, cf. 2:17, 19), but he could not release Israel from the bondage of sin or rip the idols out of their hearts. Here is the tragedy of the people of God—slavery to sin ("again did evil")—and no left-handed savior spilling the guts of foreign kings can release you from that bondage. Helplessness indeed. As noted before, it is what the apostle called being "under sin" (Rom. 3:9). Note: not sins but sin. Sin is not merely, or primarily, act but power. Being "under sin" is to be held in its clutches, bound by its chain (see the exposition of 2:19).

When my father was teaching me to ride a two-wheel bike, he would have me get on the bike while he held it, then give me a run-along shove until I was going and keeping my balance; then I rode until I crashed. I had one difficulty. I could not make turns. I could not turn the handlebars. Knowledge was not the problem; I knew what I had to do to turn. But I could not do it. One Wednesday evening my father wanted to start me off in our driveway, which was perpendicular to the highway that ran through town. I protested, since I feared I could not turn at the end of the drive and go down the sidewalk. I wanted to get my start on the sidewalk. But with that canny ability parents sometimes have to remain oblivious to their child's fears, Pop gave me my start and off I rode. Past the big pine tree, past the turn to the sidewalk, down the end of the driveway, straight into the back fender of a '51 Plymouth that was breezing into town. Again, I was well aware of what I had to do. I needed to turn the handlebars to the right and go down the sidewalk. But I could not do it. I was in bondage. I was helpless to do even what I knew I had to do. Irrational perhaps; but nonetheless real. Such, too, is the bondage of sin.

Now some church member may say: "Yes, yes; but remember, we are not a bunch of primitive Israelite idol worshipers; we are the people of God." And so was Israel. All of them circumcised, card-carrying Israelites, and in utter bondage to sin. And one may be a baptized, catechized, organized Presbyterian—yet a slave of sin. The same goes for Baptists, Methodists, whomever. That's why it is such good news to hear of "him who loves us and has set us free from our sins at the cost of his blood" (Rev. 1:5). For our real bondage does not consist of Moabites or fat kings or physical and economic oppression. No left-handed savior can break us free from our tyrant. But there is One with nail-scarred hands who can and does. The only tragedy in our story will be if, having this Savior, we do not "cry to him for help," for Yahweh has raised up for us a Savior, Jesus, who shall save *his people* from their sins.

5

A Salvation Break
(3:31)

This note about Shamgar is almost like one of those newsbreaks sandwiched between regular programming on radio or television. The writer slips him in between Ehud and Deborah in the briefest sort of way. Yet "he too saved Israel." So, if anything, we have a salvation break.

Though scholars have recently lavished some attention on Shamgar, his name is hardly a household word among Christians. (Well, who would know about you if your life were reduced to one sentence?) Shamgar has been passed over in the church year and hence doomed to oblivion. After all, who ever heard of a Saint Shamgar and All Angels' Day? Now you know we shan't be long with Shamgar for we've but one verse on him (though note Judg. 5:6). But where have you ever seen a book in which Shamgar was given a whole chapter? All by himself? Without being consigned to a footnote amidst all the furor over Ehud? This book then seeks to redress this injustice by including this chapter about Shamgar—and for Shamgar!

Shamgar has taken some vengeance upon the scholarly fraternity, for he has left us with unanswered questions. Was Shamgar an Israelite or not? His name seems to be non-Israelite; some say Hurrian, as it appears as a name in the Nuzi texts. Does "son of Anath" mean "son (worshiper?) of the Canaanite goddess Anath" or merely a resident of Beth-anath in Galilee (Josh. 1938; Judg. 1:33), or should we think of a Beth-anath down in Judah (cf. Josh. 15:59; more likely he would meet with Philistines if we place him there)? Did Shamgar knock off these Philistines single-handedly or as the leader of the farmers' militia? Should Shamgar be regarded as a kosher judge or not?[1] Shamgar was probably not an Israelite. That is about all we can know of his roots.[2]

We can be a bit more sure of his ox-goad. Like its later analogues, such an instrument might be eight feet long and up to six inches in circumference at the larger end. The smaller end was armed with a sharp prick for driving the oxen, the other end with a small spade or iron paddle for cleaning out the plow.[3] That would make quite a bayonet. And who would get up after catching the six-inch end in the jaw or solar plexus?

God's instruments of deliverance seem to have an interesting if odd collection of tools. Shamgar's ox-goad joins Ehud's dagger (3:16), Jael's hammer (4:21), Gideon's horns and torches (7:16), the woman's millstone (9:53), and Samson's jawbone (not his but a donkey's; 15:15). God's deliverances have plenty of color and interest.

However, the literal bottom line of chapter 3 is the bottom line: "He too saved Israel." So what if Shamgar was not an Israelite? What if he had Canaanite connections? What if we never dig up a biography of Shamgar? What if we never know

1. On Shamgar, see, among others, F. F. Bruce, "Shamgar," *IBD,* 3:1427–28; Robert G. Boling, *Judges,* The Anchor Bible (Garden City, N.Y.: Doubleday, 1975), 89–90; C. F. Kraft, "Shamgar," *IDB,* 4:306–7. On whether Shamgar's exploit was single-handed or as the head of some contingent, see Robert Jamieson (*A Commentary Critical, Experimental and Practical on the Old and New Testaments,* in vol. 2, *Joshua-Esther* [1868; reprint ed., Grand Rapids: Eerdmans, 1945], 78) for the former and George Bush (*Notes, Critical and Practical, on the Book of Judges* [Chicago: Henry A. Sumner, 1881], 42) for the latter.

2. We should not think that Shamgar was obscure in his own time just because we know little about him. R. K. Harrison is probably right: "From a later allusion to this hero (Judg. 5:6) it appears that his doings were evidently of such repute that events in his day were dated by reference to him, a situation that must surely have constituted the supreme accolade in antiquity. Yet despite the fact that Shamgar became a legend in his own time, the traditions surrounding his name have been reduced to a minimum by the compiler of Judges, for reasons that are not readily apparent" (*Introduction to the Old Testament* [Grand Rapids: Eerdmans, 1969], 689).

3. See Bush, *Notes,* 41, citing Maundrell.

anything about him? Do we not see here the very glory of
Israel's God? If Yahweh be the maker of heaven and earth, if
he has all resources in his hand, then can he not deliver his
people not only by many or by few (1 Sam. 14:6) but also by
disciples or by pagans? If Yahweh raises up Shamgar as a
savior for Israel, surely Cyrus should come as no surprise (Isa.
45:1–7). And it is particularly the glory of God to save by
instruments unknown or scarcely known to us. As the former
blind man exclaimed: "Now that is remarkable! You don't
know where he comes from, yet he opened my eyes" (John
9:30). We don't know anything about Shamgar and yet he
saved God's people. There is something marvelous about a God
like that, something that compels us to bow down before the
One who uses Shamgars and ox-goads.[4]

---

4. Matthew Henry nicely summed up the import of the Shamgar note: "See
here, (1.) That God can make those eminently serviceable to his glory and his
church's good whose extraction, education, and employment, are very mean
and obscure. He that has the residue of the Spirit could, when he pleased,
make ploughmen judges and generals, and fishermen apostles. (2.) It is no
matter how weak the weapon is if God direct and strengthen the arm. An ox-
goad, when God pleases, shall do more than Goliath's sword. And sometimes
he chooses to work by such unlikely means, that the excellency of the power
may appear to be of God" (*Commentary on the Whole Bible,* 6 vols. [New York:
Revell, n.d.], 2:138).

6

A Smashing Salvation
(4)

The Manner of the Story

People have their distinctive ways of telling their stories, whether they are aware of them or not. I recall my mother's manner of telling a story. When she would relate some amusing anecdote, she might introduce a particular person into her narrative. Most persons are related to somebody; so Mom would explain the network of relationships in which this person stood, sometimes explaining networks of relationships in which persons related to this person stood. The story would advance—but not far. Then, perhaps, she might refer to a place. This place also had to be explained; Mom would tell how she happened to be there, perhaps what year it was, and what chronological position this place held in respect to other places in the time line of my parents' lives. The story would creep forward. And so it would go. Almost every possible tangent was explored, explained, and exhausted. Somehow the journey tended to take the punch out of the punch line! (I am not being disrespectful to my mother's memory—this was simply the way she told stories.)

Biblical writers too have storytelling techniques, and we will appreciate and profit more from their narratives if we notice them. Judges 4 is no exception to this rule.

Unlike my mother, who relished expansion, our writer imposes a strict economy on his story. He omits all nonessential information (even though we may be curious). After Barak is briefly mentioned, Deborah announces her charge to him (vv. 6–7). Not much about Barak; no details about his journey to Deborah's palm; no greetings exchanged; no hint of whether he had taken ROTC in college.[1] Later we read that "Jael went out to meet Sisera" (v. 18). John Stek observes:

> No details are given about Sisera's flight, the course taken, the difficulties encountered, the time required, the fear that drove the fugitive on and the fatigue that slowed his pace, the hopes and expectations he entertained, or the plans he devised along the way for gaining Heber's protection. Because the outcome is affected by none of these they are passed over.[2]

Nor does our writer interweave or append any moral commentary on the action of Jael in verses 17–22. Our ethical bones may cry out for some hint, but the writer includes no overt judgment—neither rationalization, condemnation, nor exoneration. Perhaps our textbook moral questions are not the central concern. The "economics" of a biblical writer, that is, what he omits or ignores or, sometimes, condenses, will frequently disclose what he does *not* think important.

The Shape of the Story

We should note the shape as well as the manner of a biblical story.[3] Sometimes literary structure will give clues which aid proper interpretation:[4]

1. See the analysis in Jacob Licht, *Storytelling in the Bible* (Jerusalem: Magnes, 1978), 99–102.

2. John Stek, "The Bee and the Mountain Goat: A Literary Reading of Judges 4," in *A Tribute to Gleason Archer,* ed. Walter C. Kaiser, Jr., and Ronald F. Youngblood (Chicago: Moody, 1986), 71.

3. Another literary feature of Judges 4 is vocabulary pairing. Yahweh "sold" (*makar*) Israel into Jabin's power and will "sell" Sisera into a woman's hands (vv. 2, 9); Barak is to "draw out" (*mashak*) his troops on Mount Tabor, while Yahweh will "draw" Sisera and his army to the Wadi Kishon (vv. 6, 7); Yahweh will "give" (*natan*) Sisera and his troops into Barak's hands (vv. 7, 14); Barak "called out/up" (*za 'aq*) his troops, as did Sisera (vv. 10, 13); both Barak and Sisera "went down" *(yarad)* either to attack or to flee (vv. 14, 15); Jael "went out" *(yatsa')* to meet Sisera and Barak (vv. 18, 22). For additional verbal tie-ins, see Stek, "The Bee and the Mountain Goat," 66–67, 69, 74–75. The writer of Judges 4 was a first-rate wordsmith.

4. A warning: this structure makes chapter 4 look neater than it is. For example, verse 15a carries heavy theological freight and deserves to stand out more. Nevertheless, I believe this layout faithfully reflects the overall structure of chapter 4.

The sons of Israel (oppressed), 1–3
  Deborah, the prophetess, 4–9
    Barak and Sisera "call out" (*za 'aq*), 10–12/13
      Yahweh the Warrior, 14a
    Barak and Sisera "go down" (*yarad*), 14b/15–16
  Jael, wife of Heber, 17–22
Jabin, king of Canaan (subdued), 23–24

I would add the following notes on this structure: (1) The "sons of Israel" are mentioned three times in the first section; similarly, "Jabin, king of Canaan" is mentioned three times in the last section; (2) the second and sixth sections, the longest segments, pair the two women, Deborah and Jael; (3) the two captains, Barak and Sisera, carry out similar activities in sections three and five; (4) the command of Deborah in verse 14a becomes the hinge or focal point of the chapter; and (5) there is doubtless a pun in section seven, verses 23–24, when "Jabin, king of Canaan" *(kena 'an)* is now "subdued" *(kana')*.

We will briefly allude to this structure later. The structure itself, however, has something important to say; it shows us that the biblical writer was anything but sloppy in the way he wrote his story. He has carefully thought out how he wanted to tell his story; it is a piece of literary art. I include this because I want readers to appreciate the story. Now, let us look at the map; then we can hear the teaching.

The Places of the Story

The main action takes place in the north, and the writer provides a verbal map: Jabin operates out of Hazor (v. 2), ten miles northwest of the Sea of Galilee; Sisera lives in Harosheth-ha-goiim (v. 2), wherever that was—certainly in the area of Galilee or near the Plain of Esdraelon;[5] Barak hails from Kedesh-Naphtali (v. 6), which could mean the Kedesh twelve

---

5. Bible maps frequently locate Harosheth-ha-goiim at Tell 'Amr, near the base of the Carmel range in the northwest corner of the Plain of Esdraelon. But no one really knows. Yohanan Aharoni argues that it is not a place name but refers to the forested (*harosheth* = woodland) regions of Galilee (*The Land of the Bible: A Historical Geography,* rev. and enl. [Philadelphia: Westminster, 1979], 221–22); but cf. W. S. LaSor, "Harosheth-hagoiim," *ISBE* (rev. ed.), 2:618.

miles north of Hazor, although Yohanan Aharoni's suggestion
that it is Khirbet Qedish on the slopes southwest of the Sea of
Galilee makes good sense.[6] Nor must we neglect field, stream,
and hill. The battlefield in general was the Plain of Esdraelon,
a triangular plain southwest of the Sea of Galilee,[7] drained by
the unpretentious Wadi Kishon, and guarded at its northeast
apex by Mount Tabor (located ten miles southwest of the Sea
of Galilee). Enough geography for now; we hasten to the
teaching.

The Teaching of the Story

The Need for Salvation

Judges 4 is also a story of salvation, and verses 1–3 underscore the need for salvation: "The sons of Israel again did what
was evil in Yahweh's eyes." So Yahweh "sold" them to another
master, Jabin, and Jabin assigned them to his taskmaster,
Sisera, who, with his force of nine hundred iron-plated chariots, controlled (i.e., crushed) Israel very efficiently. Israel is,
again, in need of both physical deliverance (from Jabin and
Sisera) and spiritual deliverance (the bondage-to-sin theme).

Note this cycle of sinning: "again did what was evil" (=
Baal worship; see 2:11). It tells us something about sin. It is
difficult to be creative in sin; there's a certain monotony about
it; most all of it has been done before; it is simply that we
do the same thing again (v. 1). Sin is a boring routine, not a
fresh excitement. The fast lane becomes an old rut. Evil never
lends itself to originality. Hence there are two problems: the
slavery and the staleness of sin.

These verses allude to the pressurized piety of Israel. "Now
Ehud had died" (v. 1)—it was then Israel "again did what was

6. Aharoni, *The Land of the Bible*, 223–24.
7. The south/southwest base of Esdraelon's triangle runs for twenty miles
from Jokneam to Ibleam; the other two sides are equal, about fifteen miles
each, from Jokneam to near Mount Tabor and from Mount Tabor down to
Ibleam. Neither prose nor maps are much help; for Esdraelon, seeing is believing. I still remember the views from atop Megiddo and from the Nazareth
ridge. See Kenneth A. Kitchen, "Esdraelon," *IBD*, 1:476–77; and George Adam
Smith, *The Historical Geography of the Holy Land*, 22d ed. (London: Hodder
and Stoughton, n.d.), 379–91.

evil." This is a sample of what 2:19 was talking about. Take away the external restraint and Israel displays her true character. There is something wrong with religion when its degree of fidelity depends solely on outside pressures, influences, and leadership. Then we are "Christian" only because of our surroundings, or because of the expectations of Christian people around us, and lack a genuine, internal work of God.

My Latin II teacher in high school seemed to feel little urgency for teaching Latin, and class time could be whiled away in various and sundry discussions. But on one sleepy Wednesday—or whatever day it was—Mr. E. happened to step out of the room and look up the hall. At slightly less than the speed of light he darted back into the room, ordered all students to break out their Latin II books, and began expounding with evangelistic fervor a verb paradigm in the back of our book. With earnest pedagogical passion we heard him plead, "Now do you understand this, class?" Why his sudden interest in teaching Latin in Latin II class? Why, as he himself admitted, he saw Mr. M., the superintendent of schools, making his way down the hall! Pressure makes us such earnest folks.

But take away whatever influence Ehud must have exerted, and Israel shows her real colors again. That's why genuine salvation consists not of giving glowing testimonies (like deliverance from Moab, chap. 3?) but in departing from evil (2 Tim. 2:19), not in relating glorious experiences with God but in living a consistent life (1 John 2:3–5; 3:9 NIV).

The Source of Salvation

Throughout the story one finds great emphasis on the source of salvation. Deborah clearly states this in her call to Barak in verses 6–7:

> Has not Yahweh the God of Israel commanded, "Go, you shall draw out (your men)[8] on Mount Tabor, and you shall take with you ten thousand men from the sons of Naphtali and Zebulun, and I shall draw out to you, to the Wadi Kishon, Sisera, captain

8. My translation tries to retain the play on the two uses of the verb *mashak*: Barak is to draw out on Mount Tabor and Yahweh will draw out Sisera to the Kishon and to his own demise.

of Jabin's army, along with his chariots and his army, and I shall give him into your hand"?

When Deborah orders the attack, she assures Barak that "Yahweh has given Sisera into your hand; has not Yahweh gone out before you?" (v. 14). The writer himself ascribes the decisive action to Yahweh, both in verse 15 ("Yahweh threw into a panic" Sisera and Company) and in verse 23 ("So on that day God subdued Jabin king of Canaan"). "This is Yahweh's doing, / and we marvel at it" (Ps. 118:23 NJB).

We would do well to look at verse 14 again, in order to see how the saving God is described. Deborah's words in verse 14a may well be the hinge of the chapter (see the comments on structure earlier in this chapter). Note she assures Barak with a rhetorical question: "Has not *Yahweh* [emphatic] gone out before you?" She is depicting Yahweh as the warrior who fights for his people. I point out the vigor and virility of this imagery, for it is rather foreign to the contemporary church.

While Teddy Roosevelt was a student at Harvard, he taught a Sunday school class. One day a boy came to class with a black eye, admitting he had been in a fight. On Sunday no less. A bigger boy had been pinching his sister, the lad said, and he got into a fist fight with him. Teddy said, "You did perfectly right," and gave him a dollar. The vestrymen thought this was going too far and released TR from his Sunday school duties.[9]

That episode is symptomatic: there is almost an unwritten cultural law that religion and theology—and God—should always be gentle, soft, and nice. Strange then that the God of the Bible is the warrior. The Strength of Israel is not the soft, wimpy graven image of current western imagination. The only real hope of God's afflicted people is in a strong Lord who "in righteousness judges and makes war" (Rev. 19:11).

Though Yahweh is clearly the source of salvation, he frequently uses means to bring it about. Do we have any light on how Yahweh defeated Sisera? Why did Sisera abandon his chariot and hoof it from the battle (v. 15)? We have a clue when verse 15 says, "Yahweh threw [them] into a panic," for

9. Paul F. Boller, Jr., *Presidential Anecdotes* (New York: Penguin, 1982), 201.

the verb *hamam* sometimes describes situations in which God brings a thunderstorm (Josh. 10:10–11; 1 Sam. 7:10; Pss. 18:14; 144:6).[10] That's why the Wadi Kishon (vv. 7, 13) is so significant. We can see the matter more clearly if we cheat and run to chapter 5 for a moment, for it indicates that there was a rainstorm (5:4, 20)[11] and that the Kishon swelled, overflowed, and flooded the area (5:21), so that Sisera's chariots became mired in the muck and mud.[12] Hence all Sisera's tactical advantage went down the drain as Barak's infantry charged down from Mount Tabor.

Knowing how the Lord delivered his people does not diminish in the least the fact that it was the Lord who delivered them. If anything, we marvel all the more as we ponder the precise timing of God in making the clouds his chariot (Ps. 104:3).

Again, though Yahweh is the source of salvation, he frequently uses human instruments to bring his saving help— but in such a way that the instrument reveals rather than obscures Yahweh as the giver of salvation. Deborah teaches this in verse 9 when she discloses to Barak that "it will not turn out for your glory on the road you are going, for it will be into the hand of a woman that Yahweh will sell Sisera."[13]

10. See Stek, "The Bee and the Mountain Goat," 68.

11. On 5:20, see John Gray: "The reference is to a rainstorm, the stars being a source of rain in the Ras Shamra myths" (*Joshua, Judges and Ruth,* The Century Bible—New Edition [Greenwood, S.C.: Attic, 1967], 289). The Ras Shamra evidence, however, may not be as clear as Gray alleges; see the cautions of Peter C. Craigie, "Three Ugaritic Notes on the Song of Deborah," *JSOT* (April 1977): 33–37.

12. "During the Great War [World War I] experience showed that a quarter of an hour's rain on this clay soil [Esdraelon] endangered the issue of all cavalry manoeuvres" (John Garstang, *Joshua-Judges* [1931; reprint ed., Grand Rapids: Kregel, 1978], 299).

13. One should note the use of the verb *sell* (*makar*) in both verses 2 and 9; if Yahweh sells faithless Israel into the hand of Jabin, he can also sell Sisera into the hand of a woman. Incidentally, we should be cautious about seeing verse 9 as a rebuke for Barak's lack of faith in verse 8, and we should be cautious about seeing verse 8 as Barak's lack of faith. In verse 8 Barak may only be acknowledging the fact that he is but an instrument and that in this venture he will surely need God's clear direction through his servant Deborah (see Karl Gutbrod, *Das Buch vom Lande Gottes,* Die Botschaft des Alten Testaments, 3d ed. [Stuttgart: Calwer, 1965], 202). Many expositors may owe Barak an apology!

"Into the hand of a woman" is in emphatic position in the Hebrew text.

This prophecy of verse 9 is given beforehand. Hence no one could say, "It just happened to turn out that way." No, before the event, Yahweh through Deborah clearly declares that Sisera will meet his end by means of a most unusual agent (though the woman is unnamed). So then, when it occurs, there can be no doubt that it is God's doing. Moreover, the normal expectation would be that Barak (or perhaps some other outstanding warrior) would bag Sisera as his prize (cf. vv. 9a, 22). That Sisera will fall by a woman's hand shatters our human conventions and breaks all the commandments about the way things should happen (and, had he known, would have embarrassed the life out of Sisera, for nothing was more mortifying than having a woman administer the coup de grace to a warrior; cf. 9:53–54). By this unexpected and strange twist, Yahweh leaves his mark upon the occasion and testifies that what we have here is not any run-of-the-mill (human) situation.

When I was quite young, we used to watch "The Lone Ranger" on television every Saturday afternoon at one o'clock. We reveled, of course, in his bringing justice and right by outmaneuvering crooks, beating up robbers, or winning gun fights with rustlers. At the end of the day's episode the Lone Ranger (Clayton Moore with a mask) would be riding away on his white horse, Silver, while in the foreground two men conversed. One said: "Who was that masked man anyway?" To which the other replied (right before the Lone Ranger's hearty "Hi yo, Silver, away!" and the score from the William Tell Overture), pointing to the vanishing hero, "Why, that's the Lone Ranger!" At which point he would produce for his friend's perusal a silver bullet which the Lone Ranger had given him. It's all quaint and hilarious as some of us recall those Saturdays. But, according to the show, the silver bullet was the token of the Lone Ranger's presence, the mark that he had been there. Perhaps the analogy can help us appreciate Judges 4:9; when Sisera is dispatched by—of all people—a woman, that will be a clear token that Yahweh has been at work.

As he displays his glory in delivering his people, God takes pains to keep anyone from obscuring that glory. No warrior in Israel must place the Warrior of Israel in the shadows. Perhaps for personal application we could take over Deborah's words to Barak: "The road on which you are going will not lead to your glory" (v. 9 RSV). That is a necessary reminder for us—it is *Yahweh* who brings victory and we should not care which human instrument seems to shine the most therein. This word may touch some of us pastors, who, quite naturally, and perhaps idolatrously, want to have "successful" churches.

The Minutiae of Salvation

Thirdly, let us look at the minutiae of salvation in verse 11: "Now Heber the Kenite separated himself from the Kenites, from the sons of Hobab, the father-in-law of Moses, and pitched his tent as far as the oak in Za-anannim, which is near Kadesh."

Who on earth cares about that? So some unknown metal-worker pulls up stakes and moves north. So what? Neither the *Jerusalem Gazette* nor the *Hazor Herald* thought the item newsworthy. Here is a mere puny detail, a dry insertion into an otherwise interesting story.

Yet verse 11, dry as it seems, points to the providence of God. According to 1:16, the Kenites settled in the south of Judah's southern territory (near Arad). Heber separated from this group and moved north to Kedesh (like moving from Florida to Vermont, only not so far). Certainly, it appears to be nothing but a piece of geographical trivia to have Heber's change of address inserted into the story. Nevertheless, we will soon discover that Jael, the woman who nailed Sisera, was Heber's wife and that she was precisely where she needed to be when Israel's oppressor ditched his chariot and ran for his life.

The God of the Bible still injects those marvelous bits of providential minutiae into the lives of his people. In what a wonderful manner God prepares for our deliverance! Many Christians can see this as they look back and reflect on God's ways with them. There has been some little piece of divine trivia, something that seemed at the time wholly unrelated to anything, something that even escaped human notice because it was so minuscule—yet it turned out to be the vehicle of God's saving help. Not even Heber's U-Haul was outside Yahweh's plan; and a God like that surely ought to be adored.

The Problem of Salvation

Lastly, let us consider the problem of salvation in verses 17–22. Salvation a problem? Yes, for some people who read this narrative.

Some folks are bothered that the saving of Israel comes through the treachery of Jael (vv. 18–19). Sisera came into Heber's camp because a treaty bound Jabin and Heber. Therefore Sisera expected asylum here, and Jael's demeanor—invitation, solicitude, provision (vv. 18–19)—confirmed his expectations. He never knew otherwise, for, while his exhaustion plunged him into deep sleep, "Jael, the wife of Heber, took the tent peg, gripped the hammer, approached him quietly, and struck the peg into his temple, then drove it into the ground" (v. 21).[14] "So he died," obviously. Literally, a smashing salvation!

But some are loath to own it. Alas!, someone says, would that Jael could have read Charles Sheldon's book *In His Steps,* and then as she was slithering up to Sisera she would have stopped to think, "What would Jesus do?" However, Jael was born too soon to enjoy such light. Someone else claims we can still save the taint on the Scriptures here: You see, Jael's hammer points beyond itself; remember Jeremiah 23:29; Jael's hammer is the "hammer" of the word of God that brings defeat to all our sleeping tyrants. (This is the same approach that sees Ehud's dagger as the "sword of the Spirit"; see the commentary on 3:12–30.) Sorry, we can have no figurative hammers here.

Sometimes these dilemmas can be solved by remembering that we must distinguish between what the Bible reports and what it recommends, between what the Bible says and what the Bible supports. For example, the Bible may report that David had multiple wives (2 Sam. 3:2–5), but it does not thereby recommend or authorize you to do likewise. Hence, in

14. Gray (*Joshua, Judges and Ruth,* 274) points out that "among modern Bedouin pitching the tent and striking camp is women's work, so that Jael would not be awkward with the hammer."

Jael's case, it could be that the Bible does not specifically approve of Jael's act.

The problem is that the Bible *does* seem to approve Jael's act. If we castigate Jael's blow we shall have to censor Deborah's song as well, for Deborah commends Jael (5:24–27) and condemns the town of Meroz (5:23) for doing nothing. This estimate does not seem to be merely Deborah's private opinion, for Meroz is cursed by the authority of (no less than) the Angel of Yahweh.

Of course, I could be missing something, but it seems to me that the Bible itself is pro-Jael. Frankly, that does not bother me at all. Sisera, who "severely oppressed" (4:3) Israel and probably enjoyed raping captive Israelite girls (5:30), was not exactly Mr. Clean. Nor should this narrative bother you. But if it does, put the problem on the back burner for a while, for the story does not intend to raise a moral problem but to rehearse Yahweh's salvation. Perhaps we can't eliminate all the problems, but that shouldn't keep us from rejoicing in a God who lifts us out of the mud and mire, sets our feet on a rock, and puts a new song in our mouths (cf. Ps. 40:2–3). Let God worry about the mud and the mire; let us sing the new song!

7

The New Song
(5)

The Washington Redskins have just won football's Super Bowl. Today—three days after their victory—is the victory celebration in Washington, D.C. School children and government workers are granted a two-hour reprieve in order to join in the public adulation. That won't be the case, unfortunately, in Eau Claire, Wisconsin, or in Ardmore, Oklahoma, or in most all other communities. But Washington had a victory, and so there is this celebration.

Judges 5 is a victory celebration, not over athletic trivia but for divine deliverance. Deborah sings a new song to celebrate a fresh deliverance; here Israel revels in Yahweh's triumph over Sisera and his hordes.

Judges 5 presents a temptation to the interpreter. A comparison of any two English translations shows many differences in the translating and understanding of this ancient poetry. One is tempted, therefore, to be thorough, that is, discuss, explain, amplify, and (occasionally) resolve the problems in vocabulary, grammar, and rendering of the text. One might mix in a few pages on Hebrew poetry. That might prove a double loss—losing reader interest and losing sight of Judges 5. Since others have dealt with more technical matters,[1] we will concentrate on hearing the essential witness of

1. See, among others, John Gray, *Joshua, Judges and Ruth,* The Century Bible—New Edition (Greenwood, S.C.: Attic, 1967), 275–94; cf. also Richard D.

Judges 5. It will be useful, however, to see the structure before we hear the witness:

Verses 2–11c
  Bless Yahweh for willing people, 2
  Telling the story, 3
    The liveliness of God, 4–5
    The extremity of Israel, 6–8
  Bless Yahweh for willing people, 9
  Telling the story, 10–11c
Verses 11d–23
  The people and its leadership:
    the people "go down" (yarad), 11d–13
    The valiant ones, 14–15a
      The hesitant and secure, 15b–17
    The valiant ones, 18
  The kings and their battle:
    the kings "fight" (lacham), 19–23
Verses 24–30
  Blessing for the wife of Heber, 24–27
  Scorn for the mother of Sisera, 28–30
Verse 31
  Theological application

Observe that each of the three major sections centers around a basic contrast: in verses 2–11c, the explosive God and humiliated people; in verses 11d–23, daring warriors and cautious brothers; in verses 24–30, gutsy woman and poor mommy. In spite of the numerous problems Deborah's song poses, it does have this general pattern which can provide us a handle for gripping its main thrust.[2]

Patterson, "The Song of Deborah," in *Tradition and Testament: Essays in Honor of Charles Lee Feinberg,* ed. John S. Feinberg and Paul D. Feinberg (Chicago: Moody, 1981), 123–60; Alan J. Hauser, "Judges 5: Parataxis in Hebrew Poetry," *Journal of Biblical Literature* 99 (1980): 23–41; Alexander Globe, "The Literary Structure and Unity of the Song of Deborah," *Journal of Biblical Literature* 93 (1974): 493–512; idem, "The Muster of the Tribes in Judges 5:11e–18," *Zeitschrift für die alttestamentliche Wissenschaft* 87 (1975): 169–79.

  2. I have included verse 23 with verses 19–22 in my structural outline.

The Coming of Yahweh

First, Deborah gives us a lively view of the coming of Yahweh (vv. 4–5; cf. Deut. 33:2–5; Ps. 68:7–10; Hab. 3:3–4):

> Yahweh, when you went forth from Seir,
> when you marched out from the land of Edom,
> the earth trembled;
> yes, the skies dropped,
> yes, the clouds dropped water;
> the mountains shook
> > before Yahweh, the One of Sinai,
> > before Yahweh, the God of Israel.

It is difficult to know whether Yahweh's going forth from Seir and marching from Edom refer to his contemporary coming to the conflict with Sisera or whether the reference is to his ancient coming to his people in Egypt and his meeting with them at Sinai. In any case, there is a clear hint of Yahweh's delivering Israel from Egypt and preserving them in the desert when Deborah refers to Yahweh as "the One of Sinai." There, at Sinai, Yahweh had taken Israel as his own (Exod. 19); there he came and met with them; there he had placed them under his law of liberty. But Yahweh—and this is Deborah's point— is not stuck at Sinai. Rather, the God who decisively came to Israel at Sinai comes again and again to the aid of his people in their present troubles. The God who delivered them at the Sea of Reeds (Exod. 14) can rescue at the waters of Megiddo (Judg. 5:19); the God who came to Mount Sinai (Exod. 19–24) comes to Mount Tabor as well (Judg. 4:14–15). Yahweh is not set in historical concrete at Sinai; rather the One of Sinai is mobile, marching forth again and again to rescue his flock. And when he does, creation comes unglued! Earth trembles, clouds pour rain (perhaps an allusion to the rainstorm sent against Sisera), mountains shake. See Psalm 18:7–19 in context for another sample of this explosive God.

Verses 19–22 correspond to verses 11d–13, and if verse 23 is included with the former, then both sections end with *baggibborim* ("against the mighty/ warriors," or "as warriors"; translations will vary). We cannot fail, however, to see a contrast between cursed Meroz (v. 23) and blessed Jael (vv. 24–27) in the following section.

Our poem sets the hopeless plight of Israel beside this lively view of Yahweh:

> In the days of Shamgar son of Anath,
> in the days of Jael,
> caravans ceased,
> and travelers were traveling back roads;
> warriors ceased,
> in Israel they ceased,
> until you rose up, Deborah,
> until you rose up a mother in Israel.
> They would choose new gods—
> then there was fighting at the gates.
> Indeed, neither shield nor spear was seen
>   among forty thousands in Israel. [vv. 6–8]

Times were so bad folks couldn't even travel safely—they had to take the back roads because thieves and thugs freeloaded on the main highways. Israel was totally defenseless, having neither warriors (v. 7a) nor weapons (v. 8b; cf. the later situation under the Philistines in 1 Sam. 13:5–7, 19–22). Sometimes it is only when God's people see how hopeless they are (the picture of vv. 6–8) that they can appreciate how mighty Yahweh is (the picture of vv. 4–5). Desperate people (vv. 6–8) and sufficient God (vv. 4–5) are placed side by side that the former might rest in the latter. The apostle makes the same point in 2 Corinthians 1:8–9. Surely God's afflicted people should derive great comfort from knowing that the God who came to Sinai (or Golgotha) is the God who comes repeatedly to his people in distress. Omnipotence delights in encores.

The People of Yahweh

In verses 11d–23 the whole focus is on the people of Yahweh. As the structure shows (see the first part of this chapter), the primary contrast appears in verses 14–18, with glimpses of those tribes who gambled their lives (vv. 14–15a, 18) surrounding the (apparent) scorn directed at tribes who played it safe (vv. 15b–17). Hence we hear high commendation:

From Ephraim (came those) whose roots are in Amalek.[3]
After you, O Benjamin,[4] with your clansmen!
From Machir commanders went down,
and from Zebulun those who muster the troops.
And my princes in Issachar with Deborah,
yes, Issachar—like Barak—was thrust into the valley
    at his heels.
Zebulun—a people who courted death
—and so did Naphtali—
on the heights of the field. [vv. 14–15a, 18]

Within such grateful admiration, however, we meet perplexed disappointment:

Among the divisions of Reuben,
    there were great resolutions of heart.
Why did you sit between the sheepfolds
    to listen to the pipings for the flocks?
For the divisions of Reuben
    there were great searchings of heart.
Gilead dwelt on the other side of the Jordan,
    and Dan—why did he sojourn with the ships?
Asher sat by the seashore
    and dwelt by his landing-places. [vv. 15b–17]

It wasn't that Reuben didn't think about coming to Tabor. No, the Reubenites discussed the matter thoroughly; they talked a lot about it. But it wasn't a good time to leave the sheep. Perhaps the Jordan was more of a barrier than east Manasseh (Gilead) even realized; in any case, they didn't cross it. Dan and Asher evidently were preoccupied with profitable maritime trade. "I have bought a field, and I must go out and see it; I pray you, have me excused" (Luke 14:18 RSV).

Then there was Meroz (v. 23). Israel heaped a bitter curse

---

3. Judges 12:15 suggests that Ephraim's territory was formerly occupied by a clan of Amalekites; see C. F. Keil, *Joshua, Judges, Ruth,* Biblical Commentary on the Old Testament (1868; reprint ed., Grand Rapids: Eerdmans, 1950), 317.

4. An ejaculatory war cry which also appears in Hosea 5:8 (where it is used ironically in the judgment context). The cry probably reflects Benjamin's acknowledged position of leadership in tribal combat. Cf. C. F. Burney, *The Book of Judges* (London: Rivingtons, 1918), 133–34.

rather than mere scorn on Meroz, because it/they did not come "to the help of Yahweh against the mighty ones." The Angel of Yahweh himself authorized the curse. No one knows where Meroz was located, though it must have been so near the battle scene that Israel had every right to expect aid from its militia.[5] But Meroz wanted to save its life—and lost it. Thankfully, some of Israel's tribes were willing to lose their lives—and saved them.

Note the theology of the text. Though Israel's deliverance is Yahweh's sovereign and mighty work, his people are not to sit passively by: they are to participate actively in his mighty work, to come "to the help of Yahweh against the mighty ones." It speaks ill of us when we are satisfied to rest secure while our brothers and sisters are struggling and suffering. It reveals a heart unbound by the bonds of brotherly love. It is tragic when any Christian—apostle or other—has to say, "No one came to my support, but everyone deserted me" (2 Tim. 4:16). Deborah is not only a mother in Israel (v. 7); she is an instructor to the church.

The Servant of Yahweh

Thirdly, we hear Deborah lauding the servant of Yahweh in verses 24–27 and mocking the mother of Sisera in verses 28–30. The whole section is a tale of two women, a study in contrast.[6]

The picture of Sisera's mother is simply dripping with holy sarcasm. Here she is, peering anxiously through the upstairs window, squinting into the distance, demanding in suppressed fear the reason for Sisera's delay. Why hadn't she heard the clatter of his chariot horses yet? Where is her boy?

5. I take Meroz to have been an Israelite village. Some think that it was a Canaanite village bound by treaty to one of Israel's tribes. In any case, Meroz should have helped but did not.

6. Robert Alter (*The Art of Biblical Poetry* [New York: Basic Books, 1985], 45) also draws attention to the "pointed contrast between the simple Kenite tent and the Canaanite palace, with its bevy of female attendants so interested in the material benefits of war."

The suave princesses who attend Sisera's mother[7] reassure her (indeed, Sisera's mother may have been telling herself the same): You know it takes time to divide up all the spoil; and they'll likely rape some girls;[8] and think of how many lovely additions to your wardrobe Sisera will be collecting! (Oddly enough, at that very moment Sisera was in a wardrobe, Jael's—dead.) Sisera's mother resumes her vigil by the window muttering, "Yes, of course, you're right."

The primary attention, however, goes not to the mother of the oppressor but to the servant of the Lord, Jael (vv. 24–27). Meroz is cursed but Jael is blessed, because she *did* come "to the help of Yahweh against the mighty ones" (v. 23). Most of this section is a detailed, slow-motion, blow-by-blow rehearsal of Sisera's Waterloo:

> He asked for water; she gave him milk;
> she offered him curds in a lordly dish.
> She reached her hand out to seize the peg,
> her right hand to seize the workman's mallet.
>
> She hammered Sisera, she crushed his head,
> she pierced his temple and shattered it.
> Between her feet, he crumpled, he fell, he lay;
> at her feet, he crumpled, he fell.
> Where he crumpled, there he fell, destroyed. [vv. 25–27 NJB]

Note how Deborah (and Israel) itemizes every particular of Sisera's demise (e.g., Jael's reaching for the tent peg and the mallet), heaps up vicious verbs (e.g., hammered) in relating Jael's blows, and replays the last scene "at her feet" where Sisera's writhing form remains. Remember, this is a song to Yahweh celebrating his saving help (v. 3). Here Israel is delighting in and relishing that salvation, the overthrow of the tyrant Sisera (4:3).

As I have grown older, I have developed my capacity for

7. Some (e.g., Gray) think these ladies constitute Sisera's harem over which his mother, as a kind of queen mother, had charge.

8. This is the probable inference from the second line of verse 30: literally, "a womb, two wombs, per warrior." I suppose such horror usually occurred after the military conflict had been decided and the victors began their marauding through helpless Israelite villages.

enjoying certain foods. For example, if I am eating jello or ice cream or pudding, I will take a bite and—instead of gobbling it down—will savor it. That is, I run it around my mouth, up around my teeth, down around my teeth, sometimes through my teeth, silently (?) sloshing the delicious stuff around my mouth, extracting the ultimate enjoyment from each spoonful. I do the same with coffee or ginger ale. Occasionally this drives my wife to the brink of sanity, but my philosophy properly defends my practice: food is not to be consumed (merely) but enjoyed. (In case you're wondering, I am not overweight!)

That is the way Israel views Yahweh's salvation. Yahweh's deliverance is meant to be enjoyed, savored, cherished; item by item, detail by detail, blow by blow; from dish to peg to mallet to skull to feet. Someone may think that is being vicious. It is not. It is being pious. Perhaps many of us in the west cannot rejoice when God smashes oppressors because we have never been so oppressed or crushed by tyranny on a significant scale (for which we should thank God). That's why we frequently fail to appreciate texts like this; we can't really understand them from our study chairs, from our padded pews, or from our recliners beside our cozy fireplaces. Nevertheless, Deborah clearly votes for Jael, "servant of the Lord." Naturally, you can disagree. If so, you can claim more refinement but less faith.

The Kingdom of Yahweh

The final note of Deborah's song speaks of the kingdom of Yahweh:

> May all your enemies perish that way, O Yahweh!
> But let those who love him be like the sun going forth in its strength. [v. 31]

Here we have both a prayer and a call. The first line is a prayer, "Thy kingdom come." The word (Hebrew, *kēn*) I have translated "that way" (or other translations, "so") indicates that Deborah and Israel saw Yahweh's overthrowing Sisera and Company as a foretaste, a preview, a scale model of what Yahweh will do when he finally conquers "all his and our enemies" (as the Westminster Shorter Catechism, question 26, would say). As Yahweh has caused Sisera and the Canaanites to perish, so may he cause *all* his enemies to perish. That is the prayer. That is what is involved when we pray, "Thy kingdom come," for there is no relief for Christ's people until their enemies are destroyed. This is the clear witness of 2 Thessalonians 1:5–10. To pray for God's kingdom to come means that, in part, we pray like this:

> Destroy the devil's work;
> destroy every force which revolts against you
> and every conspiracy against your Word.
> Do this until your kingdom is so complete and perfect
> that in it you are
> all in all. [Heidelberg Catechism, question 123]

Yahweh's overthrow of Jabin and Sisera is clear witness that the reign of Yahweh really is coming.

Yet this kingdom word is a call, a call to fickle Israel to love Yahweh and find strength in him: "But let those who love him [Yahweh] be like the sun going forth in its strength" (v. 31b). To love Yahweh was Israel's first covenant responsibility: "And you shall love Yahweh your God with all your heart, with your whole life, and with everything you have" (Deut. 6:5). Then Moses' next words spell out how Israel was to love Yahweh with such intensity: "And these words which I am commanding you today shall be upon your heart" (Deut. 6:6). Jesus would have said, "If you love me, keep my commandments" (John 14:15). And the first commandment for Israel was "no other gods." So when Deborah sings of "those who love Yahweh," Israel—the Israel of 3:7, 3:12, and 4:1, the Israel who thinks Baal and Asherah are such a fun-loving couple— should be pricked to the heart and ask herself, "Have I loved Yahweh? Will I love Yahweh? Must I not love Yahweh? For, if I do not, will I not then belong among his enemies and stand outside his kingdom?"

8

Getting Ready
for Salvation
(6)

I would like us to swallow Judges 6 at one gulp. The chapter opens with the same dreary notice of Israel's idolatry (v. 1; cf. 2:11). This time Yahweh's scourge is Midian. We have in verses 1–6 the most detailed description of Israel's distress so far. Dire distress it was. Whenever the Israelites would plant their crops, Midian (along with Amalekites and "sons of the east") would invade and "ruin the produce of the land" (v. 4), that is, probably pillage foodstuffs for themselves and allow their livestock to pasture on the rest. They appropriated Israel's sheep, oxen, and donkeys (the equivalent of stealing a mechanic's tools). All this was what covenant breakers could expect, says Deuteronomy 28:29, 31. For seven years they left Israel no "sustenance" (v. 4) or means of sustenance. The same scourge and terror every year: invade from the east, cross the Jordan, hit the bread basket in the Plain of Jezreel, sweep southwest as far as Gaza in Philistia, practicing their clean-earth policy.

Seven years of it. You are hungry, poor, and tired. Every year, as sure as income tax, Midian's buzzards come. You're tired of rushing your family, livestock (what is left of it), and grain (if salvaged) to the hills where you live a caveman existence till the foreign locusts get bored and move on to impoverish others. Wouldn't it be wonderful to throw your wheat up into the wind out on the threshing floor, as a free man should (v. 11)? "So Israel was brought very low on account of Midian, and the sons of Israel cried out to Yahweh" (v. 6).

The Word That Criticizes Us

Now we must hear the word that criticizes us (vv. 7–10). Here Yahweh does the strangest thing; in fact, it appears ludicrous. Israel cries for relief, "and Yahweh sent a prophet to the sons of Israel" (v. 8). That would be like a stranded motorist calling a garage for assistance and the garage sending a philosopher instead of a mechanic. Israel needs deliverance and Yahweh sends a prophet; Israel asks for an act of God's power and he sends them a proclaimer of his word who rehearses Yahweh's grace (vv. 8b–9), repeats Yahweh's demand (v. 10a), and levels Yahweh's accusation (v. 10b). Hence Yahweh sends a prophet because Israel needs more than immediate relief; they need to understand why they are oppressed. They must see that "Yahweh gave them into the hand of Midian" (v. 1) because they had "not listened to [his] voice" (v. 10b).

Surely God's way with his people has not changed. Do we sometimes marvel at the "inappropriate" answers God gives to our urgent need? Like Israel, we may want escape from our circumstances while God wants us to interpret our circumstances. Sometimes we may need understanding more than relief; sometimes God must give us insight before he dare grant safety. Understanding God's way of holiness is more important than absence of pain. We may want out of a bind, whereas God wants us to see our idolatry. God means to instruct us, not pacify us.

We should not miss the kindness of God in all this. One of the kindest things God does for us is to bring us under the criticism of his word to expose the reasons for our helplessness and misery. He does this by the preaching, counsel, or reading of his word.

I was once teaching a seminary class in Old Testament poetical books. Near the time for the final exam some students were agonizing over what and how to study for the exam since we had covered so much ground. The implication was that it would be cruel not to give them some guidance. So I concocted a study guide, consisting of some sixty-five questions, which covered the material in some detail. Then, of course, the problem was: such a vast amount of material to be studied! Was that also cruel? I think not. I think it was sheer professorial kindness. They knew exactly what to study and how much and how thoroughly. The amount of study may have brought pain, but the fact that they had utter clarity about their responsibility was most gracious of me, even if I do say so myself. So it is when God teaches us, when his word criticizes and corrects and imparts solid wisdom instead of instant deliverance.

The Grace That Holds Us

Secondly, we must see here the grace that holds us. There is something strange about the prophet's preaching in verses 8b–10. He didn't finish his sermon. Let us set down the content of his proclamation:

> *Introductory formula*
> Thus says Yahweh the God of Israel
> *Rehearsal of Yahweh's grace*
> I brought you up from Egypt,
> and I led you out from the house of slaves,
> and I delivered you
> from the hand of the Egyptians and
> from the hand of all your oppressors,
> and I drove them out from before you,
> and I gave you their land.
> *Reminder of Yahweh's stipulation*
> And I said to you,
> I am Yahweh your God;
> You must not fear the gods of the Amorites
> in whose land you live.
> *Accusation*
> But you have not listened to my voice.

The next thing we know the Angel of Yahweh comes and sits under the oak at Ophrah (v. 11). That is wholly unexpected. After hearing the prophet accuse in Yahweh's behalf, "But you have not listened to my voice," we expect him to go

on to his punch line, which would normally be an announcement of judgment. For example, in Jeremiah 11:9–11, Yahweh
makes a threefold accusation against Judah and Jerusalem
(v. 10) and immediately launches into "therefore . . . I am
bringing evil upon them" (v. 11). Or try Jeremiah 25:1–11,
where the prophet accuses Judah of not listening to Yahweh
(vv. 3–7), and then with his dreadful "therefore" proceeds to
announce that Yahweh will bring "all the tribes of the north"
and Nebuchadnezzar of Babylon against Judah (vv. 8–11). The
problem with this prophecy in Judges 6 is that after verse 10b
we are all tensed for the proper "therefore," which does not
come. The judgment that should be announced is omitted.
Instead the Angel of Yahweh goes to coax a man to deliver
Israel.

That is why I have called this section "the grace that holds
us." How like the God of the Bible whose covenant love is so
"mighty" over us (Ps. 103:11, in the Hebrew)! When he "ought"
to destroy he delivers yet again; when he has every right to
shatter he nevertheless prepares to save. How "slow to anger"
(Exod. 34:6) indeed! How loath he is to strike his people (Lam.
3:33) even when justice begs for it. That is why Ephesians 2:4
grips us so. There we are lifeless (because dead in trespasses
and sins, Eph. 2:1), helpless (because toadies to Satan and our
own desires, 2:2–3a), hopeless (because children of wrath,
2:3)—"But God, who is rich in mercy . . .!" (Eph. 2:4). As I said
previously, no one could ever have invented a God like this; it
would be too much for guilty, sane folks to hope for, a God who
bridles his judgment to hold us in his grace. He is the God who
displays himself on the pages of Judges 6.

The Promise That Equips Us

Thirdly, we must hear, in verses 11–24, the promise that
equips us. The promise is simply, "Yahweh is with you" (v. 12).
Such a promise raises all sorts of problems for Gideon. If
Yahweh were with them, why was Gideon beating out wheat
in this winepress (v. 11)? If Yahweh were with them, why did
the Midianite wave come over them every year? If Yahweh
were with them, where were all his anti-Egyptian-like deeds?
If Yahweh were with them, why had he abandoned them to

Midian (v. 13)? Incidentally, Gideon's perspective in verse 13 shows how necessary it was for Israel to have the prophetic interpretation of verses 8–10. Sometimes we must be told:

> No, the arm of Yahweh is not too short to save,
> nor his ear too dull to hear,
> but your guilty deeds have made a gulf
> between you and your God.
> Your sins have made him hide his face from you
> so as not to hear you. [Isa. 59:1–2 NJB]

Gideon still protests against Yahweh's commission. Gideon is utterly inadequate: his clan is the weakest in Manasseh; he is the youngest in his father's house (v. 15). Against Gideon's inadequacy Yahweh stacks his adequacy—and it is simply the same promise of verse 12 only in its classic form. Everything that Gideon needs is supplied in this brief statement: "But I will be with you" (v. 16).

The statement has a history. It seems to be Yahweh's trump card placed down in front of either unwilling or hesitant servants. In face of Moses' resistance, Yahweh had insisted, "But I will be with you" (Exod. 3:12).[1] After Moses' death had apparently left a giant hole in Israel's leadership, Yahweh had reassured Joshua with "As I have been with Moses, I will be with you" (Josh. 1:5). In all their dilemmas, quandaries, and crises, this has ever been the word of the covenant God to his servants (Gen. 28:15; 46:4; Deut. 20:1; Ps. 23:4, Isa. 41:8–10; 43:2, 5; Matt. 28:20; Acts 18:9–10).

"But I will be with you." Basically, God has nothing else or more to offer you. You can go through a lot with that promise. It does not answer your questions about details. It only provides the essential. Nothing about when or how or where or why. Only the what, or, better, the Who. "But I will be with you." And that is enough.

Gideon, however, needs assurance that this promise is really *God's* promise: "Give me a sign that it is really you talking to me" (v. 17b NIV). Gideon evidently had some clue

---

1. For some of the Moses-Gideon parallels, see Barry G. Webb, *The Book of the Judges: An Integrated Reading,* JSOT Supplement Series 46 (Sheffield: JSOT, 1987), 148.

about the dignity of his Visitor; his respectful "sir" (v. 13) becomes "Lord" (v. 15), according to the traditional Hebrew text. Gideon shows how highly he values Yahweh's *promise* by wanting to be sure it is *Yahweh's* promise. There must be no mistake, no illusion. He must know it is God's word or at least that it comes with God's authority.

Gideon proposed that his offering become the laboratory for God's assuring sign. His Visitor agreed to wait (v. 18). The day was certainly not cluttered with appointments and deadlines (cf. Abraham's preparing a "morsel of bread" for his visitors in Gen. 18:1–8!). Gideon did not hurry to his favorite fast-food outlet. It takes time to butcher and prepare a young goat and to bake unleavened bread (v. 19). But with meat in a basket and broth in a pot Gideon at last returns. He arranges the items as his Guest directs. The Angel of Yahweh touches the meat and bread with the tip of his staff—fire (v. 21b), disappearance (v. 21c), realization (v. 22).

Here is an amazing paradox. Gideon must have assurance of Yahweh's promise (v. 16), but, when the assurance comes, it terrifies rather than fortifies him ("Oh no, Lord Yahweh, for I have seen the Angel of Yahweh face to face!" [v. 22]).[2] He must have assurance but there is a problem with the assurance. This assurance does not settle but alarms him.

We western Christians do not understand Gideon's agony (v. 22). Such talk is strange to us. We long to reach our warm hand through the print of our Bible page, pat Gideon's shoulder, and soothe him with "Don't worry, brother Gideon, God's not really scary like that—if only you had a New Testament . . . ." A pained, perplexed look would come over

---

2. The narrative makes clear the identity of the Angel of Yahweh with Yahweh himself (see vv. 11, 12, 14, 16). Cf. Gerhard von Rad (*Old Testament Theology,* 2 vols. [New York: Harper and Row, 1962], 1:287): "The most interesting [stories/narratives] are those which are not really able to distinguish between Jahweh and his angel, and which therefore do not take the angel as only a messenger, but as a form of manifestation of Jahweh himself. The angel of Jahweh is Jahweh himself, appearing to human beings in human form. In consequence—the chief passages concerned are Gen. xxi.11ff. and Jg. vi.17ff.—the story-tellers speak of Jahweh in one sentence, and then again of the angel of Jahweh in the next. In Gen. xxii.11, xxxi.11ff. and Ex. iii.2ff. too, the angel who speaks is identical with Jahweh." See further, J. Barton Payne, *The Theology of the Older Testament* (Grand Rapids: Zondervan, 1962), 167–70.

Gideon as if he had just heard a theological ignoramus. And so he did. This sort of talk (v. 22) is strange to us, because we have no real sense of the terror and awesomeness of God, for we think intimacy with God is an inalienable right rather than an indescribable gift. There is nothing amazing about grace as long as there is nothing fearful about holiness. But, thankfully, Gideon knew better. Nothing is more assuring than God's "I will be with you"; nothing is more overwhelming than the fact that it is *God* who says it. It is only God who can speak peace to the trembling (vv. 23–24).

The Demand That Commits Us

In verses 25–32 Yahweh lays down the demand that commits us. He tells Gideon:

> Take your father's bull, the second bull, seven years old, and tear down the altar of Baal which belongs to your father, and the Asherah pole beside it you must cut down. And you shall build an altar, ready for sacrifice, to Yahweh your God on the top of this fortress; and you shall take the second bull and offer it up as a whole burnt-offering, using the wood of the Asherah pole you cut down. [vv. 25–26]

Why such a demand? Because two altars cannot coexist side by side. You cannot have an altar to Yahweh (v. 24) and an altar to Baal (v. 25). They are mutually exclusive.

The demand placed on Gideon was meant as a paradigm for Israel. Yahweh was preparing to deliver them. But Israel must be properly prepared for such deliverance. God cannot safely trust his good gifts to those not fully given to him. When our little boy comes, bawling, into the kitchen with knees skinned up from a headlong fall on the driveway, we don't simply slap a giant two-inch-wide Band-Aid over the mess. Rather, we cleanse the grit and gunk out of the wound before the Band-Aid goes on. And that is Jesus' way. He did not hand the rich man a decision card and tell him to check the box beside "follow me." Instead he exposed the moral man's transgression of the first commandment and called on him to smash his idol— then he could follow Christ (Mark 10:21). There can be none of this double-heartedness—not for Gideon, nor for Israel, nor for the rich young ruler, nor for us.

Such is Yahweh's demand on Gideon and Israel. If Yahweh is to be their Savior, Baal must go. Baal may be tolerant, but Yahweh is jealous. There can be no "limping between two opinions" (1 Kings 18:21). To pray "Grant me chastity and continence, but not yet" (as Augustine did while still a Manichean) is to have already decided the issue. Judges 6 and Matthew 6 agree: no one can be a slave of two masters (Matt. 6:24). For Gideon and for us those times come when our commitment to the living God can no longer remain hidden, when we must declare ourselves, when we must burn our bridges and, if need be, stand alone against the religious, social, cultural expectations of the community.

Gideon "did as Yahweh had commanded him" (v. 27). Some may blame Gideon for demolishing Baal's altar by night, fearing relatives and city fathers. I doubt that it matters. Did God tell him to do it by day? Did God tell him he couldn't be afraid? Or did God simply tell him to do it? Evidently, obedience was essential and heroism optional.

Nothing had so shaken Ophrah in all the village's history! What a furor as the town councilmen sipped their warm goat's milk in the town gate that morning! Lord Baal's altar wrecked, Lady Asherah's pole hacked to pieces and used for firewood—they'd never known such sacrilege. Wait'll they catch the rascal who did it.

Somehow word leaked out and the village fathers pay Joash a call, demanding he turn over his son for execution. Crises sometimes cause people to talk sense—at least Joash found it so:

> Will *you* fight for Baal
> or will *you* save him?
> Whoever fights for him—
> let him be put to death by morning!
> If he is God,
> let him fight for himself,
> since someone has pulled down his altar. [v. 31]

The writer of Judges must have smiled as he recorded the biting satire of Joash's words. (Only Elijah's, 1 Kings 18:27, will be more pungent.) "If Baal is God," so ran Joash's new theology, "he doesn't need any help from Ophrah's town council to maintain his honor; he should be perfectly able to zap my son himself."[3] So the issue presses Israel: either continue to prop up Baal (v. 31) or worship at the altar of Yahweh (vv. 24, 28).

The Assurance That Settles Us

Next year. Same song. Next verse. Midian and Company flood into the Valley of Jezreel (v. 33). Same old story. But this year there is a new twist: "The Spirit of Yahweh put on Gideon" (or: "clothed himself with Gideon," v. 34), and in the Spirit's power Gideon summons his own clan and Manasseh and several other tribes (v. 35) to assemble for conflict. The Spirit's power, however, is joined to human weakness, and so we must observe, lastly, the assurance that settles us (vv. 36–40).

We must pay particular attention to the last of verses 36 and 37 in this episode, to the words *as you have said*. Gideon wants to be assured of Yahweh's promise to save Israel through him. Gideon wants to be more sure of Yahweh's sure word. He is hesitant, not unbelieving. It is not the absence of faith but the caution of faith we see here.[4]

Cautious it is. After Yahweh granted the sign of the wet fleece and the dry ground, Gideon asked for a reverse—dry

3. Joash's retort reminds us of one by John Knox. When Knox was a slave in the galleys, he was ordered to reverence a painted figure of the Virgin Mary. He threw it into the river with the comment: "Let our Lady now save herself: she is light enough; let her learn to swim" (A. M. Renwick, *The Story of the Scottish Reformation* [Grand Rapids: Eerdmans, 1960], 44).

4. I cannot agree with expositors who charge Gideon with sin in asking for this sign. Leon J. Wood even asserted that the "significance is that Gideon was not really seeking to know the nature of God's will, but to have God's will changed. He simply felt that the problems were too great to proceed, and, therefore, what God had previously said must somehow be wrong" (*Distressing Days of the Judges* [Grand Rapids: Zondervan, 1975], 213). I cannot see how one could know that unless one were inside Gideon's head. If we expositors would be a bit more incarnational in our approach we would be slower to critique trembling Gideons. "God says it; I believe it; that settles it" may be snazzy bumper-sticker theology, but it doesn't always neatly cover the struggles of believing experience. For a similar positive evaluation of 6:36–40, see H. W. Hertzberg, *Die Bücher Josua, Richter, Ruth,* 2d ed., Das Alte Testament Deutsch (Göttingen: Vandenhoeck und Ruprecht, 1959), 194.

fleece and wet ground. As C. J. Goslinga has said: "This would be even more striking and marvelous, since it is in the nature of wool to absorb moisture. The second sign would therefore go against nature and demonstrate God's power to do what seems impossible to men even more clearly."[5]

Granted, Gideon's is a unique situation. Yet there is, I think, a theological spillover from this text for all God's flock. God is not ashamed to stoop down and reassure us in our fears. (Would we, if we were thinking, call our three-year-old "sissy" or "chicken" because he was afraid of a big neighborhood dog?) He is patient with our weakness. God doesn't mind humbling himself in order to bolster our fragile faith, our wavering grip on his word. He is so eager to do just that that he has provided a table instead of a threshing floor, and bread and wine in place of a fleece.

5. C. J. Goslinga, *Joshua, Judges, Ruth*, Bible Student's Commentary (Grand Rapids: Zondervan, 1986), 332–33.

9

Strength Made Perfect in Weakness
(7:1–8:21)

Advertising keeps selling images. Television beer commercials associate a certain beer with hearty, robust construction workers, as if to suggest that drinking such-and-such beer puts you in the class of the macho and the physical. Cigarette ads do the same; magazine and billboard preach that smoking one brand is for durable, tough, outdoorsy types, while another brand puts you in the class of the suave and debonair. Usually, it would be fair to say, both our advertising and our passions prefer the types that are poised, assertive, assured, daring, self-sufficient, even cocky (so long as it's not overdone).

Perhaps that's why we have trouble understanding the Bible. The Bible is not obsessed, as we are, with our image. In fact, the Bible frequently cuts cross-grained to this whole mentality. God usually calls servants, not heroes, and many of his servants simply don't fit the mold that Madison Avenue has taught us to prize. Gideon is a case in point.

The weakness of Gideon and of Israel pervades chapters 6–8. One can trace this theme in Israel's total helplessness (6:2–6), in Gideon's lack of status and relative obscurity (6:15), in his fear of family and townspeople (6:27), in his need for additional assurance (6:36–40), in the radical reduction of his army (7:2–8), in his fear of the battle and need for additional encouragement (7:10–15), in his soft answer to Ephraim (8:1–3), in his troops being weary and unsupported by fellow Israelites (8:4–9), and—perhaps—in his refusal of kingship (8:22–23). Gideon is not the conventional hero.[1] Instead he—and Israel— are presented in their weakness. This weakness theme functions as a foil for the writer's major point that—if one may paulinize—Yahweh's power is made perfect in weakness (cf. 2 Cor. 12:9), something even the church finds hard to believe.[2] F. F. Bruce's paraphrase of 2 Corinthians 12:9 nicely sums up the primary thrust of the Gideon materials: "My power is most fully displayed when my people are weak."[3]

The Necessity of Weakness

First of all, Yahweh insists on the necessity of weakness in 7:1–8.[4] Yahweh teaches this lesson at the Spring of Harod (v. 1), located at the base of the Gilboa range.[5] Several miles to the north Midian's hordes spread themselves on the Hill of Moreh (at the east end of the Plain of Esdraelon and about fifteen miles southwest of the Sea of Galilee) and on into the valley.

1. Leland Ryken, *The Literature of the Bible* (Grand Rapids: Zondervan, 1974), 66–67. See also H. W. Hertzberg, *Die Bücher Josua, Richter, Ruth*, 2d ed., Das Alte Testament Deutsch (Göttingen: Vandenhoeck und Ruprecht, 1959), 191–92, 194–95, on the weakness theme.

2. I would stress that Gideon's and Israel's weakness is not a false weakness induced by mere modesty. Weakness is their real condition. So in Christian experience it is important to define what weakness is not. It does not mean that you are a glob of spiritual jello that flops at God's feet; it does not mean that you whine a lot, or that you look pale or have the flu. You may not feel weak at all. It has little to do with how you feel. You do not feel weak; you *are* weak, that is, you are stripped of all human resources and are forced to lean upon God alone.

3. F. F. Bruce, *An Expanded Paraphrase of the Epistles of Paul* (Exeter: Paternoster, 1965), 155.

4. The references to the "camp of Midian" in both verses 1 and 8b set this passage off as a distinct unit. There is a subtle contrast between 7:1–8 and 6:36–40. In 6:36–40 Gideon speaks to Yahweh about assurance, which Yahweh grants; in 7:1–8 Yahweh speaks to Gideon to bring weakness. Thus Yahweh assures Gideon and then weakens him. See C. F. Keil, *Joshua, Judges, Ruth,* Biblical Commentary on the Old Testament (1868; reprint ed., Grand Rapids: Eerdmans, 1950), 343.

5. There may be a word-play between the name of the spring (*ḥerōd*, v. 1) and the trembling (*ḥarēd*, v. 3) of Gideon's troops.

Verse 2 must eat its way into the grooves of our gray matter. This verse—and not the so-called vigilance of the "lappers"— is the key for interpreting this section. I know such a statement reeks of slaughtering a hermeneutical sacred cow, a cow loved dearly not only in Sunday school stories and in sermons but also in serious commentaries. But the fact is that any virtue or noble qualification the lappers are said to show must be read into the text; the text itself does not hint of any virtue in lapping or of any implicit vice in kneeling to drink water. Let us review the text again.

In line with Deuteronomy 20:8 all the fearful ones were sent home, a ploy that shaved Gideon's army from thirty-two thousand to ten thousand (v. 3). In Yahweh's strange view, there were still too many (v. 4); hence Yahweh will "test" (or "refine") them for Gideon as they drink water. There would be two groups: ones who lapped with their tongues like a dog laps and those who got down on their knees to drink (v. 5). Result: three hundred lappers; the rest were kneelers (v. 6).[6] Then comes Yahweh's announcement: "With the three hundred lappers I will save you" (v. 7).

It is amazing how virtuous the lappers become in the view of expositors. They are heralded as the vigilant, watchful ones who lean down, scoop a little water, always with their eyes on the enemy (which may yet have been several miles to the north!), while the kneelers are the careless, who think only of their thirst.[7] For example, one expositor (who shall remain anonymous) concludes:

6. In verse 5 one is said to lap "with his tongue," whereas in verse 6 the ones who lap do it "with their hands to their mouths." Some believe that "with their hands to their mouths" can only describe the way the kneelers drank and so argue that we must transpose the phrase to the end of the verse to meet this requirement (see NEB and Goslinga). Others (e.g., Keil) explain "lapping with their hands to their mouths" as only a more distinct expression for "lapping with his tongue."

7. If with Goslinga one assumes "putting their hands to their mouths" (v. 6) describes the kneelers, the scenario is different but the approach is the same: "The 300 threw themselves flat on the bank, hastily gulped down a little water, and had already returned to their ranks when the others had just kneeled down. The 9,700 did not show the same alacrity; they took their time and remained on their knees long enough to draw up several handfuls of water" (C. J. Goslinga, *Joshua, Judges, Ruth,* Bible Student's Commentary [Grand Rapids: Zondervan, 1986], 335).

God saw how untrustworthy would be those thousands who carelessly indulged under the lure of the flesh, over against the three hundred who exemplified a spirit of vigilence [sic] and disciplined life in the Spirit. Thus were selected the strong and resolute, the men who could be trusted under rigorous conditions, those who did not think of themselves before the enemy's unexpected assault. This is ever the divine principle of selection for service. As Gideon, so the church in this day is served well by the minority group ready and vigilant [sic].

The problem with this kind of exposition is that it has no basis in the text. The text does not hint at any virtue or vice in how one guzzles water. The water-drinking episode was simply Yahweh's mechanism for further reducing Gideon's army. The attention lavished on the quality of the three hundred actually obscures what the text is trying to say, for when verse 2 stresses the necessary weakness of Israel, one doubts if it means to laud the vigor of this minority. The three hundred are the sign of Israel's weakness, not the epitome of her strength.

If we are to rightly hear this passage, we must hear verse 2: "The people who are with you are too many for me to give Midian into their hand, lest Israel should glorify themselves against me by saying, '*My hand* has saved me.'" In other words, because of the tendency of God's people to glorify their own efforts, to trust in their proven methods, to credit their own contributions, to think well of their cleverness, Yahweh frequently insists that his people be reduced to utter helplessness, so that they *must* recognize that their deliverance can only be chalked up to Yahweh's power and mercy.

Does not 7:2 speak to us? Does it not tell us there is a certain deviousness in God's people, a tendency to steal God's praise? Does it not teach us that sometimes he cannot trust us with his work unless we realize how inadequate we are to do it? This may explain why God frequently chooses such unlikely instruments.

Few would ever have suspected William M'Culloch of kindling a revival. He was parish minister in Cambuslang (Scotland) about 1740. A scholarly pastor excelling in languages, especially Hebrew, he had, nevertheless, little gift for the pulpit. His own son described him as "not a very ready speaker

. . . not eloquent . . . his manner [was] slow and cautious." In fact, he was called an "Ale-minister," which meant that, when he rose to speak, a number in the audience left to quench their thirst at the local tavern.[8] Yet God chose to use William M'Culloch's ministry as the means of revival at Cambuslang, some time before George Whitefield visited there. Now I cannot divine the divine ways. But I wonder if God was pleased to use William M'Culloch in order to make clear that the Cambuslang work could not be explained by eloquence or human dynamism but only by the Spirit of God. The necessity of weakness—that is often Yahweh's method.

Before going on, I want to point out how consistent the victory report (7:16–22) is with the theme of weakness (7:1–8). The plan seems ingenious—dividing into three groups, smashing jugs, brandishing torches, blowing rams' horns, bellowing the war cry. Yet for all that, the three hundred men remain primarily hornblowers; verse 21 insists that "each man stood in his place around the camp," while verse 22 explains the Midianite mayhem as Yahweh's doing ("Yahweh set each man's sword against his companion"). The victory was Yahweh's work—the three hundred did not attack but pursued (v. 22b).[9]

The Encouragement in Weakness

Next, verses 9–15 show us the encouragement in weakness. Here is God's assurance.[10]

Gideon is a most unheroic hero. Yahweh orders him to attack Midian's army (v. 9) yet offers him a preliminary option: "but if you are afraid to go down, you and Purah your servant go down to the camp, and you shall hear what they are saying, and after that your hands will be strengthened, and you shall

8. Arthur Fawcett, *The Cambuslang Revival* (London: Banner of Truth, 1971), 38–39.
9. The precise path of the Midianites' flight in verse 22b is difficult to trace because location of the sites mentioned is uncertain; for example is Abel-Meholah west or east of the Jordan (cf. S. Cohen, "Abel-Meholah," *IDB*, 1:5)? Apparently, they fled south/southeast seeking to cross the Jordan.
10. God himself provides fresh assurance for Gideon in 7:9–15; this should keep us from faulting Gideon for seeking it in 6:36–40.

go down against the camp" (vv. 10–11a). "If you are afraid . . . ."
Afraid? Gideon? Certainly! "So he went down, he and Purah
his servant, to the edge of the army in the camp" (v. 11b). Here
is not your conventional, crusty, immovable man of steel. Gideon is no fearless all-pro linebacker, no General Patton and
John Wayne rolled into one huge ball of true grit. "So he went
down."

Eavesdropping pays off. One can almost hear the conver-
sation. One Midianite private says to another: "Hey [quite a
good rendering for the Hebrew *hinnēh* here], I've had a dream;
see, a loaf of barley bread comes rolling into the camp of Midian, and it comes to a tent, smacks into it, and it falls—it
turned it upside down . . ." (v. 13). His sidekick knew what it
meant: "This can only be the sword of Gideon son of Joash, a
man of Israel; God has given into his hand Midian and all the
army" (v. 14). Gideon worshiped (v. 15). Yahweh was right;
his hands were strengthened (v. 11).

There is a certain irony in this episode: God's word comes
through the oddest channel—a Midianite private. But this
shouldn't surprise us, since he also made a murderous high
priest his prophet (John 11:49–52), mocking priests and theo-
logians his evangelists (Mark 15:31),[11] and a pagan governor
his stellar witness (John 19:19–22).

We can trace Yahweh's concern in his words: "Arise, go
down" (v. 9); "but if you are afraid to go down . . ." (v. 10);
"and afterward your hands will be strengthened" (v. 11). The
Lord knows the fears of his servants, knows how scared we
can be in our various circumstances. "He [emphatic] knows
our frame" (Ps. 103:14). Yet God is not so strict as to be harsh
when we tremble; he does not ridicule us for our fears; he never
mocks us because we are fragile.

In light of this, we may need to alter our current stereotypes
of what a servant of Christ is (or, is like). We sometimes dupe
ourselves into thinking that a real servant of Christ is only
someone who is dynamic, assured, confident, brash, fearless,
witty, adventuresome, or glamorous—with one or two appearances on a Christian television network. Don't think you are

---

11. A little thought should convince any Christian that "he saved others;
he cannot save himself" (Mark 15:31) is some of the best news he has ever
heard!

unusable because you don't have that air about you. Christ takes uncertain and fearful folk, strengthens their hands in the oddest ways, and makes them able to stand for him in school or home or work. We must not forget how the writer of Hebrews describes those we sometimes call the "heroes of faith": "They were weak people who were given strength to be brave in war and drive back foreign invaders" (Heb. 11:34 NJB).

The Cause of Weakness

Now the weakness theme takes a new twist. There is a necessary weakness (see my first observation in this chapter); there can also be a detrimental weakness, as in 7:24–8:21. Here God's people are the cause of weakness. Weakness is brought about by fragmentation among God's people.[12] Gideon, as it turns out, has to fight three conflicts: with Baal, chapter 6; with Midian, chapter 7; and, sadly, with Israel, chapter 8.

Gideon had called upon the tribe of Ephraim to race to the Jordan, control access to it as far as Beth-barah, and thus prevent the Midianites' eastward escape (7:24).[13] So they did, collecting in the process two princely heads and adding a rock and a winepress to the list of historical markers (7:25). Then they vent their anger on Gideon. Who did he think he was, initiating hostilities with Midian without consulting Ephraim (8:1)? Ephraim was a prima donna among the tribes, a corporate Diotrephes (3 John 9). They could claim Joshua among their number (Num. 13:8), and, in any case, they never tire of asserting their hegemony (Judg. 12:1–6). But Gideon's quick-witted proverb (8:2) and common-sense psychology (8:3) administer the strokes needed, and Ephraim's temperature cools. It is nothing but Ephraim's pride that fuels the dispute.

12. Other examples of the fragmentation-of-Israel theme can be found in 5:15b–17; 12:1–6; 15:10–13; chaps. 19–21. I have a detailed discussion in "A Proposed Life-Setting for the Book of Judges" (Ann Arbor: University Microfilms, 1978), 66–76.

13. The location of Beth-barah is not known; some would place it near where the Wadi Farah joins the Jordan, which is opposite and a little south of the point where the Jabbok empties into the Jordan from the east. For the general picture, see Yohanan Aharoni and Michael Avi-Yonah, *The Macmillan Bible Atlas*, rev. ed. (New York: Macmillan, 1977), 54, map 76.

With Succoth (8:4–7) and Penuel (8:8–9)[14] resistance was more passive than active, generated by fear rather than pride. Gideon has crossed to the eastern side of the Jordan; his three hundred are "faint yet pursuing" (8:4). When Gideon asks Succoth for provisions, the town leaders reply, "Are the palms[15] of Zebah and of Zalmunna in your hand already that we should give food to your army?" (8:6), which, being interpreted, means "No!"

One can partly understand their refusal. If the leaders of Succoth (or Penuel) give aid to Gideon's army and if Gideon, for whatever reason, should fail to eradicate the Midianite menace, they would invite reprisals on themselves as soon as the Midianites were able to recoup. And, unlike the western tribes, Succoth and Penuel have no Jordan Valley to provide at least a partial buffer from swift attack. These towns were directly exposed to Midianite attack. Prudence—so they held—dictated their opposition to Gideon. Or was it faithlessness? It can be difficult to distinguish the two. Must our safety always be the ultimate consideration? Could Succoth and Penuel not see that Yahweh had granted a signal victory and that they could assist in completing it? The story is ironic: the towns avoid Midian's wrath but suffer under Gideon's wrath (8:13–17). Since they sided with Israel's enemies, they were treated as Israel's enemies (vv. 13–17 in light of vv. 10–12 and 18–21).[16] It is tragic when judgment must include Yahweh's people and begin at his sanctuary (cf. Ezek. 9:6 in context).

14. Succoth and Penuel were located east of the Jordan near the River Jabbok. For more detail, see S. Cohen, "Succoth," *IDB,* 4:449, and "Penuel," *IDB,* 3:727.

15. The term may allude to the practice of dismembering conquered enemies. If so, the men of Succoth are sarcastically asking if Gideon has already vanquished the Midianite kings and cut off their hands, and can produce them as proof of his victory.

16. The towns also *acted* like Israel's enemies, for Gideon says they "scorned" him (v. 15). The Hebrew verb *(haraph)* means to taunt, mock, or insult. Expositors usually allow that Gideon's measures against Succoth and Penuel were justified but sometimes view his execution of Zebah and Zalmunna (vv. 18–21) as personal vindictiveness. I do not think so, for verse 19 implies that Zebah and Zalmunna did not kill Gideon's brothers in battle but that they had an option to spare them, which suggests they deliberately killed them after taking them captive.

Gideon then is not supported by Yahweh's own people, who are concerned for either their own status (Ephraim) or their own security (Succoth and Penuel). With a remarkable victory needing to be clinched, the pride of Ephraim and the fear of Succoth and Penuel are both stupid and wrong. A passion for recognition and safety destroys the cohesion Israel needed.

Here is instruction for us: sometimes the people of God are a great disappointment. (If you don't know that, you may not survive in the church.) Don't allow God's people to disillusion you; at least be prepared for it. And watch out that it is not *your* passion for status (Mark 10:35–45) or *your* pursuit of security (1 Tim. 6:17; cf. 2 Tim. 4:16) that disturbs the unity and saps the energy of the church.

When General Sherman relieved the siege of Knoxville in the War Between the States, the ragged, hungry Federals knew they would soon have provisions again. Railroad connections with Chattanooga were restored, and half the army flooded to the station to meet the first train. It was a ten-car freight train, which, by someone's bureaucratic botch, was loaded with nothing but horseshoes.[17] Horseshoes do not provide sustenance for famished soldiers, nor do bickering and division in any way nourish God's Israel. Though Christ's power is "most fully displayed when [his] people are weak," we must take care that we ourselves are not the cause of such weakness.

---

17. Bruce Catton, *This Hallowed Ground* (Garden City, N. Y.: Doubleday, 1956), 301.

10

It's Tough to End Well
(8:22–32)

I remember how disappointed I was as a child in the kings of Judah. Whether I read in my Bible story book or in the text of Kings and Chronicles, I mentally grieved over kings like Asa, Jehoshaphat, Uzziah, and Hezekiah who, though basically faithful, all marred that fidelity in some way before the end of their reigns (e.g., 2 Chron. 16; 18:1–19:3; 26:16–23; 2 Kings 20:12–21). I was uniformly disappointed; it was tough, I concluded, to end well.

Disappointing Leadership

Gideon appears to fall into the same pattern, and in this section we meet disappointing leadership. Before developing this point, however, we must try to make sense out of Israel's request (v. 22) and Gideon's refusal (as it is frequently called, v. 23) of kingship.

The men of Israel[1] ask Gideon to establish a dynasty: "Rule over us, you, your son, and your grandson as well" (v. 22). Although the verb for "become king" (*malak*) is not used (*mashal,* to rule, occurs instead), the Israelites clearly intend a hereditary regime. Gratitude stands behind their offer: "for you have saved us from the hand of Midian." One might accuse

---

1. I doubt that all Israel is meant—probably only those tribes west of the Jordan who enjoyed most relief from Midian's demise.

them of an idolatrous tendency. Should they not have ascribed their salvation to Yahweh (7:2) rather than to his instrument? But the matter is not so simple. They may only be expressing a proper esteem for Yahweh's servant, a gratitude that was lacking at a later point (8:35).

The really sticky question is what to make of Gideon's answer (v. 23): "I will not rule over you, nor will my son rule over you; *Yahweh* will rule over you." What does Gideon mean? Is this a "brusque refusal," showing that the "whole notion of monarchy was rejected as improper" and that "the very idea of monarchy was anathema to true Israelites"?[2] Or, was Gideon's refusal only apparent? Perhaps it was a veiled acceptance of kingship?[3] If so, Gideon is not so much rejecting kingly rule in itself as underscoring the form it must take (not really I—or my descendants—but Yahweh must rule). The context, after all, does contain some evidence of royal status: Gideon's role as religious innovator (vv. 24–27), his keeping a sizable harem (v. 30), dubbing his concubine's son "My father is king" (Abimelech, v. 31),[4] and Abimelech's propaganda that rule would surely pass to or continue in Gideon's family (9:1–

2. John Bright, *A History of Israel,* 3d ed. (Philadelphia: Westminster, 1981), 167, 182.

3. G. Henton Davies, "Judges VIII 22–23," *Vetus Testamentum* 13 (1963): 151–57.

4. Verse 31b is literally, "he appointed his name Abimelech." The terminology refers to renaming (see Robert G. Boling, *Judges,* The Anchor Bible [Garden City, N.Y.: Doubleday, 1975], 162). Scholars, however, either seem almost to conspire against admitting that Gideon would have dubbed this son "my father is king," or they claim that, if he did, "my father" must refer to Yahweh rather than to Gideon. C. J. Goslinga (*Joshua, Judges, Ruth,* Bible Student's Commentary [Grand Rapids: Zondervan, 1986], 353 n) is certain that Abimelech could not mean "my father [= Gideon] is king," "since Gideon certainly would never have given such a name." How can he know that? One wonders if scholars have not gratuitously assumed that Gideon was consistent and therefore have tended to squeeze verse 31 into their interpretation of verse 23. Martin Buber's attempt to see the name as Abimelech's chosen designation for himself is a very unnatural way of reading verse 31 (*Kingship of God* [New York: Harper and Row, 1967], 74). I agree with Barry G. Webb: "The name Abimelech (My-father-is-king) is an ironic comment on the contradiction between Gideon's public pronouncements and private practice" (*The Book of the Judges: An Integrated Reading,* JSOT Supplement Series 46 [Sheffield: JSOT, 1987], 154).

5). I lean toward this latter view, though I prefer to call it a qualified, rather than a veiled, acceptance.[5]

Whether we prefer a trenchantly anti-monarchical Gideon or a mildly pro-monarchical Gideon, we meet, in either case, inconsistency and disappointment. If he refused kingship, he nevertheless hankered after it (e.g., in giving the name "My father is king"). If in some way he accepted it, he disappoints us in his lack of discretion, in his giving opportunity for further apostasy (v. 27b). Most Christians know the struggle to make our practice (v. 27) as good as our theology (v. 23). It is ever our danger that after being used of God in some way, we mouth humility but practice pride. We may know occasions of the Spirit's power (6:34) and yet lack the Spirit's wisdom.

This shadow of inconsistency and of disappointment frequently hangs over God's servants. Gideon was hardly a rare exception. This is not to excuse the sins or errors of the leaders of God's people. But let it temper our expectations, let it cushion our despair, and let it lift our gaze to the Leader of God's elect, who does not disappoint (cf. 1 Pet. 2:6), in whom is no sin (1 John 3:5), and against whom no charges can be brought (John 8:46). We will never find perfection of office except in our Lord Jesus Christ. Realizing this can save us from cynicism that may come from disappointing servants of Christ.

Disastrous Ingenuity

Secondly, verse 27 tells us of a disastrous ingenuity. Gideon fashioned an ephod out of the spoils he requested, and "all Israel went like prostitutes after it." Such false devotion lured and trapped Gideon and family in its clutches.

The ephod was part of the high priest's attire (see Exod. 28:1–35; 39:1–26), a sleeveless tunic worn over his other garments. It was made of costly and colorful materials—gold, blue, purple, scarlet, fine linen. Attached to the ephod was a breastplate in which twelve precious stones (representing Isra-

5. Yet the evidence is not conclusive. Arthur E. Cundall points out that verse 29 strongly suggests Gideon retired into private life—a strange twist for new royalty (*Judges,* Tyndale Old Testament Commentaries [London: Tyndale, 1968], 121).

el's twelve tribes) were set in four rows. There was a pocket or pouch in the breastplate which contained the Urim and the Thummim (Exod. 28:30), objects used to discover Yahweh's will on particular matters (see Num. 27:21). Since the breastplate was attached to the ephod, requesting the priest's ephod meant to ask for Yahweh's direction by Urim and Thummim (see 1 Sam. 23:9–12; 30:7–8). Although some prefer to see Gideon's ephod as an image (e.g., Moore), there is no need to do so. It is most natural to view it as a priestly vestment intended as a means of obtaining direction from Yahweh.[6]

Ordinarily, the ephod would be with the current high priest wherever the ark and tabernacle were located. We have, however, little data about the location of the tabernacle during the conquest and settlement. Apparently, it was usually at Shiloh (Josh. 18:1, 8–10; 19:51; 22:9, 12–14; Judg. 18:31; see also 1 Sam. 1–3) though occasionally at Bethel (Judg. 20:27–28). Yahweh had provided priest and ephod at the sanctuary; here Israel's leaders and people could receive direction and guidance (cf. Num. 27:21). If Yahweh gave uniquely direct guidance to one of his servants (as to Gideon in chaps. 6 and 7) in some circumstances, that did not authorize that servant to assume he should become an ongoing, alternative channel of divine guidance for Israel. I suggest this was the essence of Gideon's action in verse 27; Gideon would become a channel of Yahweh's direct guidance in addition to the priest and ephod Yahweh had already provided. Whatever else can be said, the center of the matter seems to be that Gideon hankered after more than what God had given for declaring his will. And Israel loved it with a godless passion (v. 27).

Christians today do not deal with ephods, high priests, or tabernacles and yet may have this same thirst for more—hankering for more than what God has already given for our

6. On the ephod generally, see R. K. Harrison, "Ephod," *ISBE* (rev. ed.), 2:117–18; on the ephod in Judges 8:27, see Goslinga, *Joshua, Judges, Ruth*, 351. For background, see W. F. Albright, *Yahweh and the Gods of Canaan* (Garden City, N. Y.: Doubleday, 1968), 200–203. Uncertainties surround the Urim and Thummim; for a careful treatment, see C. Van Dam, "Urim and Thummim," *ISBE* (rev. ed.), 4:957–59. Keil has some balanced observations on Judges 8:24–27; see his commentary.

sustenance, nurture, direction. We subtly suggest God has furnished us inadequately. (Maybe Psalm 23:1 is not really true!) We are not content merely to walk obediently to the Scriptures, trusting God's providence and goodness to direct us in the proper path. No, we must have more—a specific, direct word from God about what we should do in our particular problem. So we come up saying, "The Lord said to me that I should . . ." or "The Holy Spirit spoke to me, telling me that . . . ."[7]

I would even suggest we go ephod-making in the way we ignore God's provision of the Lord's covenant meal as the means of Christian renewal. We plan, organize, and concoct "revivals," seminars, retreats, or encounters, or we pressure congregations to come forward and rededicate their lives to Christ. All the while we neglect what God has provided: the Lord's Supper.

> Evangelists frequently give invitations to a public rededication of Christians to the Lord. The communion is God's instrument for rededication which has stood from the very first. Each time it is served it is a clarion call to every Christian present to offer himself once again to the Lord.[8]

I am not saying that Christian retreats, for example, are an exercise in idolatry; I am saying that Christians no less than Israelites have a passion for enriched, extraordinary experiences while virtually ignoring the rich, normal means of grace God has provided.

7. Then you are really adrift if you somehow get the wrong direction. In one of my father's pastorates there was a zealous man who wanted to speak to another man in the congregation about his spiritual state. He came to the latter's farm and asked the wife if her husband was home. No, he had gone off somewhere. Well, the Holy Spirit had told him that he should come over and talk to her husband. To which the absentee's wife responded: "If the Holy Spirit told you to come talk to my husband, the Holy Spirit would've made sure my husband was at home!"

8. Alan Dan Orme, *God's Appointments with Men: A Christian's Primer on the Sacraments* (Athens, Ga.: University Church Press, 1982), 54.

Tragic Loss

Finally, we meet a tragic loss implied in verse 28. "The land had rest forty years in the days of Gideon." This means the land had rest from war (see Josh. 11:23 and 14:15 where the same verb, *shaqaṭ*, occurs). No enemy incursions, no invaders raking the land of its produce, no pillaging in villages.

There is reason to underline 8:28. It is the last rest note in Judges (see 3:11, 30; 5:31). After verse 28 the land no longer recovers its rest. This is a gift Israel loses, an enjoyment she forfeits. Contrary to some, Judges does not follow a recurring cycle of rebellion, repentance, rescue, and rest, but charts the progressive disintegration of a people who will not serve the God who saves them.[9] People who by persisting apostasy despise Yahweh's gift will find that gift withdrawn.

When I was in fourth grade my father instituted a new thing. He gave me an allowance. Money had to be carefully budgeted in our family, yet he gave me five dollars a month. I was astounded. The only requirement was that I tithe the amount to the church. But that left $4.50. My father likely expected me to save a good bit of that amount, allowing it to sit in the little can in his filing cabinet where I was to keep my funds. Ah, but there was Herr's Grocery Store down by the traffic light with a superb inventory of candy, gum, and junk for pennies, nickels, and dimes—the delight of any carnal child. I had $4.50 and my friend Dick. We delighted ourselves in fatness for two or three months. Then, I suspect, Dick's mother became suspicious and probably made my father suspicious. Suddenly, there was no more allowance. Privilege abused—and removed.

So it is with Israel; after this the land will no longer recover its rest. Judges will show you that Yahweh's mercy is deep (see the comments on 2:18) but not easygoing; it is tender but will not be trampled. The word it preaches is not "though it makes him sad to see the way we live, he'll always say, 'I forgive' " (a la the sentimental song of the fifties) but "do you despise the riches of his kindness and forbearance and long-

9. Note my comments on 3:11; see also J. P. U. Lilley, "A Literary Appreciation of the Book of Judges," *Tyndale Bulletin* 18 (1967): 97–99, and Webb, *The Book of the Judges,* 158, 175–76.

suffering, ignorant of the fact that the kindness of God leads you to repentance?" (Rom. 2:4).

It *is* tough to end well. Any believer knows that. "He will keep you strong to the end" (1 Cor. 1:8 NIV)—that is one's only assurance. But in Judges it will get worse; wait till "My-father-is-king" becomes king.

11

Brambleman, Destroyer of Israel
(8:33–9:57)

Several months ago our family was driving west on our way to Kansas when traffic on our side of the interstate slowed, crawled, stopped, and waited. As we inched our way along we at last came to the cause of the bottleneck—a car had caught fire and now sat there almost totally gutted. In highway driving we often think of driving defensively, watching out for the other fellow. The danger, we assume, is from the outside. But not always. What about that skeleton of charred, smoking rubble on the interstate? There must have been something from within that destroyed it. An electrical malfunction, perhaps; who knows? Ruin can come from within as well as from without.

Nor did it require a foreign invader to ravage and destroy Israel. Naturally, Moabites, Canaanites, and Midianites could do it; but so could Abimelech, the Destroyer of Israel, who arose from within Israel. That is what Judges 9 shows us with its fascinating array of scenes from the big payoff (v. 4) to the woman who had a crush on Abimelech (v. 53).

This is a long narrative; hence I want to outline its structure and content so we can see at a glance how the story develops; then we can get to its teaching.

Summary, 8:33–35
The treachery of Abimelech and Shechem, 9:1–6

The Peril of Forgetting

Our narrative proclaims the peril of forgetting:

When Gideon died, the sons of Israel turned back and went like prostitutes after the Baals; they made Baal-berith their god; and the sons of Israel did not remember Yahweh their God who kept delivering them from the hand of all their enemies around them; and they did not act faithfully with the house of Jerubbaal (Gideon) in light of all the good that he had done for Israel. [8:33–35]

When the text condemns Israel for not remembering Yahweh, it is not suggesting that Israel forgot the identity of Yahweh nor even that they could no longer list the enemies from whom Yahweh has rescued them. It means that what they knew of Yahweh exercised no control over them, held no grip on their loyalties. They could still answer catechism questions about Yahweh but that knowledge did not determine their commitment. Whatever factual, intellectual information about

Yahweh they retained did not keep them from adopting Baal-berith as their god.

In the latter months of 1947, sometime before the British mandate in Palestine expired, Jamil Mardam, the prime minister of Syria, joined other Arab leaders in planning a coordinated military attack on Israel as soon as the new Jewish state was born. Ironically, all that winter Mardam's wife made her regular visits to Jerusalem, where she received treatment from her Jewish doctor.[1] Apparently, the benefit Mardam's wife received from a Jewish source had no impact on how he himself planned to deal with the Jews. There was no connection; that is, he "did not remember" in the biblical sense of the phrase.

But not only did Israel forget Yahweh; they forgot Gideon too (8:35). Had they treasured Gideon and his work they would have dealt loyally with Gideon's family. The writer places much emphasis on Israel's ingratitude toward Gideon, alluding to it in his introduction (8:35), in Jotham's address (9:16–20), and in the theological explanations (9:23–24, 56–57).

Though the Bible forbids God's people to deify God's servants (e.g., Acts 10:25–26; Rev. 19:10; 22:8–9), it commands us to esteem them highly (1 Thess. 5:12–13; cf. 1 Tim. 4:12). Christians frequently show more skill using the critical knife than tendering grateful thanks to parents, pastors, mentors, friends, or educators who have labored to lead them in the grace and wisdom of God.

For a number of years I have profited immensely from the works of a certain biblical scholar and pastor. About two years ago a conviction began to nibble at my conscience: you have received much help from his writings; you have never expressed your thanks to him; you really ought to do that. I was able to compile what looked like a sufficient overseas address, and so I sent off a letter informing him of the help and encouragement he had given me in the Scriptures and thanking him for it. This may appear puny beside Israel's ingratitude toward Gideon, but the principle is the same. When we ignore the instruments of God's grace we demean the Giver of that grace. In the text apostasy from Yahweh and

---

1. Larry Collins and Dominique Lapierre, *O Jerusalem!* (New York: Pocket Books, 1972), 39, 330.

ingratitude toward Gideon occurred together. On this matter of remembering and forgetting, see the comments on 2:11–13.

The Problem of Leadership

Secondly, observe how 9:1–21 emphasizes the problem of leadership.

If only Gideon had not had a concubine in Shechem (8:31)! But he did, and Abimelech, the son of that concubine, was both ambitious and treacherous. Abimelech asked his mother's relatives to put a bug in the ears of Shechem's city fathers. The gospel according to Abimelech was: "I don't want to scare you, but you don't want seventy men—all Jerubbaal's sons—trying to rule over you, do you? How less chaotic if only one of his sons rules you—me! By the way, I *am* related by blood to you men" (see vv. 1–2). The favorite-son argument won the day. The city fathers weigh out good pagan money with which Abimelech hires a gang of stupid but brutal thugs; he visits Ophrah and solemnly butchers Gideon's seventy sons (vv. 4–5). With all pomp and circumstance the men of Shechem install Abimelech as king (v. 6).[2] Why? Because "he is our brother" (v. 3). Blood is thicker than brains.

The scene is amusing. We watch the solemnity and ceremony of Abimelech's coronation—all the local politicians have that grave and profound look on their faces which needs to remain there until they adjourn to the Hilton for the party. Suddenly, an irreverent yell, somewhere between tenor and baritone, profanes the occasion: "Hey, you guys, listen to me!" (cf. v. 7). All eyes turn toward Mount Gerizim (oddly enough, the mount of blessing, Deut. 27:12–13, Josh. 8:33); there Jotham, Gideon's youngest son, the one who escaped, is perched ready with a story.

Jotham has caused interpreters to flounder on his fable.[3]

2. How ironic that this occurs "by the oak of the pillar at Shechem" (RSV) where both Jacob (Gen. 35:4) and Joshua (Josh. 24:1, 26) affirmed fidelity to Yahweh; now Abimelech uses the place to sanctify his treachery under the auspices of Baal-berith.

3. It is immaterial whether Jotham created the fable himself, or adapted a current popular tale, or culled it from the collection of some Late Bronze Age Aesop.

Some think that Jotham's fable is an ideological or political statement; it shows or reflects how vigorously true Israelites rejected the institution of kingship. This view hears the olive, fig, and vine (vv. 9, 11, 13) saying, "Should I give up my useful, productive calling [whether rich oil, sweet fruit, or cheering drink] to take on the fruitless—albeit royal—task of swaying over the trees?"[4] I think this view claims too much.[5] Indeed, I hold that the climax (vv. 14–15), and not the preliminary scenes, carries the heaviest freight; the main concerns are the stupidity of the trees (v. 14) and the uselessness (except for bringing disaster!) of the bramble (v. 15). The fable does not stress the worthlessness of kingship but the worthlessness of Abimelech; the concern is not that the worthy candidates depreciate the offer of kingship but that a bramble accepts it. The problem is not kingship but the character of the king and his cronies, as Jotham makes clear in verses 16–20.[6] Jotham's theme is the foolishness and peril of accepting clearly unqualified leadership. Brambles make good fuel but poor kings; they burn better than they reign.

People have a strange tendency to accept bramble-leadership, a fact which continues to baffle us. William L. Shirer

4. Perhaps the verb *hadal* (to cease, stop) in verses 9, 11, 13 should be taken as a simple stem and as a strict perfect, in which case the botanical voices would be saying: "Have I stopped yielding" my rich oil, sweetness, or new wine? (so NJPS). On this variation they would be saying, "So you think that since I am no longer productive I should turn to politics?" Hence, some infer, Jotham's fable holds kingship up to ridicule, as though it were an activity open only to those who had outlived their usefulness.

5. Assuming the historicity of the situation, Jotham may well have intended his fable to address only the problem at hand (Abimelech) and not to proclaim an anti-monarchical ideology.

6. I have discussed the matter more fully in "A Proposed Life-Setting for the Book of Judges" (Ann Arbor: University Microfilms, 1978), 106–13; see also Eugene H. Maly, "The Jotham Fable—Anti-Monarchical?" *Catholic Biblical Quarterly* 22 (1960): 299–305. Some claim that "to wave [or sway] over the trees" (vv. 9, 11, 13; the verb is *nu'a*) is meant in a derogatory sense, that is, the olive, fig, and vine have more productive pursuits to follow than to discharge such a useless function (so John Gray, *Joshua, Judges and Ruth*, The Century Bible—New Edition [Greenwood, S. C.: Attic, 1967], 319). This, however, imputes undue significance to the mere imagery of the fable, for this verb describes only what trees ordinarily do (see Isa. 7:2), especially when the wind catches them.

saw this in September 1934, at the Nazi Party celebration in Nuremberg.

> The words he uttered, the thoughts he expressed, often seemed to me ridiculous, but that week in Nuremberg I began to comprehend that it did not matter so much what he said but how he said it. Hitler's communication with his audiences was uncanny. He established a rapport almost immediately and deepened and intensified it as he went on speaking, holding them completely in his spell. In such a state, it seemed to me, they easily believed anything he said, even the most foolish nonsense. Over the years as I listened to scores of Hitler's major speeches I would pause in my own mind to exclaim: "What utter rubbish! What brazen lies!" Then I would look around at the audience. His German listeners were lapping up every word as the utter truth.[7]

And history will see yet more of this. Jesus knew this strange perversity of man that ignores God's true Führer but is duped by chintzy imitations: "*I* have come in my Father's name, and you do not receive me; if another should come in his own name, you will receive *him!*" (John 5:43).

But our anxiety does not center on bramble-leaders within history in general but among God's people in particular. Woe to Israel—or a section of it—when it covenants with an Abimelech!

We should hold Jotham in proper esteem. He is no mere spinner of fables but an instructor of the church. What care God's people should take in seeking and selecting their leaders.

I remember as a young pastor working within a denominational body in which, when the time came to nominate new elders, the primary question was—Would so-and-so serve as an elder? We have two elders going off the session, and we need two more. Who can we get to accept it? One seldom if ever heard any reference to 1 Timothy 3:1–7 or to Titus 1:5–9. No one ever seemed to say: "Here are the biblical qualifications for eldership. Now who is there among us who seems

---

7. William L. Shirer, *The Nightmare Years 1930–1940,* vol. 2 of *Twentieth-Century Journey: A Memoir of a Life and the Times* (Boston: Little, Brown and Company, 1984), 127–28.

to conform to these standards?" Imagine my amazement when in several years I discovered a body of believers who had the revolutionary idea that 1 Timonthy 3 and Titus 1 actually applied to contemporary church government! What if no one was biblically qualified for the office of elder? Then you didn't have elders. You borrowed one or two from a neighboring congregation until under the teaching of the Word and the work of the Holy Spirit you saw men growing into the biblical shape of the office of elder. All this may seem a vast distance from Mount Gerizim and the olives and the brambles—but it's not.

The Process of Judgment

Finally, we can see how verses 22–57 display the process of judgment.

Though we don't relish an episode of judgment, we must admit that this account is an interesting story. The men of Shechem install gangs of ambushers on the highways around Shechem to rob travelers passing by (v. 25). This will give Abimelech a political black eye—what sort of king is this who cannot even guarantee safe transit across his territory? And then Gaal and Company come to town (vv. 26–29). Gaal had gall all right, at least when he was fortified with a little alcohol. Grape harvest was a naturally joyous time and all the more so when the harvesters gathered for happy hour in Baalberith's temple. Gaal found that a little Shechem Lite went a long way. He denounced Abimelech[8] and offered to lead a revolt against him. He had lots of support there in Baal's Bar.

Zebul, Abimelech's local henchman, informed Abimelech of the growing anti-Abimelechian sentiment and specified precisely when and how Abimelech should move to quell the revolt (vv. 30–33). By about 3:00 A.M., I imagine, Abimelech had his four companies of troops waiting in position around Shechem. Then there is that classic scene at the city gate. One can almost see it! Gaal arrives about six o'clock at the city

8. Verse 28 is very difficult, as the reader can see in the variety among English versions. Yet there is no doubt about the general tone—Gaal is fomenting revolt. I wonder if the text is so difficult because Gaal was half-drunk when he spoke!

gate, munching on his doughnut and sipping his coffee from the convenience store. Abimelech's men started forming their attack, and Gaal remarked to Zebul about how men were coming down from the hills. Zebul made a disarming comment, maybe something like: "How long has it been since you've seen your ophthalmologist, Gaal?" (cf. v. 36). Gaal squints and exclaims, "No, Zebul, those *are* men!" (cf. v. 37). Zebul has his trump card ready: "Where is your mouth now?" (v. 38). He must have practiced that line all night—such a delicious moment.

Abimelech had no trouble dispatching Gaal and his supporters (vv. 39–41). I suspect the residents of Shechem thought the next day would be like any other Tuesday. Many of them had not been among Gaal's hotheads and therefore did not count on any reprisals against them. Gaal bit the dust yesterday. Things are back to normal now. Let's farm. But Abimelech still fumed. No sooner had they reached their fields than a group of Abimelech's guerrillas sealed off escape into the city (v. 44) and two other groups massacred the workers in the field. Then they demolished the city (v. 45).

The city leaders escaped to what they hoped was the safety of the temple tower.[9] Abimelech, however, who decided to play follow-the-leader (v. 48), started a huge brushfire, either burning up or smoking out his prey (v. 49).

Perhaps Thebez[10] had also revolted against Abimelech. Abimelech successfully attacked. The last resistance was the fortress tower (vv. 50–51). Abimelech's pragmatism told him that what worked at Shechem would surely work at Thebez, but as he leaned over to ignite the fire, he discovered—too

9. The leaders of Shechem escaped to "the *seriaḥ* in the temple of El Berith" (v. 46). Some think the *seriaḥ* was an underground chamber (see NASB on vv. 46, 49), while others take it as a "stronghold," that is, a fortress tower (see Robert G. Boling, *Judges,* The Anchor Bible [Garden City, N.Y.: Doubleday, 1975], 181). I prefer the latter.

10. Thebez surely was not far from Shechem, but whether it should be identified with Tubas, nine miles northeast of Shechem, or perhaps with Tirzah, about six miles northeast of Shechem, cannot be determined; cf. Yohanan Aharoni, *The Land of the Bible: A Historical Geography,* rev. and enl. (Philadelphia: Westminster, 1979), 265.

late—that a certain woman had a crush on him (v. 53).[11] It was all over; now Israel was at peace again (v. 55).

The story is so interesting in itself that we might forget what is really taking place—divine judgment. We must view all of verses 22–57 in light of Jotham's double-edged curse in verse 20; fire came from Abimelech to destroy the men of Shechem and fire came from Shechem and consumed Abimelech. One episode; double destruction. Lest we miss the point the writer frames this last section with unmissable statements that here *God* was instigating and executing his judgment on Abimelech and Shechem (vv. 23–24, 56–57). I append several observations.

There is a certain quietness about the judgment. It is well we have the clear statements of verses 23–24 and 56–57 or we might not realize what is taking place. The whole episode seems so natural, from the highway robberies to Gaal's blathering, from Zebul's intelligence work to Abimelech's vengeance. The writer describes even the last blow in almost laconic terms: "and a certain woman threw an upper millstone upon Abimelech's head" (v. 53 RSV). So unconstrued. Simply a matter of course—apparently. God's judgment works so gradually here; there is no smell of fire and brimstone; Sinai is not shaking with smoke and thunder.

We once had a basketball goal in our back yard. The backboard was composed of pressed board and was not highly weather-resistant. On a particular day after a particular shot, the right side of the backboard came loose and hung down. That was only the final result. The process of decay had been going on for months as the backboard rotted away around the heads of the bolts that held it in place, until the bolts no longer held anything and that last shot jarred the backboard loose. Sometimes God's judgment is like that; it works so silently and unobserved. We need to beware of thinking that God avenges only when he makes a racket.

11. One can just imagine a husband panting beside his wife as they run to refuge in the Thebez tower, exasperated that his wife insists on lugging her upper millstone along. Doubtless she responded: "Now, dear, you never know when you might need a good millstone!"

Again, there is a certain irony about this judgment. As Jotham declared (v. 20) and the story reported (vv. 22–57), Abimelech destroyed Shechem and the men of Shechem destroyed Abimelech (with a little help from Thebez). That is, evil destroyed evil. God frequently judges in this way, using evil men to destroy evil men, evil nations to wipe out other evil nations. Judges 9 teaches us something very important: there is no fellowship in evil; evil has no lasting cohesion; it does not care for its own (it only *uses* its own). You can see this in living color in Revelation 17:16–17, which depicts how the Antichrist and his cronies will hate and consume the very anti-God culture they had nourished.

Lastly, there is a certain comfort in this utter humiliation of Abimelech. In the mentality of the time there was no worse fate than being dispatched by a woman.[12] That's why Abimelech pleaded for his armor-bearer to finish him off (v. 54); at least then the newspapers couldn't officially say a woman killed him. His armor-bearer obliged; but what difference did it make? Here lies Abimelech, the destroyer of Israel (see esp. v. 5). Here lies a firm comfort for God's beleaguered people: God destroys the destroyers of his people. The rulers of this age have never learned that whoever touches the flock of Yahweh touches the apple of his eye (cf. Zech. 2:8) and therefore places himself under God's sword or millstone. Similarly, if God's people are God's sacred temple (1 Cor. 3:16, where the "you" is plural in Greek), how careful the church's teachers and members must be not to destroy that temple by teaching error or brewing strife (cf. 1 Cor. 3:17).

Judges 9 shows Israel that destruction can come from within as well as from without, from Israel as well as Midian. Yet even Judges 9 preaches a word of hope to Israel: God does not abandon his people to their Abimelechs but keeps his people from utter destruction.

---

12. In one sense this unnamed woman in verse 53 is as much a deliverer of Israel as Jael (chap. 4).

12

A Couple of Minors
(10:1–5)

I doubt that Tola and Jair are on your list of favorite Bible characters. We don't know enough about them to make them favorites. One usually learns more about a person from a newspaper obituary than we can gather from these brief verses. So Tola and Jair are sometimes called minor judges—as opposed to major judges like Ehud or Deborah or Gideon, about whom we have more detail and who are the subjects of more extensive narratives. Tola and Jair are minor judges because they receive less ink, less space in the story, a fact which does not mean they were of no importance.[1] In fact, there was probably little difference in function between the major and the minor judges.[2]

1. We have the same situation in the way we distinguish between major prophets (Isaiah, Jeremiah, Ezekiel) and minor prophets (Hosea through Malachi). The minor prophets are minor not in the significance but in the shortness of their books.
2. For support of this position, see Alan J. Hauser, "The 'Minor Judges'—A Re-evaluation," *Journal of Biblical Literature* 94 (1975): 190–200; E. Theodore Mullen, Jr., "The 'Minor Judges': Some Literary and Historical Considerations," *Catholic Biblical Quarterly* 44 (1982): 185–201; and F. C. Fensham, "Judges, Book of," *ISBE* (rev. ed.), 2:1156–57. This position rejects the previously dominant view of Martin Noth, who held that the minor judges were proclaimers of the law while the major judges were "charismatic" military deliverers - *The History of Israel,* 2d ed. [New York: Harper and Row, 1960], 101–3, 107).

A Hint of Yahweh's Goodness

What do we know about Tola? Actually, not much; only his pedigree ("son of Puah, son of Dodo," v. 1),[3] his tribe (Issachar), his residence ("Shamir [location unknown] in the hill country of Ephraim," v. 1), his tenure (judged twenty-three years, v. 2), and his death and burial place (in Shamir). However, verse 1 is careful to state that Tola arose "after Abimelech to save Israel." Here we have a clear hint of Yahweh's goodness. We don't know just how Tola was to save Israel, whether by establishing a period of stable administration or by some military victory.[4] But his saving work—whatever it was—came "after Abimelech," after the destroyer of Israel had done his worst, after the chaos he caused, after the infamous treachery against Gideon's family—after that Yahweh raises up Tola for a saving mission. That is, I would say, typical of Yahweh. He does not allow blasting to go on for ever, does not allow his people to be trampled ad infinitum; but it is his way after the Valley of the Shadow to anoint our heads with oil, after sorrow and sighing to grant joy and gladness. Yahweh is the gracious God who never allows "Abimelech" to be the last word for his people.

A Picture of Man's Tendency

Then there was Jair—a judge for twenty-two years and with thirty sons on thirty asses over thirty cities (vv. 3–5).[5] The scene is Gilead to the east of the Jordan, a few miles southeast of the Sea of Galilee.[6] If in Tola's regime we find a hint of

3. The fact that Tola's descent is given indicates he was likely a man of some prominence.

4. Robert Boling (*Judges*, The Anchor Bible [Garden City, N. Y.: Doubleday, 1975], 187) and Barry G. Webb (*The Book of the Judges: An Integrated Reading*, JSOT Supplement Series 46 [Sheffield: JSOT, 1987], 160) take "save" here as referring to the establishing of a peaceful administration, though I think it alludes to military deliverance since that is the consistent connotation of *yasha'* (to save) in the Book of Judges (see Hauser, "'Minor Judges,'" 199).

5. In the Hebrew of verse 4 there is a word-play between the words for "asses" and "cities," both being written so they sound the same yet with diverse meanings; something like "peace" and "piece" in English.

6. Arthur E. Cundall, *Judges*, Tyndale Old Testament Commentaries (London: Tyndale, 1968), 137. For the possible location of Kamon (v. 5) see Boling, *Judges*, 48–49, 188.

Yahweh's goodness, we may see in Jair's a true picture of man's tendency.

We must be careful here. The text only depicts Jair's wide influence through his thirty sons; it does not necessarily imply there was anything wrong with that. Indeed, Israelite theology taught that numerous sons were a gift from Yahweh and a means of protection from enemies (Ps. 127:3–5). However, Jair's thirty sons (and who know how many daughters he sired?) imply he had multiple wives. This text records no specific displeasure about this. Yet when we heard of Gideon's seventy sons, the writer gave the explanation, "for he had many wives" (8:30), a circumstance that at least made the Abimelech fiasco (chap. 9) possible. Gideon's fertility also displayed the usual trappings of kingship in spite of official denials of it (8:22–23).[7] The writer seems to have put a certain negative cast over that situation. Hence I suggest we may regard Jair with the same concern.

We need not begrudge Jair his success, his influence, his evidently peaceful administration. Yet surely we understand him. In all our ways there is this subtle urge to secure our position, to display our status, to extend our influence, to guarantee our recognition. Christ's servants seldom care to be servants (see Mark 10:35–45). We have never gotten over the garden (Gen. 3:5)—our program to unseat the true King has a way of slipping out from behind our largest fig leaves.

7. The Torah specified that any future Israelite king "must not multiply wives for himself" (Deut. 17:17). The reason for this was not so much to prevent self-aggrandizement but apostasy; if a king married pagan princesses to seal political agreements, his heart would "turn aside" from Yahweh (see Peter C. Craigie, *The Book of Deuteronomy,* New International Commentary on the Old Testament [Grand Rapids: Eerdmans, 1976], 256).

13

The Kindness and the Severity of God
(10:6–16)

I've had a bad day; I had a flat tire on the freeway."
If a husband said that to his wife, she would probably acknowledge that such an inconvenience does place a blot upon one's day. But suppose he said: "I've had a bad day; I fell in the shower and cracked a rib, got sick on my cornflakes, ripped my pants on the latch of the car door, had a flat tire on the freeway; a passing truck hit a nearby mud puddle as I was changing the tire and splattered my suit. The highway patrol stopped me for speeding; the boss read me the riot act for being late; and, when I went off to get a drink and cool off, someone had spiked the water fountain and it squirted me in the face." His wife would surely concur; he *really* had had a bad day.

Judges 10:6 is like that second statement. It does not—like some of the previous statements in Judges (see 3:12; 4:1; 6:1)—merely state the fact that Israel again committed apostasy; it says they really committed apostasy. Here the writer piles up his statements so that you will see how intensely and totally Israel had fallen away from Yahweh: "Now the sons of Israel again did what was evil in Yahweh's eyes, and they served the Baals and the Ashtaroth, the gods of Aram, the gods of Sidon, the gods of Moab, the gods of the sons of Ammon, and the gods of the Philistines; so they abandoned Yahweh and they did not serve him." Here is faithlessness stacked high. Israel's state is not merely critical but disastrous.

Yahweh meets intense apostasy with severe retribution, a double oppression by Philistia and Ammon (v. 7; the Ammonite threat takes up chaps. 10–12, the Philistine will hit the press in chaps. 13–16), who "shattered and crushed" (v. 8) Israel.[1] The Ammonites not only stomped Israel throughout Gilead but even made forays west of the Jordan against Judah, Benjamin, and Ephraim (vv. 8b–9a). Israel was desperate (v. 9b).

Hear Yahweh's Threat

Now you must perk up your senses, because you must hear Yahweh's threat (vv. 11–14). Israel is so desperate that they not only cry out to Yahweh for help but also include in their cries some sort of confession of sin (v. 10; see the comments on 3:9 regarding za'aq, to cry out). Surely these are the lines God longs to hear, but evidently Yahweh had heard this song and dance before:

> Did I not save you from the Egyptians, from the Amorites, from the sons of Ammon, and from the Philistines?[2] And the Sidonians, and Amalek, and Maon [or, Midian?] pressed you hard, and when you cried out to me, I would save you from their hand. But *you* abandoned me and kept serving other gods; therefore I will not save you any longer. Go on and cry out to the gods you have chosen—let *them* save you in the time of your distress. [vv. 11–14][3]

"You cried out to me, I would save you . . . but you abandoned me." Same song, sixteenth verse. The theology of bomb-shelter religion teaches that—of course—God will help you in your need, that he is—helpfully enough—incredibly naive and hopelessly soft. He's like a great warm vending machine in the

---

1. The verb *shattered (ra'aṣ)* occurs but one other time in the Old Testament, in Exodus 15:6, where it describes Yahweh's shattering of the Egyptian enemy.

2. The text of verse 11 is somewhat difficult, but I am assuming that a form of the verb *yasha'* (to save), which does occur in verse 12, is implicit in verse 11.

3. The last clause might also be translated: "*they* will save you," so long as we hear the biting sarcasm with which it is spoken.

sky into which you need only drop a token or two of repentance before he spits out the relief you currently crave. Religion is a great game—you only need to know a few rules. And Yahweh is a great God—if you happen to need him and want to use him.

Yahweh must destroy these false images we fashion of him. Israel apparently assumed that whenever things became too bad she could always go back to Yahweh; and he says that she cannot. There is a difference between a prodigal who comes to his senses and returns home and a whore who pleads for her husband's security only until she finds someone else to take her on.

"I will not save you any longer." You have, Yahweh seems to say, chosen gods; go to those gods in your jam; they'll save you!—but don't come yammering back to me in one of these repentance acts. Israel's sin in Judges is not a cycle but a plunge, which, persisted in, will place her beyond Yahweh's help. Israel must awake to her peril. Yahweh is saying that Israel is on the edge of becoming an abandoned people. Sheer tragedy is when people become so accustomed to the mercy of God that they despise it—even, and especially, in the act of seeking it.

Unfortunately, we can hear the reaction of the proverbial New Testament Christian to this. "Yes," he agrees, "the Old Testament people of God stood under this dire threat of placing themselves beyond God's grace, but threats like that no longer apply since Jesus' death and resurrection." Simon of Samaria was a New Testament Christian; at least he had believed and been baptized and loved to accompany Philip the evangelist (Acts 8:13). Simon also held that religion was for fun and profit, especially profit, and recognized that the Holy Spirit was very marketable (Acts 8:18–19), which merited him Peter's rebuke: "Your silver perish with you, because you thought you could obtain the gift of God with money! You have neither part nor lot in this matter . . . . You are in the gall of bitterness and in the bond of iniquity" (Acts 8:20–21, 23 RSV). Christians must beware of their tendency to make God safe; when we do so we end up worshiping something other than the Holy One of Israel.

See Yahweh's Heart

Secondly, you must see Yahweh's heart; and you see it in verse 16b, which the Jerusalem Bible nicely renders, "He could bear Israel's suffering no longer."

We must be careful here. It is all too easy to view verse 16b as if it were the natural result of verses 15–16a: "The sons of Israel said to Yahweh, 'We have sinned! Do to us whatever you want; only please deliver us this time.' And they put away the foreign gods from among them and served Yahweh."

Hence some may surmise, "True, Yahweh threatened to cease saving Israel, but then they *really* repented and so Yahweh relented; when they put away the foreign gods they showed how sincere they were, and this moved Yahweh to compassion." That is, I would hold, a wrong reading of the text for two reasons. First, Israel's previous cryings out to Yahweh (v. 12b) may well have involved the putting away of foreign gods, for Yahweh's complaint (v. 13) "is not that Israel has failed in the past to back up its cry by putting away its other gods, but rather that on each previous occasion, after deliverance has been granted, Israel has abandoned him for these gods again."[4] The second reason is that verse 16b itself does not tie Yahweh's compassion to Israel's repentance but to her misery or suffering.

"He could bear Israel's suffering no longer." Our hope does not rest in the sincerity of our repentance but in the intensity of Yahweh's compassion.[5] It is very difficult for us to imagine how much Israel's misery moves Yahweh. It is as if he cannot stand to see his people—even his sinful people—crushed. In all their affliction he is afflicted (Isa. 63:9). That is why we have this seeming tension between judgment and grace in Scripture, a tension not merely in the texts of Scripture but in

4. Barry G. Webb, *The Book of the Judges: An Integrated Reading*, JSOT Supplement Series 46 (Sheffield: JSOT Press, 1987), 46.

5. I am not saying that repentance is unimportant; however, we must learn, for example, from Joel 2:12–14 that repentance is a divine demand (vv. 12–13a) but that it places its hope in divine grace rather than in human sorrow (v. 13b) and recognizes that any benefit received is not properly coerced but freely given (v. 14). Repentance may be a condition but not a cause of God's restored favor.

the character of Yahweh himself, for he is the God whose holiness demands he judge his people yet whose heart moves him to spare his people. If it is a tension, its origin is in the bosom of God himself.

"He could bear Israel's suffering no longer." Many Christians, especially those who have a lively sense of God's severity but little of his kindness, should meditate on this text. You must see Yahweh's heart. And don't forget where he showed it to you: in the Old Testament, the book of the grace of God.

14

Despised and Rejected by Men
(10:17–12:7)

I remember one of my earlier forays into plumbing. Something was wrong with our bathroom lavatory and I thought it was probably located in the trap. I rejected hiring a plumber in order to save expense. The problem was not, as it turned out, in the trap, but in the process I became acquainted with pipe-joint compound, using it liberally in my ineffective repairs, so that when the real plumber came, he nearly had a coronary unassembling my work. But the health of the bona fide plumber is not at issue. The *real* problem with the whole affair was having to eat humble pie—having to beg a plumber's help after I had, in principle, rejected him.

The elders of Gilead knew little about plumbing but were familiar with the taste of humble pie. What could they do? The Ammonites were about to attack (10:17) and Gilead was caught in a leadership vacuum (10:18). They could only go to the one despised and rejected by men, to Jephthah, the man nobody had wanted (11:1–3). An outlaw will be their savior.

The Instrument of Salvation

We will look at the Jephthah materials under our broad theme of salvation (cf. the use of *yasha'*, to save, deliver, in 10:12, 13, 14), and, clearly, 10:17–11:11 places Jephthah on center stage as the instrument of salvation.

The parenthetical material of 11:1–3 gives us the vital background about Jephthah. His problem was not his military ability but his mother. Gilead, Jephthah's father,[1] had an affair with a prostitute; Jephthah was born; Jephthah was the one who suffered. Gilead and his wife also had legitimate sons, who (by the time they were smart enough to think of inheritances) banished Jephthah since he, obviously, didn't "belong" (11:2). Jephthah fled to the land around Tob,[2] where the dregs collected themselves around him, a band of freebooting guerrillas led by a social outcast (11:3).

If we are to appreciate the figure of Jephthah, we must consider the similarity of structure between 10:6–16 (Israel and Yahweh) and 11:1–11 (Gileadites and Jephthah). I need not describe it if the reader will work through table 14.1 with reference to the biblical text. The parallels between Israel's way with Yahweh and Gilead's way with Jephthah seem too close to be accidental. When the Israelites are in a jam they cry to Yahweh to bail them out (10:10), as the elders of Gilead do to Jephthah (11:5–6). Both Yahweh's reply (10:11–14) and Jephthah's (11:7) show that they know someone is trying to use them.[3] The way the Gileadites treat Jephthah is an acted parable of the way Israel approaches Yahweh.

We pause to reflect on this parallel. In its own way it suggests that "a slave is not above his lord; if they persecuted me, they will persecute you as well" (John 15:20; cf. Matt. 10:24–25). Even from God's professing people a servant of God may have no right to expect better treatment than the Lord himself receives. Certainly Jephthah fared no better than Yahweh.

A similar pattern occurs in the case of Israel and Jesus. On

1. I take the Gilead of 11:1–2 as a namesake of his ancestor (Num. 26:29).
2. Tob is usually identified with et-Taiyibeh, over ten miles east of Ramoth-gilead and Edrei, near the sources of the Yarmuk River.
3. After tracing out this structural pattern, I discovered that Matthew Henry had noticed it long ago (1708!), at least in general: "The particular case between the Gileadites and Jephthah was a resemblance of the general state of the case between Israel and God at this time. They had thrust God out by their idolatries, yet in their distress begged his help; he told them how justly he might have rejected them, and yet graciously delivered them. So did Jephthah" (*Commentary on the Whole Bible*, 6 vols. [New York: Revell, n.d.], 2:190).

Table 14.1   The Structure of Judges 10:6–16 and 11:1–11

Theme	Chap. 10	Chap. 11
Rejection	v. 6	vv. 1–3
Distress	vv. 7–9	v. 4
Repentance	v. 10	vv. 5–6
Objection	vv. 11–14	v. 7
Appeal	vv. 15–16a	v. 8
Acquiescence	v. 16b	vv. 9–11

Pentecost Peter accuses Israel: "You, with the help of wicked men, put him to death by nailing him to the cross" (Acts 2:23 NIV); he then turns around and calls them to "repent and be baptized, every one of you, in the name of Jesus Christ so that your sins may be forgiven" (Acts 2:38 NIV, 1973 ed.). They must seek succor from the very One they had cast out. Moreover, Jesus seems to say that in connection with his second coming Israel will again welcome the Rejected (Matt. 23:39).[4]

What is most striking, however, is that Yahweh will use this man—son of a harlot (v. 1),[5] rejected by his brothers (v. 2), a leader of thugs (v. 3)—to relieve Israel. Jephthah's situation was no fault of his own; he was more victim and sinned against. He could hardly help his being the leader of the Tob Raiders, an existence unlikely to nourish careful ethics or social graces.

Jephthah was, for whatever reason, a loser. Yet the Spirit of Yahweh came upon this loser (11:29), and Yahweh gave the

4. See, for example, Robert H. Gundry, *Matthew: A Commentary on His Literary and Theological Art* (Grand Rapids: Eerdmans, 1982), 474; and George E. Ladd, *A Theology of the New Testament* (Grand Rapids: Eerdmans, 1974), 200.

5. We cannot be sure whether the stricture of Deuteronomy 23:2 (no bastard to enter the assembly of Yahweh) would have applied to Jephthah, for there "bastard" (*mamzer*) may be used more specifically and not refer generally to all born out of wedlock. See S. R. Driver, *A Critical and Exegetical Commentary on Deuteronomy*, The International Critical Commentary (Edinburgh: T. and T. Clark, 1895), 260–61; and Peter C. Craigie, *The Book of Deuteronomy*, New International Commentary on the Old Testament (Grand Rapids: Eerdmans, 1976), 297.

Ammonites into his power (11:32). "But God chose" what men had rejected (cf. 1 Cor. 1:27; 1 Pet. 2:4).

It was the same with Alexander Whyte, well-known minister of Free Saint George's, Edinburgh, in the late nineteenth century. What an outstanding preacher, writer, educator the Free Church of Scotland had in Alexander Whyte! But no one would have guessed as much in 1836, when Janet Thomson brought him into this world—born out of wedlock. But God chose. . . . Maybe some day we will see it enough times in Scripture that we will cease to be surprised at the unlikely instruments God uses to deliver us.

The History of Salvation

Now that the sparring with the elders of Gilead (11:5–11) has ended, Jephthah can begin the conflict with the king of the Ammonites, which, at first, is a conflict of words. This we might call the history of salvation (11:12–28), for a large part of it (vv. 15–27) consists of Jephthah's rehearsing how Yahweh gave Israel the land east of the Jordan.

Why are the Ammonites attacking? According to their king, "because Israel took my land when he came up from Egypt, land from the Arnon as far as the Jabbok and to the Jordan" (v. 13). So Jephthah and Israel were to restore the land peaceably.

Jephthah's answer comes in verses 15–27. The first half of it (vv. 15–22) is explanation, a review of what actually happened in years past. Jephthah's point is: "Look, let's get the facts straight." For this reason he rehearses how, after leaving Egypt, Israel carefully respected both Edom's and Moab's land rights, asking special permission of both to traverse their respective territories (v. 17). Permission denied. Israel did not attack in retaliation but circled around Edom and Moab (v. 18). At that point they petitioned Sihon, king of the Amorites, with headquarters in Heshbon, for the privilege of passing through his land (v. 19), a chunk about fifty miles long between the Arnon and Jabbok rivers and about twenty miles wide from the Jordan east.[6] Sihon, however, did not send a memo but brought his army to attack Israel. Yahweh gave Israel the victory and so Israel possessed Sihon's former territory.

"Now, my dear Ammonite brother," says Jephthah, "it's time for inferences" (vv. 23–27). First, the argument from history. Yahweh drove out the Amorites (v. 23) and Israel possessed the land of the Amorites (vv. 21, 22). The land at that time belonged to neither Moab nor Ammon. Jephthah is saying: "What do you mean calling it *your* land [v. 13]? It wasn't yours; it was Amorite. Quit your history twisting."

Next, the argument from theology. "Yahweh, the God of Israel, dispossessed the Amorites from before his people Israel . . . and all that Yahweh our God dispossessed from before us— that's what we will possess" (vv. 23–24; see also v. 21). Yahweh gave Israel Sihon's land. It's as simple as that. A divine gift. So, Jephthah implies, "You'll simply have to be content with whatever Chemosh your god has given you" (v. 24a).

Let us go on a brief tangent. This reference to Chemosh has troubled some. Does this mean Jephthah thought Chemosh was a real god on the same level as Yahweh? No more than the psalmist did when he praised Yahweh as "a great King above all gods" (Ps. 95:3), for he knew—as well as his fellow worshipers—that "all the gods of the peoples are idols" (Ps. 96:5 RSV). In any case, when Jephthah calls on Yahweh as the true Judge (v. 27), he makes it clear that he does not think Yahweh and Chemosh stand on the same level; for Jephthah only Yahweh, not Chemosh, is judge.[7]

---

6. For your mental map: (1) The River Arnon (11:18) flows into the eastern side of the Dead Sea at about the midpoint; the Arnon was the northern boundary of Moabite territory. (2) The River Jabbok (11:22) empties from the east into the Jordan at a point not quite halfway up from the Dead Sea to the Sea of Galilee. (3) Heshbon (11:19), Sihon's center of operations, is usually located at Tell Hesban, about fifteen miles east of the northern tip of the Dead Sea; cf. L. T. Geraty, "Heshbon," *ISBE* (rev. ed.), 2:699–702. (4) We do not know the exact location of Jahaz (11:20). (5) Aroer (11:26), modern 'Ara'ir, stands about fifteen miles east of the Dead Sea on the north side of the River Arnon; see Kenneth A. Kitchen, "Aroer," *IBD*, 1:117–18.

7. Karl Gutbrod, *Das Buch vom Lande Gottes,* Die Botschaft des Alten Testaments, 3d ed. (Stuttgart: Calwer, 1965), 240.

Some still wonder if Jephthah had his facts straight. He is speaking to an Ammonite and yet says "Chemosh, your god" (v. 24). Didn't Jephthah know that Chemosh was the god of Moab and that Milkom (or Molech) was the god of Ammon? Barry G. Webb's close attention to the text helps to dissolve this difficulty:

> The words 'your god Chemosh' are rather startling in view of the consistent distinction in the Old Testament between Milcom/Molech as the god of Ammon and Chemosh as god of *Moab*. What is clear from the content of Jephthah's argument as a whole, however, is that he recognizes his opponent as legitimate ruler of *both* Ammon *and* Moab. Thus to his opponent's charge that Israel took away '*my* land' (v. 13) Jephthah replies that it took away 'neither the land of Moab nor the land of the Ammonites' (v. 15). In vv. 25–26 Jephthah addresses his opponent as successor to the kings of Moab (including Balak ben Zippor). . . . The natural inference is that Jephthah recognizes Ammon's title to 'the land of Moab' as being as legitimate as Israel's title to 'the land of the Amorite'.[8]

There is, then, no real incongruity in Jephthah's identifying Chemosh as the god of the Ammonite king. Moreover, there is some evidence from the Ebla Texts which suggests that Chemosh's sway was acknowledged far beyond Moab and Ammon;[9] and there is other evidence that indicates Chemosh and Milkom may be identical or local manifestations of the same "source deity."[10]

Jephthah also marshals what we might call the argument from precedent (v. 25). He says in effect: "Think about Balak, son of Zippor, king of Moab, when Israel was ready to enter the land promised. Did he ever fight Israel, alleging that Israel had grubbed land from Moab? If that wasn't Balak's problem it shouldn't be yours either." A check of Numbers 22:6 shows that Balak did want to defeat Israel and drive them away—if

8. Barry G. Webb, *The Book of the Judges: An Integrated Reading,* JSOT Supplement Series 46 (Sheffield: JSOT, 1987), 56.

9. William Sanford LaSor, "Chemosh," *ISBE* (rev. ed.), 1:641.

10. Peter C. Craigie and G. H. Wilson, "Religions of the Biblical World: Canaanite (Syria and Palestine)," *ISBE* (rev. ed.), 4:97.

only he could get them cursed in kosher style first. But in fact Balak did not fight them; and even though he wanted to drive them from "the land" (Num. 22:6), there is no evidence that his desire arose from thinking Israel had taken his land. Apparently, he saw their proximity and strength as a threat.

Finally, Jephthah presses the argument from silence (v. 26). Israel has been living, Jephthah chides the Ammonite, in this land for three hundred years, living in Heshbon, Aroer, and the villages around. Now if this is "your land" as you say, if this is such a disputed area, why does it only become a hot issue in our day and age? If this is such a sore spot, why hasn't someone else yelled about it in the last three hundred years? Why are you raising a stink now?

These are Jephthah's arguments; this is Jephthah's case. The Ammonite, not Jephthah, was in the wrong (11:27). But the Ammonite was in no mood to be confused by the facts (11:28).

Just because the Ammonites are bullheaded is no reason for us to follow their lead. If they refuse to listen to this little history of salvation (vv. 15–27), that is no reason for us to have uncircumcised ears. Jephthah makes it clear that Israel's triumph east of the Jordan was Yahweh's gift and doing (vv. 21, 23, 24), and, if they were to retain that gift, Yahweh alone could decide that (v. 27). Ammonites may prefer to remain dense; but Jephthah's little history of salvation should kindle gratitude and trust in true Israelites. Yahweh's defeating Sihon and giving Israel his land may not be as exciting or familiar to us as the Red Sea, smoking Sinai, or crumbling Jericho; but this also constitutes a chapter of Yahweh's great salvation (see Ps. 136:17–22 in context of the whole psalm).

The Tragedy of Salvation

In the last two sections of the Jephthah materials we meet the tragedy of salvation (11:29–40; 12:1–7). Both episodes center around words, the one a vow, the other a password. In the former the tragedy apparently arises from zeal, in the latter certainly from pride.

Let us try to sense the mood the writer creates in the vow narrative (11:29–40). He briefly notes that Yahweh's Spirit empowers Jephthah and traces Jephthah's movements under that power toward the foray with Ammon (v. 29). He then alludes to something that had taken place, which, as it turns out, will overshadow the rest of the story:

> Now Jephthah had vowed a vow to Yahweh; he said: "If you will certainly give the sons of Ammon into my hand, it shall be that the one who goes forth who will come forth [lit.] from the doors of my house to meet me when I come back in victory from the sons of Ammon, it shall belong to Yahweh, and I shall offer it [lit., him] up as a burnt offering." [vv. 30–31]

The writer next summarizes in briefest outline the victory Yahweh gave Jephthah (v. 32), along with something of the geographical movement and extent of the victory (v. 33).[11] "So the sons of Ammon were subdued from before the sons of Israel" (v. 33b). That remark makes short literary work of the Ammonites. We would be happy to have had a few wild, chilling scenes from the battles; but the writer compresses all of that to the barest of facts because he wants to focus on what comes from this vow Jephthah has made. It is as if the writer wants to swallow up victory in sorrow; almost as if he disposes of the Ammonites because he is preoccupied with what Jephthah's vow will bring. Oddly enough, the day will be far more bitter for the victor (Jephthah) than for the vanquished. In any case, the Ammonites must take a back seat. All attention falls on Jephthah as he approaches home.

Tragic Zeal

Let's continue to follow the story; we'll come to questions and difficulties later. The reader gasps even before Jephthah can. "Why, his daughter was coming out to meet him with tambourines and dances!" (v. 34)—as Miriam and her girls celebrated the deliverance at the sea (Exod. 15:20).[12] But the joy at Mizpah would be short-lived. Isaac too casts his shadow over this text—he was also the yahîd (the "only one" and

---

11. The sites of Minnith and Abel-keramim remain unidentified; on Aroer, see n. 6.

12. As noted, for example, by A. R. Fausset, *A Critical and Expository Commentary on the Book of Judges* (London: James Nisbet, 1885), 195.

therefore precious; *yeḥîdah* is the feminine used of Jephthah's daughter in v. 34) destined as a burnt offering (Gen. 22:2). However, as Webb points out, Yahweh remains silent through all of this; there is no voice from heaven intervening to stay Jephthah's hand (as in Gen. 22:11–14).[13] (Not that heaven approves Jephthah's activity but simply that there is no relief from above.) The story thuds heavily on, from the submission of Jephthah's daughter ("do to me according to what has gone forth from your mouth," v. 36 RSV) to the report of his action (he "did with her according to his vow which he had made," v. 39 RSV), with the two months' reprieve (vv. 37–39a) only switching the inevitable into slow motion.

It sounds as though I think Jephthah actually offered up his daughter as a sacrifice. That is correct. That is, I believe, the most natural reading of verses 30, 31, and 39. I do not say that the writer (let alone Yahweh) approves of it; he never says he does. He simply reports the matter. I do not say we understand all that is involved, for biblical writers frequently refuse to elaborate on what we are curious about, and, in any case, we cannot get inside Jephthah's head. I do not wish to duplicate other discussions but the matter merits some attention.

First, did Jephthah expect a human to be first to meet him when he returned? Probably. Strictly speaking, Jephthah's words in verse 31 can be rendered, "*What*ever comes forth . . . to meet me" rather than "whoever," in which case one could say Jephthah had in mind an animal sacrifice. But "coming forth to meet" someone is a purposeful action more naturally associated with a human agent.[14]

Secondly, would Jephthah—could Jephthah—have intended to offer a human sacrifice? I think there are two errors we need to avoid here. One is to think that Jephthah was such a

13. Webb, *The Book of the Judges,* p. 69.

14. The New American Standard Bible renders verse 31: "whatever comes out of the doors of my house to meet me . . . shall be the LORD'S, or I will offer it up as a burnt offering." That is, Jephthah keeps his options open: if a person meets him, he dedicates him/her to Yahweh; if an animal, he offers it in sacrifice. Though the translation "*or* I will offer it up" is possible, it is not the more natural. I would venture no one would think of it unless driven to seek an escape from a (perceived) ethical difficulty in the text.

primitive bumpkin that he did not realize human sacrifice was wrong according to Israel's law (Lev. 18:21; 20:2–5; Deut. 12:31; 18:10). No one is claiming he had a master's degree in Pauline ethics, but his speech (11:12–28)—even if he used a speechwriter—shows he is no early blob on some scale of moral evolution.

At the same time we must beware of being so cocksure that Jephthah would never have offered a human sacrifice. Some writers regard it as inconceivable that a God-fearing man like Jephthah would ever perform such an act. I think it is conceivable. And I think we must be careful of our conceptions, that is, we should not attribute to Jephthah a certain complex of piety which may reflect the way we prefer to think of him rather than what the text warrants.

How God-fearing was Jephthah? Certainly Jephthah was a Yahweh-worshiper, knowledgeable in Yahweh's history with Israel, and—I should think—acquainted with Yahweh's law. But that does not mean Jephthah observed the law he knew. We have already rejected his being a moral ignoramus; yet we must acknowledge that guerrilla life and gross companionship (11:3) hardly enhance social graces or nourish personal ethics. I have a problem with those who claim Jephthah would never have sacrificed his daughter because that would have been against Yahweh's law: they automatically assume that Jephthah was consistent with what he knew. But how do we know that Jephthah was consistently consistent? Is it not just as conceivable that, in spite of what knowledge he had, he convinced himself that such a sacrifice, given the emergency, might be not only entirely proper but also deeply pious?

A third question is: Wasn't it assumed that if such a vow involved a human life it was to be fulfilled by some sort of lifelong dedication to Yahweh? Some argue for this in the present case. They note that Jephthah's daughter and her companions weep over her virginity (vv. 37, 38) rather than her impending death. Moreover, after Jephthah carries out his vow, verse 39 states that she had never had sexual relations with a man. That, so it is held, is a strange thing to say if her father sacrificed her but makes perfect sense if she was locked in to a celibate life of devotion to Yahweh, perhaps at the worship sanctuary.[15]

Some scholars have pointed out that women evidently did serve at Israel's worship center (Exod. 38:8; 1 Sam. 2:22).[16] They have also noted that according to Leviticus 27:1–8 a man might vow a person to Yahweh. Hence they infer that Jephthah vowed his daughter to Yahweh and that he fulfilled that vow through her lifelong celibate service at the sanctuary.

There are problems, however, with such a reconstruction. The vowing of persons in Leviticus 27:1–8 has nothing to do with serving at the sanctuary. Each person had a value assigned him/her, which the person who made the vow paid to the priest, thus no doubt redeeming that person. Moreover, the idea of virginity or celibacy fits nowhere. There are no grounds for assuming that the women of Exodus 38:8 and 1 Samuel 2:22 were virgins. If Jephthah's daughter had to serve the rest of her life at the sanctuary, why would she have to remain unmarried? Is that a clause of Jephthah's vow the writer omitted? So I agree with Matthew Henry: "Besides, had she only been confined to a single life, she needed not to have desired these two months to bewail it in: she had her whole life before her to do that, if she saw cause. Nor needed she to take such a sad leave of her companions. . . ."[17]

Someone will say that the view I advocate makes the episode very sad indeed. It does. I think that is what the writer wants us to see. The Ammonites have been whipped; but the sky in Gilead is very, very gray.[18] Some of our most solemn

---

15. Actually, the stress on her virginity in verses 37, 38, and 39 fits well with the literal sacrifice view; she weeps over her virginity because death will cut off from her any hope of bearing seed. With her (v. 34b) Jephthah's line will vanish.

16. But no one knows if such service was the result of a vow.

17. Henry, *Commentary*, 2:197.

18. The reader may find discussions of Jephthah's vow in George Bush, *Notes, Critical and Practical, on the Book of Judges* (Chicago: Henry A. Sumner, 1881), 162–65; C. J. Goslinga, *Joshua, Judges, Ruth,* Bible Student's Commentary (Grand Rapids: Zondervan, 1986), 391–96; and Leon J. Wood, *Distressing Days of the Judges* (Grand Rapids: Zondervan, 1975), 287–95. All of these take the nonliteral view.

commitments may be stupid. We will return to this tragic element.

Tragic Pride

We have the second tragic episode in 12:1–7. Some are not even content to sit at the right hand and the left in the kingdom but insist on occupying the center throne. That description fits the tribe of Ephraim to a T.

Ephraim crosses the Jordan, meets Jephthah at Zaphon (a town east of the Jordan in the river valley and north of Succoth), and berates him for fighting Ammon without consulting Ephraim, without asking their assistance. "What about us? Why did you ignore us when you fought Ammon? Why didn't you call *us* to go with you?"[19] That is Ephraim's gripe; they are somebodies and you don't treat somebodies like that.

Jephthah, having been a nobody (cf. 11:1–3), was likely unimpressed with somebodies. In any case, Jephthah retorted that he *had* summoned the Ephraimites (vv. 2b–3a) and they had left him in the lurch. What Ephraim did not do, however, Yahweh did (v. 3b).

Ephraim may have been expecting something more like the psychology of Gideon (8:1–3) than the sword of Jephthah (12:4a). Jephthah never used much psychology in Tob (11:3) and probably saw no need to begin now, especially when Ephraim began flinging racial slurs at his Gilead men (12:4b). Jephthah and Company cut down and scattered the Ephraimites, occupied the crossing-places on the Jordan,[20] then waited to play Password with Ephraimite stragglers wanting to go west (12:5–6).

How vivid those "shibboleth" episodes must have been. Here comes an Ephraimite fugitive to one of the fords and tells the Gileadite guards, "I want to cross over." Ah, yes, well, you are not an Ephraimite, are you? Oh no, I'm a Reubenite going to visit some friends on the west bank. Fine, that's okay. Now

---

19. Ephraim's "us" is emphatic in the Hebrew text of 12:1.
20. Twice before Ephraim had successfully manned the crossing-places against the enemy (3:27–28; 7:24–25); here they are on the receiving end.

will you please say "shibboleth?"[21] Certainly; "sibboleth." It
was like someone denying he was a native of Virginia and then
being asked to say, "I went out about the house." We are most
accustomed to the idea: we detect a New Englander when he
tells us he "parked the car," a southerner by how he handles
his long-i vowels (as in "five"), and a western Pennsylvanian
when he calls a narrow, flowing stream a "crick" instead of a
"creek." So every Ephraimite who played Bible Password that
day lost.

Again (see 8:1–3), it is Ephraim, in his pride, who fragments
Israel. The Ephraimites always feel they must dominate, they
must control, they must be recognized. Nor is it a peculiarly
Ephraimite or Israelite problem. It flourishes in the Christian
fellowship. How *we* want to be the ones to score the Christian
points, to be known as the ones on Jesus' varsity squad. How
difficult it is for me to rejoice in God's saving work when I am
not the Christian celebrity in the middle of it. We don't like
to play the Christian game unless people will appropriately
stroke our egos for doing so.

Ammon is subdued. But there is the grave of Jephthah's
only child. And there are the lifeless forms of once-cocky
Ephraimite militia. Whether from excessive zeal (11:30–31) or
stubborn pride (12:1) tragedy overshadows the salvation
Yahweh gave (11:32b–33). I would wager that the writer
meant to paint it so; I think he wants us to see Yahweh's
deliverance tinctured by human foolishness and human arrogance. It is as if even the winners can't have a clean win. We
have salvation here but a marred salvation. The writer is suggesting that if we seek a perfect salvation we will have to look
to One greater than Jephthah.

The writer of Judges seems intent on stressing this imper-
fection in the salvation that comes through the judges—at
least through some of them. It is an integral part of the way
he depicts the progressive fragmentation of Israel throughout
his book. I can best summarize this with a self-citation:

21. "Shibboleth" means either "flowing stream, torrent" or "ear of grain."
On the incident see Willem A. VanGemeren, "Shibboleth," *ISBE* (rev. ed.),
4:476.

Another indication of the disintegration process may be detected in the basic pattern used in combining the accounts of the so-called major judges. These accounts may be divided into two groups of three, the first group consisting of Othniel, Ehud, and Deborah and Barak, with Gideon, Jephthah, and Samson composing the second. The narratives dealing with the first group are, in general, relatively brief, lack any extensive personal details about the judge (e.g., about his/her domestic life), and contain no negative connotations about their subjects. By contrast, the accounts about the second group are more extensive and detailed, provide more intimate glimpses of the characters of the judges, and convey negative evaluations (explicit or implicit) about some aspect of their activity. In this last regard it is particularly interesting to note that each narrative cycle of the second group ends in grievous tragedy. Gideon sows the seed of fresh apostasy (8:24–27) and sires Abimelech whose reign of terror will bathe Abiezer in its own blood (ch. 9). Jephthah's success comes at the high price of the sacrifice of his only child and daughter. And Samson's flippant self-sufficiency [16:7, 11, 13, 20] has already prepared the reader for the sight of his mutilated body (16:21) and the discovery of his corpse among the rubble of Gaza's temple (16:30). The contrast in this three-plus-three pattern, especially with its general movement from positive to negative overtones, fits perfectly with the scheme of progressive disintegration. . . .[22]

Jephthah does remind us of Jesus; he was despised and rejected by men (11:1–3; Isa. 53:3). But there is something lacking in the deliverance he could bring; the full and perfect salvation will come only through Immanuel (Matt. 1:21–23). How appropriate that I should write this the day before the first Sunday in Advent.

22. Dale Ralph Davis, "A Proposed Life-Setting for the Book of Judges" (Ann Arbor: University Microfilms, 1978), 71–72.

15

A Judges' Directory?
(12:8–15)

Each year my own denomination publishes a yearbook. One section of this floppy paperback is called the ministerial directory, which gives a just-the-facts summary on each teaching elder (birth, marriage, children, education, and so on). One can't find much human-interest material in such summaries—the bare-facts approach makes that impossible.

We seem to have discovered a judges' directory in 12:8–15 (include v. 7, on Jephthah, if you like). We have notices about Ibzan, Elon, and Abdon with the barest amount of information: origin,[1] family data (though not for Elon), years of judging, death, and burial place. Our curiosity gets frustrated when the Bible is so skimpy.

The Selectivity of God's Word

Our frustration can prove instructive, for a passage like this certainly underscores the selectivity of God's word. We crave more detail, some flesh on the bones of Ibzan, Elon, and Abdon's lives. No stirring deeds recorded, no gripping stories, no miracles—unless Ibzan's having thirty sons and thirty

---

1. Ibzan was likely from the Bethlehem in Zebulun (Josh. 19:15), perhaps seven miles northwest of Nazareth. Elon's burial place is also in Zebulun (v. 12) though the site is uncertain; it should not be confused, however, with the Aijalon fourteen miles northwest of Jerusalem. Abdon's Pirathon (v. 15) is likely Far'ata, about six miles southwest of Shechem.

daughters and apparently retaining his sanity qualifies for such. We would like to have stories for them as for Deborah or Gideon or Jephthah. But we don't. This does not necessarily mean there were no stories to tell. It means only that the Bible has not told them. We must beware of thinking that Ibzan and Company were obscure or unimportant. Hardly. Ibzan's numerous sons and daughters and the marriage network he arranged (v. 9) show he was a man of social stature and political clout.[2] The same goes for Abdon (v. 14). Yet the Bible does not elect to give us more biography.

We don't know why the Bible tells us so little about Ibzan, but by telling us so little about Ibzan (and Elon and Abdon) the Bible tells us a lot about the Bible. It tells us that its purpose is not to tell us about every Ibzan, Elon, and Abdon. The Bible is saying that its focus is not on man's life but on God's action. The Bible is theo-centric. That does not mean that man does not count but that man is not the center. Even though Gideon, for example, may receive three chapters, the writer's purpose is not to relate Gideon's eventful life (not even his problems, struggles, victories, or failures in themselves) but to depict Yahweh's saving activity. For this reason I question the validity of much biographical preaching and Bible studies billed as character studies of biblical figures. Almost by their very nature, by their chosen starting points, such efforts begin by looking in the wrong direction. It is as if Scripture cries, "Behold your God!" (cf. Isa. 40:9), and we reply, "Thank you, but we have found something more interesting to us." And if a little frustration over Ibzan and associates makes us aware of this danger, they will not have lived in vain.

The Enigma of God's Providence

Secondly, these verses highlight the enigma of God's providence. The story of Jephthah, who has but one child and becomes, apparently, childless, is sandwiched between Jair with his thirty sons (10:3–5) and Ibzan with a total of sixty children (12:8–10). Abdon's total of seventy descendants

2. See the discussion of 3:31 (Shamgar), n. 2.

(12:14) also emphasizes the contrast. Many have noted this striking difference. Matthew Henry put it succinctly:

> What a difference was there between Ibzan's family and that of his immediate predecessor Jephthah! Ibzan has sixty children and all married, Jephthah but one, a daughter, that dies or lives unmarried. Some are increased, others are diminished: both are the Lord's doing.[3]

Once we see this we almost automatically ask, "Why?" Why does God give to one and withhold from another? Why does Yahweh give and take away? Why does he order our affairs with such differences? We cheer the providence of God when the angel warns Joseph and the child Jesus escapes Herod's clutches (Matt. 2:13–15). But what about the other toddlers in Bethlehem? Why didn't God spare them from Herod's butchers (Matt. 2:16)? Could not the God who spared Jesus have also shielded these from the sword? If the king's heart really is in the hand of the Lord (cf. Prov. 21:1), why didn't he give Herod a fatal coronary for Epiphany?

Or there is Acts 12. Peter, chained in prison, was soon to face the axe of Herod Agrippa. The very night before Death Day, an angel of the Lord set Peter free (Acts 12:6–11). Such a narrow escape! Such a marvelous providence! Such an answer to the church's prayers—the folks at the prayer meeting couldn't even believe it (vv. 5, 12–17)! But—same chapter—what about James? You know, the brother of John. Agrippa's sword dispensed with him (vv. 1–2). Why does James perish while Peter enjoys a miracle? Could not the God who rescued Peter from Agrippa's chains have delivered James from his sword? There it is again, side by side: marvelous prov-

---

3. Matthew Henry, *Commentary on the Whole Bible,* 6 vols. (New York: Revell, n.d.), 2:200–201. Barry G. Webb points out the direct contrast between Jephthah and Ibzan: "The tragic story of Jephthah and his one daughter, an only child, is followed by this note about a judge who had *thirty* daughters and brought in a further thirty daughters from outside his clan as wives for his thirty sons! Of all the judges, daughters are mentioned only in connection with these two, Jephthah and Ibzan. After Jephthah's barrenness comes Ibzan's fulness; the contrast serves to underscore the tragic barrenness suffered by Jephthah in consequence of his vow" (*The Book of the Judges: An Integrated Reading,* JSOT Supplement Series 46 [Sheffield: JSOT 1987], 161).

idence and mysterious providence. How anyone could think God is boring is beyond me.

Jephthah and Ibzan, the toddlers and the Christ child, James and Peter—repeatedly we face this enigma. We cannot claim to know why God so works (that does not mean we cannot ask "why?"). We can only bow before the One whose understanding is unsearchable (Isa. 40:28) and confess that though it is unsearchable it nevertheless must be understanding. We can, however, avoid foolish responses to this enigma—like imagining that if the parents of the Bethlehem toddlers had prayed more fervently, or if James had had stronger faith, God would have preserved them. And we can keep from inflicting such nonsense on others. We don't like to be without an explanation. But faith is willing, if need be, to be baffled, to bow and worship in the dark. That is the witness of Jephthah and Ibzan.

The Absence of God's Rest

Third, I submit that these verses may allude to the absence of God's rest (see the previous comments on 8:28). The text specifies that each of these men judged Israel over a specific number of years (vv. 9, 11, 14). I want to look at this matter in the context of the whole book.

There are three major types of time formulae in the Book of Judges:

1. The number of years Israel serves foreign oppressors (3:8, 14; 4:3; 6:1; 10:8; 13:1). These notices occur in connection with the narratives of each major judge.
2. The number of years the land enjoyed rest (3:11, 30; 5:31; 8:28). These no longer occur after Gideon.
3. The number of years a leader judged Israel, a sort of term-of-office notice (10:2, 3; 12:7, 9, 11, 14; 15:20; 16:31). These all occur after the Gideon cycle.

Is there any connection between the last two formulae? If the "land had rest" formula ceases after Gideon and the "he judged _____ years" formula occurs only after Gideon, might the writer be suggesting that the latter is a substitute for the former? Perhaps a poor substitute at that? Could the writer be implying that Israel in her ongoing apostasy has forfeited God's rest even though there is yet a semblance of normalcy in that certain leaders still manage to judge? If so, Israel is the land that no longer enjoys a divine gift but knows only a human activity. Life goes on but the quality of time is different. Life among Yahweh's people may seem about as usual but the appearance deceives (Rev. 3:1). Something is absent, missing. Once you see this you are hardly shocked when Ichabod arrives (1 Sam. 4:21–22).

The Deaths of God's Leaders

Finally, we can observe how these entries note the deaths of God's leaders. We have already met with death notices for Joshua (2:8), Othniel (3:11), Ehud (cf. 4:1), Gideon (8:32), Tola (10:2), and Jair (10:5). It doesn't strike us, however, until we begin to see death-in-concentrate, until we meet these brief sequential entries and hear the staccato fact being drummed into us:

Then Jephthah the Gileadite died . . . (v. 7)[4]

Then Ibzan died . . . (v. 10)

Then Elon the Zebulunite died . . . (v. 12)

Then Abdon the son of Hillel the Pirathonite died . . . (v. 15)

Now we feel like Judges 12 is beginning to batter us like Genesis 5, a chapter that keeps hammering us with "and he died . . . and he died."

We soon realize that this doesn't merely concern Israel's judges or Scripture's antediluvians—there is also an obituary with our names on it.[5] Yet God has raised up a Leader in Israel who "continues forever"; death cannot terminate his tenure nor annul the benefit he brings his people (Heb. 7:23–25). Indeed, he has "broken the power of death" (2 Tim. 1:10 NEB).

---

4. I am including the note about Jephthah since it immediately precedes the other three.

5. "Death, the lot of man, at last claims his due of the great and the good, and whatever else we may hear of any man, we are sure to hear one thing—that he died: unless indeed our own departure hence anticipates his" (George Bush, *Notes, Critical and Practical, on the Book of Judges* [Chicago: Henry A. Sumner, 1881], 173).

16

Samson the Savior Is Born
(13)

It is Advent as I write this, and "Silent Night" is enjoying its annual resurrection. But, somehow, our chapter title would not be a fitting close to the second stanza. We celebrate the birth of a far greater than Samson. That fact, however, should not cause us to take Samson lightly (no one ever did!). He, too, was a savior; at his birth a savior was born. Such is the keynote of chapter 13. As soon as Manoah's wife is told she will bear a son, she hears of his mission: "And he [emphatic] will begin to save Israel from the hand of the Philistines" (v. 5). This text is the hermeneutical star that must go before us as we work through the Samson materials. True, Samson will only begin to save, but even that constitutes him a savior. The theme is still salvation (see the introductory comments on 3:7–11). There is one danger. Samson is such a rollicking, entertaining, break-the-mold fellow that we may become preoccupied with him. We must not allow our focus on the savior God raises up to eclipse the God who saves. Therefore, we want to develop the teaching of Judges 13 in terms of what Yahweh is doing.

The Grace Yahweh Maintains

We should see, first of all, how verse 1 hints at the grace Yahweh maintains. Here, in one sense, is the same tedious

159

refrain: "And the sons of Israel again did what was evil in Yahweh's eyes, so Yahweh gave them into the hands of the Philistines for forty years." That is all. The next sentence introduces us to Manoah and his childless wife (v. 2). We have a sequence of three elements: Israel's apostasy (v. 1a), Yahweh's judgment (v. 1b), and the beginnings of another story of Yahweh's deliverance (vv. 2ff.). There is something missing, something we have come to expect. There is no statement between verse 1 and verse 2 about Israel "crying out" to Yahweh in their distress (cf. 3:9, 15; 4:3; 6:6–7; 10:10).

We have already argued that Israel's "crying out" to Yahweh did not in itself involve repentance (see the discussion on 3:9 and footnotes there). It is a cry for help in trouble rather than a confession of sin. Yet here in 13:1 their cry is missing. Here then is Israel—in the power of Baal (cf. v. 1 with 2:11) and Philistia; an Israel who not only does not cry out in repentance from sin but also does not even cry out for relief from misery. They have, apparently, grown accustomed to servitude; in fact, in the Samson cycle, they are content with it, are surprised should anyone suggest otherwise (see 15:11).

Once you see this Israel you marvel at this Israel's God. What does he do when he has a people who refuse to forsake Baal and have no desire to forsake Philistia? A people grown so used to bondage they don't even have sense to call out for relief? At least here the very God who judges them (v. 1b) begins to work their deliverance—anyway (vv. 2–5). That is grace—grace greater than all our sin, than all our stupidity, than all our density.

Nor can any Christian fail to rejoice in such a "grace-shuss" God (we don't always see the connection if we spell it correctly!). For if Yahweh's help were given only when we prayed for it, only when we asked for it, only when we had sense enough to seek it, what paupers and orphans we would be.

The Place Yahweh Begins

We cannot help but notice, secondly, the place Yahweh begins (vv. 2–5). We are introduced to Manoah the Danite (v. 2a) and to the big fact about his wife—"she was barren; she had not had a child" (v. 2b). Even the Angel of Yahweh seems to rub it in with his first words to her: "Look, you are barren; you have not given birth" (v. 3). Then she heard wonderful words of life, words like "pregnant," "birth," and "son." Words that meant shattered hopes; but the Angel of Yahweh spoke them as certain facts. It was all part of a whole program: "See, you are going to be pregnant and give birth to a son; a razor must not go up on his head for the lad is to be a Nazirite to God from the womb; and *he* will begin to save Israel from the hand of the Philistines" (v. 5).

This motif of the barren woman is a familiar pattern in Scripture. Sarah anguished over her childlessness (Gen. 11:30–21:1). Rebekah's first twenty years of marriage were childless (Gen. 25:19–26). Rachel was both barren and green with envy until she at last bore Joseph (Gen. 29:31–30:24). Then in post-Samson time we meet Hannah (1 Sam. 1) and Elizabeth (Luke 1).

Here in Judges 13 the woman is both barren and anonymous. We don't even know her name. She is Manoah's wife and becomes Samson's mother, but her name is not given us. To her sterility the Bible has added obscurity.

Yahweh often begins precisely there—in human obscurity and hopelessness, where there is no human energy or ability to serve as a starter. Samson's birth is another instance of "God's way of prefacing an exceptional work with exceptional difficulties."[1] Yahweh will bring salvation out of nothingness.

Vance Packard in *The Hidden Persuaders* tells of homemakers' problems with cake mixes in the days when such mixes first appeared. Cake-mix packages would warn not to add milk but "just add water." Some housewives would add milk anyway as their special touch and be disappointed when cakes or muffins fell. Some cake mixes would also prohibit adding eggs since eggs and milk had already been added in dry form by the manufacturer. Women interviewed in depth studies were disturbed: "What sort of cake is it if you just need to add tap water!" The marketing needed to be changed. The mixes needed to tell the homemaker that she and the mix together could produce the cake. A white cake mix box now

---

1. Derek Kidner, *Genesis: An Introduction and Commentary,* Tyndale Old Testament Commentaries (London: Tyndale, 1967), 151.

proclaimed, "You add fresh eggs."[2] The message was: you do have a contribution you can make.

There are times, however, in Yahweh's history with his people that he refuses their help and will not allow them to add their touch. Instead he brings his salvation or relieves their distress in the face of impossible human odds. He displays his power precisely when and where they can contribute nothing, and all in order to lift our eyes to himself, so that we will have no illusions or delusions about where our help is found. That's why in the days when the Philistines ruled, the Angel of Yahweh paid a visit to a nameless, childless woman.

The Prayers Yahweh Hears

The story continues in seemingly predictable and unexceptional form:

> Then Manoah prayed to Yahweh: "Please, Lord, the man of God whom you sent—please let him come again to us, and let him teach us what we are to do for the lad who is to be born." And God heard the voice of Manoah, and the Angel of God came again to the woman—she was sitting in the field and Manoah, her husband, was not with her. [vv. 8–9]

Manoah probably wanted confirmation of the Visitor's words and certainly instruction (v. 8b) for a child with such a mission. We have grown so accustomed to the flow of biblical narratives that we fail to see the little miracle here, the prayers Yahweh hears. "And God heard the voice of Manoah"—we have read such clauses so frequently that they no longer strike us. But the psalmists never take it for granted (Pss. 5:1–2; 28:1–2; 65:2). We may have relegated God's hearing our prayers to our "of course" category, but biblical pray-ers do not regard it as so routine. Rather, Yahweh's hearing is the most crucial matter for all prayer.

Maybe prayer is like garbage. I regard taking out the garbage as part of the daily tedium of life, and it is something I

2. Vance Packard, *The Hidden Persuaders* (New York: Pocket Books, 1958), 66.

leave, whenever possible, for other household members to do. Of course, I am wrong. Taking out the garbage should be viewed as a daily sacrament, for garbage in itself is a sign of provision. Potato peelings, apple cores, and squash seeds are silent witnesses that our Father is still feeding us. So garbage is not a tedious detail but a divine blessing. We can miss that because it is so routine. I guess our problem is that we don't think theologically about garbage.

When God listens to the voice of Manoah, or to our voice, we must never respond with a yawn. We will trivialize prayer whenever we forget the repeated miracle it involves, the gracious condescension of the King of glory, who stoops down to listen to our verbs and nouns, our adverbs and questions, our groans and tears.

The Limits Yahweh Imposes

When the Angel of Yahweh appeared again, Manoah's wife fetched her husband; Manoah asked his questions and received the same information his wife had been given previously. By the end of verse 14 the prenatal instructions have been stated three times (vv. 4–5, 7, 13–14) with some variation. Manoah wants to honor the Visitor with an elaborate meal (v. 15). Offer declined. If, however, Manoah wants to offer a burnt offering, he must offer it *to Yahweh* (v. 16). Manoah tries again: What is the Guest's name, for when his prediction comes true they will want to give him proper recognition (v. 17). Again, the Angel of Yahweh fences: "Why now are you asking about my name?—it is wonderful!" (v. 18). Here are the limits Yahweh imposes.

What did the Angel of Yahweh mean when asserting that his name was "wonderful"? We can catch the idea from the use of the term in Psalm 139:6. There the psalmist is being overwhelmed by God's intimate, detailed, comprehensive knowing of him—his activities, his purposes, his words (before they're spoken!). He revels in pondering God's gentle pressure behind and in front of him and God's warm hand upon him. How can one react to that except with some sort of frustrated delight? "That knowledge is too wonderful for me—it is so high I cannot reach it!" (Ps. 139:6). By "wonderful" he means "it's beyond me"; he is saying, "It is so grand I can't pull it all in." So here in Judges 13:18. The Angel of Yahweh is saying, "My character, my nature is 'too much'; it is beyond you—you simply can't take it all in." Manoah's second request is refused. The name is not given. Manoah must stay within certain bounds; he must abide within stipulated limits. His Visitor—though he does not yet realize it (vv. 16, 21)—is far more than he can take in.[3]

We still stand, to a large degree (in spite of, e.g., John 1:14, 18; 14:7–9), in Manoah's situation. There is a mystery, a depth, a surpassingness about God that we can never fathom, comprehend, or touch (cf. Rom. 11:33). This does not mean we cannot know God; it means that though we may know God truly we do not know him exhaustively. He has given us sufficient but not complete knowledge of himself. There are still limits imposed; we do not have total knowledge of his character and ways. We may be *new* creatures in Christ but we remain new *creatures* in Christ. All of which should lead God's people to genuine humility.

There are some matters God keeps from us. For example, he frequently does not divulge the explanation or reason for particular trials or afflictions. We may inflict our theories of the Lord's rationale upon other believers or be confident that we clearly discern God's purpose in our own predicaments. But if we recognize that Yahweh's character and ways are wonderful, we may find ourselves more often baffled by him than sure of him. We will edge toward a cautious humility in estimating his designs and find a holy reticence chastening our remarks to other saints in the throes of distress.

The Fear Yahweh Arouses

Fourthly, we cannot fail to see the fear Yahweh arouses (vv. 19–23). Manoah brings his sacrifice with its grain offering, offers it to Yahweh, and then Yahweh, or perhaps the Angel of Yahweh, does something wonderful (v. 19; the text is some-

---

3. Manoah cannot be blamed for his limited perception—he does not yet know (v. 16b) what he will soon know (v. 21b). On the Angel of God/Yahweh, mentioned twelve times in chapter 13, see the exposition of Judges 6, n. 2.

what difficult but the idea seems clear). That wonder is
described in verse 20: when the flame went up from the altar
the Angel of Yahweh ascended in the flame of the altar. The
writer twice insists that "Manoah and his wife were watching"
(vv. 19, 20). It was a real, observable event.

They fell to the earth (v. 20); light dawned (v. 21); fear rose
(v. 22). Manoah concluded: "We will surely die, for we have
seen God" (v. 22). Manoah was simply stating a biblical axiom.
Long ago Yahweh had explained why Moses must rest content
with an indirect view of his glory: "You are not able to see my
face, for man will not see me and live" (Exod. 33:20). Being
too near God was not cozy but fatal. Manoah apparently felt
they had seen too much, had been too close.

We must wipe those patronizing smiles off our faces. Christians sometimes have a tendency to read passages like this
with their condescending, silent commentary: "Well, of course,
Manoah was only an Old Testament believer and didn't understand." On the contrary, Manoah understood perfectly—and
trembled. We must allow Manoah to be our teacher. We must
not pooh-pooh his reaction as understandably naive. (In any
case, when believers are naive they are usually close to the
truth.) Manoah may have been wrong in his inference, but he
was right in his instinct, for where did we ever get the idea
that the presence of God is not dangerous? Have we really
bought Santa Claus theology? Has God somehow become safe
because we live in A.D.? Were the disciples still too primitive
to realize that the divine presence did not require human trembling (Luke 9:34)?

We need, nevertheless, the rest of the picture. Side by side
with the fear expressed by Manoah stands the comfort declared
by his wife in her "faith-full" reasoning: "If Yahweh had meant
to kill us, he would not have accepted a burnt offering and
oblation from us, he would not have let us see all this and, at
the same time, have told us such things" (v. 23 NJB). Surely
then, his wife reasons, Yahweh does not mean to consume but
to preserve us. Manoah had the reverence but not the comfort,
the fear but not the joy. We need a properly balanced response
to the presence of God; saints easily err to extremes in this
matter.

One school year one of our sons had a rather solemn teacher.

Never, according to report, any frivolity in her classroom. School was on the glum side. Then one day Seth came home and announced: "Mrs. Blank [the name has been changed to protect the living] laughed today for the first time this year! It was 1:56 and 43 seconds." When laughter can be so distinctly noted and accurately clocked one might surmise there is far too little of it. Not that one should open the floodgates of levity, but it wouldn't hurt to let them spring a leak now and then. There should be a proper balance, a faithful tension.

This should be true of our response to Yahweh's presence in our regular worship. Some can shudder but never smile before God. Some of us have reverence without assurance. Others can so focus on God's nearness that they risk turning warm intimacy into cheap familiarity. But the Bible keeps us in bounds: "Rejoice with trembling" (Ps. 2:11).[4] Hence we must also allow Manoah's wife to teach us, and she would want us to realize that "even when he overwhelms us with awe-inspiring glimpses of His majesty, it is not in order to destroy, but to assure us of His power, as well as His will, to save."[5]

The Pattern Yahweh Follows

Let us not leave this chapter without observing the pattern Yahweh follows. Verses 24b–25 contain all we know of Samson's childhood. Most all of chapter 13 is Samson's nativity story, concentrating on the circumstances of his birth. Chapter 14 opens with a grown Samson romping off to obtain a wife. There are only these two sentences (13:24b–25)—a very terse summary—relating in any way to his childhood. Obviously, the writer is not interested in giving us a full biography or he wouldn't have omitted all the details of Samson's childhood. Just as obviously he thinks Samson's birth story is very important or he wouldn't have devoted such attention to it.

4. You will not find this rendering in, for example, the Revised Standard Version or the New English Bible, but the text of Psalm 2:11–12 is not as uncertain as the footnotes in the Revised Standard Version decree.

5. A. R. Fausset, *A Critical and Expository Commentary on the Book of Judges* (London: James Nisbet, 1885), 223.

Interestingly, Jesus' story follows the same pattern. Both Matthew and Luke devote significant space to Jesus' roots, birth, and infancy (Matt. 1–2, though Jesus is probably a toddler in chap. 2; and Luke 1–2) and, certainly, to his public ministry. But we have nothing about his childhood except that snatch in Luke 2:41–52.

There is nothing like chapter 13 in the rest of Judges. Samson's is the only nativity story. We are given details about Jephthah's roots (11:1–3), but that is nothing like chapter 13.

Why then this pattern? Why would the writer single out Samson's nativity and make such a point of it? Because he wants to show that, at least in this case, Yahweh didn't merely raise up a deliverer who was, as it were, already available (as, e.g., Othniel or Ehud, 3:9, 15); rather, he grew one—from scratch. It is crucial that we see this, lest we think Yahweh's salvation is always an ad hoc, Band-Aid affair, a piece of divine crisis management instead of a plan that Yahweh has had in view far in advance. This is exactly what staggers and gladdens us about the Greater-than-Samson who ransomed us at such cost—"He was marked out before the world was made, and was revealed at the final point of time for your sake" (1 Pet. 1:20 NJB). It boggles the imagination let alone the mind to think that something before "in the beginning" could be for my sake. Even Judges 13 wants us to jump up and sing the doxology.

17

Secrets
(14)

Happily, we have the reader's edge. We are in on all these secrets floating around chapter 14. We know all four secrets. Some form of the verb *higgîd* (to tell) occurs fourteen times in the Hebrew text (vv. 2, 6, 9, 12 [twice], 13, 14, 15, 16 [thrice], 17 [twice], 19). The whole chapter then is about telling, or, I should say, not telling. It's all about what people don't know.

Structurally, the chapter divides by means of another verb, *yarad* (to go down), used five times (vv. 1, 5, 7, 10, 19), each of the first four sections centering on a secret (see table 17.1).

The Secret of Yahweh's Purpose

As we focus on the teaching of this chapter, we must take some time to think about the secret of Yahweh's purpose (esp. v. 4).

Manoah and his wife were upset. They'd had another go-around with Samson, their strong-willed child. Samson had been to Timnah.[1] He had seen a girl.[2] He was determined. His father must arrange for the marriage.

---

1. The site is probably Tell el-Batashi, not quite five miles west of Beth-shemesh, a little over twenty miles straight west of Jerusalem.
2. "A woman I have seen in Timnah" is a literal translation of Samson's statement in verse 2. The emphasis is on "woman." Had Samson been an American he would have said: "Let me tell you, I saw a *woman* in Timnah!"

169

Table 17.1   The Structure of Judges 14:1–20

Vv. 1–4	Samson goes down to Timnah and sees a woman	Secret of Yahweh's purpose
Vv. 5–6	Samson—with father and mother—goes down to Timnah	Secret of slaying the lion
Vv. 7–9	Samson goes down and talks with the woman	Secret of the honey
Vv. 10–18	His father goes down to the woman and Samson puts on a drinking feast	Secret of the riddle
Vv. 19–20	Samson goes down to Ashkelon and kills thirty Philistines	Climax: the power of Yahweh's Spirit

Father and mother were shattered. They had lived in the hope of his birth (chap. 13) and now this. You can imagine the scene. "But she's a Philistine," Manoah half-pleaded, half-roared. Surely the Angel of Yahweh hadn't had this in mind (13:5). "Get her as my wife," Samson persisted (v. 2). Father and mother explode: "Isn't there any girl in all Israel who could please you, that you have to go off to Philistia to find a wife? Samson, that girl's a *pagan*!" Samson looks Manoah in the eye, his words come out deliberately through clenched teeth: "Get *her* for me" (v. 3, emphasis in Hebrew). His reason? "For she is right in my eyes" (v. 3c, literal translation).[3] Grief and misery in one home in Zorah that evening. "But his father and his mother did not know that this was from Yahweh, for He was seeking an occasion against the Philistines" (v. 4).

We must discuss the interpretation of verse 4. As the reader can see, I take the clause *he was seeking* to refer to Yahweh. It is, however, frequently taken as referring to Samson, as if all the hoopla over the Philistine girl was a cover-up for Samson's real purpose.[4] In that case the secret is Samson's. Yet in

3. "It is true that the only marriages expressly prohibited in Ex. xxxiv.16 and Deut. vii.3, 4, are marriages with Canaanitish women; but the reason assigned for this prohibition was equally applicable to marriages with daughters of the Philistines" (C. F. Keil, *Joshua, Judges, Ruth,* Biblical Commentary on the Old Testament [1868; reprint ed., Grand Rapids: Eerdmans, 1950], 409).

4. So Goslinga, Bush, Keil, and Fausset.

my view the "he" is almost certainly Yahweh. First, "Yahweh" is the nearest and most natural grammatical antecedent for "he" in the sentence. Secondly, Samson appears to be driven only by his own glands ("for she is right in my eyes," v. 3) rather than by any hidden anti-Philistinism. Someone could claim that Samson's words in verse 3 are merely his way of concealing his true motives from his parents. But not likely— even the narrator indicates that Samson's pleasure rather than his purpose carried the day ("she was right in the eyes of Samson," v. 7). Samson is a typical Judges man (17:6; 21:25), high on doing his own thing. Verse 4 then tells us of Yahweh's—not Samson's—secret. Yahweh is after an opportunity for striking the Philistines; he seeks grounds for opening a quarrel.[5]

Here would have been real comfort for Samson's parents had they known; they didn't realize this situation was "from Yahweh"; they couldn't see that Yahweh "was seeking an occasion against the Philistines." This does not mean they were wrong to object to Samson's desires and action. Nor does it mean that Samson's desires were virtuous or that his bullheadedness was right. It means that neither Samson's foolishness nor his stubbornness is going to prevent Yahweh from accomplishing *his* design. Yahweh can and will use the sinfulness or stupidity of his servants as the camouflage for bringing his secret will to pass.

Ehud Avriel took three months (1947–48) looking for a ship to transport some of his purchases to Palestine. At last he was able to hire the *Nora,* a tramp steamer in the Yugoslavian port of Brno. To all eyes his shipment consisted of Italian onions—six hundred tons of them. British customs agents would not likely sniff around that cargo for long! Which was the idea—six hundred tons of Italian onions covered the real cargo, a shipment of Czech rifles Avriel had purchased for the Haganah, Israel's army.[6]

---

5. Seven English versions (NASB, NIV, JB, NJB, TEV, NEB, and NJPS) explicitly indicate Yahweh as the subject of "was seeking," as do, for example, Gutbrod, Moore, and Myers (*IB*) among commentators. See also James A. Wharton, "The Secret of Yahweh: Story and Affirmation in Judges 13–16," *Interpretation* 27 (1973): 55.

6. Larry Collins and Dominique Lapierre, *O Jerusalem!* (New York: Pocket Books, 1972), 175.

This text then should hold out some hope for God's people. Frequently, all we can see are the onions of a situation. The sin or the smell of disappointment seems to dominate the scene, seems to cover our whole map. But perhaps that is only the cover for Yahweh's secret work; perhaps our greatest comfort is hidden in what we don't know or can't see; perhaps it is "from Yahweh," who has his own saving design to work either through or in spite of yuck and muck. Many Christian parents have stood in the sandals of Manoah and his wife. They have, though realizing their own sinful inadequacies, faithfully taught, prayed for, disciplined, and loved a son or a daughter only to see that child willfully turn from the way of the Lord. No one can deny it is anything but devastating. Yet no one should forget verse 4: "But his father and his mother did not realize it was from Yahweh." What we don't know may yet prove to be our deepest comfort.

The Sign of Yahweh's Strength

Like it or not, we must go by the vineyards of Timnah and meet this lion (vv. 5–6)! Fortunately, Samson has preceded us and dealt with the lion. But dead lions should not be ignored; therefore, we must see in this episode the sign of Yahweh's strength.

The writer does not merely include this episode so that we will have the needed background for Samson's later riddle (vv. 12–14). The incident is important in its own right. The lion comes roaring toward Samson and the Spirit comes rushing upon him, and in the Spirit's strength the lion could just as well have been a young goat, so easily did Samson tear it apart.[7] Samson's strength comes from the Spirit of Yahweh. This is not the last time Yahweh's Spirit will "rush" upon Samson (see 14:19; 15:14).[8] The mangled lion is meant as Yahweh's sign to Samson. It shows him what Yahweh can and will do through him. It should show him that the God who

7. We can't be sure from verse 5 just how long Samson's parents were with him on this trek down to Timnah, but verse 6 clearly indicates Samson was alone when the lion attacked. We see Yahweh's protection of his servant here, for Samson's life was obviously in danger.

8. The same verb (ṣalaḥ, to rush) is used of the Spirit's empowering of Saul (1 Sam. 10:6, 10; 11:6; cf. 18:10) and of David (1 Sam. 16:13).

makes him able to tear up lions can also empower him to ter-
rorize Philistines. Here is a preview of what Yahweh can do
through Samson.[9]

We must not ignore such previews. David argued that if
Yahweh made him able to wipe out the lions and bears that
attacked Jesse's sheep, he would also give him guts and skill
to knock off the King Kong of Philistia (1 Sam. 17:34–37).
Mark suggests that if the disciples had understood the feeding
of the five thousand they would not have been astounded at
Jesus' presence on the lake (Mark 6:51–52). No, you needn't
expect lions to come roaring out of vineyards; but you should
notice this pattern in God's ways. He will, by some smaller
episode of deliverance or provision, show you how adequate he
is so that you will be encouraged to rely on him in upcoming
and possibly more demanding circumstances.

The Weakness of Yahweh's Servant

In verses 10–18 the shadow begins to fall—ever so
slightly—over the Samson stories, for the weakness of
Yahweh's servant appears. Here is a hint of what is to come.
We have just seen his strength in verses 5–9 and, immediately,
we are faced with his weakness.

As readers we have to admit we rather enjoy the drinking
feast (for that is the meaning of the Hebrew *mishteh,* v. 10) at
Timnah.[10] After all, we know about the lion and the bees and

9. See the comments of S. G. De Graaf, *Promise and Deliverance,* 4 vols.
(St. Catharines, Ontario: Paideia, 1978), 2:43, and C. J. Goslinga, *Joshua,
Judges, Ruth,* Bible Student's Commentary (Grand Rapids: Zondervan, 1986),
422.

10. Samson may have already compromised his Nazirite status by eating
honey from the lion carcass (unclean food because it was in contact with something dead) and by throwing a drinking party (though, if someone wants to
be picky, the text does not say Samson himself imbibed). The Nazirite restric-
tions were: no grapes, no razor, no death (see Num. 6:1–21 for details). Paulus
Cassel, however, argued that Samson "was not at all such a Nazarite [sic] as
the sixth chapter of Numbers contemplates. The introduction to his history
clearly shows that definite prescriptions concerning food and drink were given
only to his mother; concerning himself, nothing more is said than that no
razor is to come upon his head. It is only upon this latter obligation, as the
history shows, that the strength of his Nazariteship depends" (*The Book of
Judges,* Lange's Commentary on the Holy Scriptures, in vol. 2, *Numbers-Ruth*
[1865; reprint ed., Grand Rapids: Zondervan, 1960], 196).

the honey, and thus we can enjoy the Philistines' sweating lest they lose the bet. We are in on the secret. We have come down with Samson to Timnah; we know what even his parents don't know. No wonder we enjoy this story—we have superior knowledge.

Since the Philistines generously provide thirty companions for the groom, Samson proposes some additional entertainment. "Let me riddle you a riddle" (v. 12a) and let us make a bet (vv. 12b–13). In western parlance the stakes would be thirty sets of underwear and thirty new suits. If the Philistines win, each of them can sport a new "Easter" outfit at the next Dagon festival. If the Philistines lose, Samson will own the swankiest wardrobe in the country! The Philistines are game. Samson announces his teaser (v. 14):

> From the eater came forth something to eat,
> from the strong came forth something sweet.[11]

The war of wits may be challenging for a while, but even jolly fellows become frustrated, edgy, and irritable after three days of futility (v. 14b). They don't mind freeloading at someone's party, but why should *they* be forced to subsidize this Israelite barbarian's finery? At last[12] and in desperation they caucus with Samson's wife: Is your daddy's fire insurance paid up? Do you want us to make things hot for you? Have you invited us here to clean out our bank accounts? Then be your old seductive self and worm that riddle out of your husband— or we'll riddle you (see v. 15). A little pressure on the bride.

11. On riddles see James L. Crenshaw, *Samson: A Secret Betrayed, A Vow Ignored* (Atlanta: John Knox, 1978), chap. 3.

12. Most all English versions follow the Septuagint and Syriac in verse 15 by reading "on the fourth day" rather than "seventh" as the Hebrew text has it. This construction gives what *appears* to be a more consistent picture: three days of frustration (v. 14); threatening the bride on the fourth day (v. 15); and a general statement of seven days' bridal pressure on Samson when, at last, he yields. However, retaining "on the seventh day" in verse 15 (with the Hebrew) poses no direct conflict with the bride's weeping on Samson for seven days in verse 17. In that case one assumes that "the woman had already come to Samson every day with her entreaties from simple curiosity; but Samson resisted them until the seventh day, when she became more urgent than ever, in consequence of this threat on the part of the Philistines" (Keil, *Joshua, Judges, Ruth,* 412).

Suddenly Samson's wife finds herself caught in a no-win wedding celebration. She must cry now or she will really cry later. So the waterworks and the you-don't-love-me act begin (v. 16). Samson at last caves in under her desperate cajoling. As expected, "he told" is followed by "she told" (v. 17). Before the deadline the Philistines play their honey-and-lion trump card (v. 18a). But Samson is no dummy; he knows sweet honey and strong lions come only from talking heifers (v. 18b)!

Since many of us have heard Samson's whole story before, we cannot help seeing the present episode as a foreshadowing of Samson's telling a far more sacred secret to Delilah in chapter 16. The occasion of his failure was the same in both cases: "she pressured him" (the same Hebrew verb, $\bar{suq}$, occurs in both 14:17 and 16:16). Already in chapter 14 we see a worrisome weakness in Yahweh's strong servant. The point should not be lost on any of Yahweh's servants. Awareness of our weakness is the beginning of safety, as later Samsons have also discovered the hard way (cf. Matt. 26:31–35).

The Beginning of Yahweh's Deliverance

Finally, verses 19–20 describe the beginning of Yahweh's deliverance.

Seems that everyone in Ashkelon[13] dialed 911 at once. Samson had come. Samson had struck down and stripped thirty of Ashkelon's leading citizens, appropriated their attire, and carted it off to Timnah, where he threw it all down among his tipsy companions and stalked off in a fury for Zorah.

Our impulse is to attribute the slaughter at Ashkelon to Samson serving "in the flesh" (whatever that means). But the text will not allow us to do that. It insists that "the Spirit of Yahweh rushed upon him" and so he "went down to Ashkelon and struck down thirty men." Now the Spirit is not giving Samson power to tear up lions (vv. 5–6) but to strike down Philistines. Here now was the occasion Yahweh was seeking (v. 4). Here is the climax of the story (see the discussion on

13. Ashkelon was located on the Mediterranean coast about midway between Ashdod and Gaza (to the north and south, respectively) and approximately twenty-five miles southwest of Timnah.

structure at the beginning of the chapter), for even Yahweh's secret is coming into the open. The text then is clear: what we are dealing with is not Samson's temper but the Spirit's power. If this seems brutal, we must simply live with it. We have already seen that when Yahweh delivers his people he does not always dip his saving acts in Clorox and sprinkle them with perfume. To be delivered from evil will frequently be messy.

If we are not offended at how vicious Samson's deed is, we may stumble over how small it is. If Yahweh is saving Israel, what difference can thirty Philistines make? Yahweh promised only that Samson would *begin* to save Israel from the Philistines (13:5). Here in Ashkelon is the beginning of that beginning. We must not despise it.

I have seen this principle operating in the personal situations of God's people. For example, a family receives a mammoth blow, the sudden death of a spouse and/or parent. Reeling from grief, the one left goes plodding on in confusion. As weeks and months go by, God does not close up the gaping wound or eradicate the dull ache; but the one stricken can frequently relate a small providence here or point to a timely provision there, which, though very small, points to the fact that God's care still hovers near. God's true people always treasure even the smallest of his deliverances.

"And he went up to his father's house" (v. 19b). After Samson "went down" all through the chapter (vv. 1, 5, 7, 19; cf. v. 10), he finally "went up." And Samson's wife is given to the best man. Everything seems solved. All is quiet in Timnah tonight.

18

The Battle of Jawbone Hill and Other Stories
(15)

Did I say all was quiet in Timnah? Well, it *was*. However, on one lovely day in May, there's a knock on the door. There stands Samson, young goat (in lieu of flowers) under his arm, a twinkle in his eye, and he's in the mood for love. Samson never bears grudges for long; now—he tells his wife's father—it's time to make up in the bedroom. Doubtless his daddy-in-law felt an Excedrin headache coming on along with a sick churning in his stomach. No, Samson couldn't go to bed with his daughter. Yes, they might be pagans, but even Philistines have some standards, and, you see, he had married off his daughter to Samson's best man. Samson had seemed so angry, you know, that he just didn't think Samson would ever. . . . Now her younger sister. . . . Samson's furious look and seething departure promised that it wouldn't be quiet in Timnah for long. At 14:20 things had returned to normal, but now (15:3–5) a whole can of worms—or shall we say, foxes?— had been opened.

This pattern occurs throughout chapters 14–16. In every episode the Philistines will seem to reach a solution to their problem, only to see that solution dissolve because of something Samson does. A Philistine would call it a solution-failure pattern. Tracing this structure takes us beyond chapter 15 itself, but in order to appreciate the episodes in chapter 15 we must lay out this solution-failure structure for chapters 14–16 as a whole.

For convenience chapters 14–16 can be divided into six main episodes. Each episode is structured around these two basic elements: a Philistine success followed by a Samsonite disaster. The outline is this:

Episode 1   14:5–20
   Solution—answer to riddle
   Failure—slaughter at Ashkelon
Episode 2   15:1–6a
   Solution—Samson gone, peace restored, girl given to best
     man
   Failure—flaming foxes
Episode 3   15:6b–8
   Solution—burn up Timnite woman and father
   Failure—slaughter by Samson
Episode 4   15:9–17
   Solution—Samson bound, handed over
   Failure—"Jawbone Hill"
Episode 5   16:1–3
   Solution—Ambushing the playboy
   Failure—portable gates
Episode 6   16:4–30
   Major pattern:
   Solution—hair shaved
   Failure—tragedy at Dagon's Place
   Subsidiary patterns:
   Solution/failure—7 bowstrings   (16:6–9a/9b)
   Solution/failure—new ropes   (16:10–12a/12b)
   Solution/failure—loom   (16:13–14a/14b)
   Solution/success—razor   (16:15–19a/19b–21)

Hence the dual pattern of solution-failure or success-disaster persists through every anecdote in the three chapters. It even furnishes the structure for the subsidiary vignettes making up the solution portion of the climactic sixth episode. The pattern is then broken in the fourth vignette when the Philistines bind and blind their shaven trophy (16:19b–21). Yet the general pattern remains unbroken, for 16:22–30 goes on to show that, once again, Philistine success was in fact non-success.

The Humor of Yahweh's Salvation

Let us jump from structure into teaching without taking our feet out of the structure. Chapter 15 (indeed all of chapters 14–16) depicts the humor of Yahweh's salvation.

A thoughtful review of these episodes indicates that they are a biting satire against the Philistines. So they triumphantly answer Samson's riddle (14:17–18)? They win the bet and lose thirty fellow citizens (14:19). They are the winning losers! Does everything seem peaceful in Timnah? Samson's foxy antic will insure that the Philistine Cooperative Association's elevators will be near empty (15:4–5).[1] No, it's not funny for the foxes (or jackals), but, looking at the episode in general, I'm sure an Israelite would find it at least mildly humorous. Or the Philistines are cocksure they have their foe at their mercy (15:14a)—until Samson is suddenly beating sense into their heads with an ass's dentures (15:14b–15). Dear reader, you needn't be so glum; don't be so concerned about the Philistines; think how your Israelite brother would react to the story; go ahead and laugh a little.

The whole of chapters 14–16, therefore, constitutes one long Israelite joke on the Philistines. The story is full of subtle but powerful irony, humor at its best. Every move the Philistines make, though temporarily successful, proves—due to Samson—disastrous. He plays with them. Though the narrative has no interest in whitewashing Samson (see chap. 16), nevertheless even in his downfall he will make the Philistines appear as bungling stooges (see the discussion of 16:22ff.). In general, the theme of the episodes may be summarized as "the stupidity of the Philistines."

Some readers may think it irreverent to find such humor in the Bible. They may suppose that if there is such humor, it must be confined to the way the story is told; surely, the humor has nothing to do with the theological thrust of the text. I

---

1. See W. M. Thomson, *The Land and the Book,* 2 vols. (New York: Harper and Brothers, 1873), 2:340–41.

disagree. The Bible uses humor when it has a very sober point to make. The humor is not only human but also divine.

The Philistines are the enemies of Yahweh's people. Here their stupidity is held up for ridicule; here they are made the laughingstock of Israel. Why? To show us the peril of being an enemy of Yahweh's people (even of his *sinful* people), for Yahweh makes fools of those who seek to ruin and crush his people. The awesome fearfulness of Israel's God! His enemies—and theirs—are kids' stuff for him; he toys with them and makes his people able to laugh at them (cf. the discussion of 3:12–30). It is a ghastly thing to make oneself the object of divine laughter (see Ps. 2:4 in context).

Perhaps this Philistine principle, this solution-failure syndrome, was operating in March 1941. (I say "perhaps" because I have no supernatural revelation in order to be more definite.) No sooner had Hitler concluded the necessary agreements with Yugoslavia for making that nation usable to the Nazi cause than a coup overthrew that government and established a new regime in Belgrade. The new government was willing to sign a nonaggression pact with the Nazis but clearly would not accept mere puppet status. In any case, the coup in Belgrade threw Hitler into a rage. He acted decisively and hastily; Yugoslavia would be destroyed militarily and as a nation, overrun with "unmerciful harshness." Goering's bombers were to level Belgrade. They did. For three days and nights they scanned the capital at rooftop level (Belgrade had no anti-aircraft guns), wiping out seventeen thousand civilians, wounding many more, leaving the city a pile of rubble. Hitler's term for it: Operation Punishment. Nothing succeeds like success—and power.

Or was it a case of the "stupidity of the Philistines"? Some have argued that the Führer's decision to crush Yugoslavia was the "most catastrophic single decision in Hitler's career." The reason? In order to stomp on Yugoslavia Hitler had to delay his projected attack on Russia for four to five weeks. Later the deep snow and frigid Russian winter hit Hitler's forces three or four weeks short of what the Nazi generals said they needed for final victory in the Soviet Union. Napoleon could have told him that Russian winters may be more deadly than Russian weapons.[2] Hitler's very success contained his disaster; his solution prepared his failure. Did the Real Führer (Ps. 2:4) sit laughing?

The Lethargy of Yahweh's People

A story can be both humorous and tragic.[3] The Samson narrative has its touches of the latter., Samson's prank with the fox fire moved the Philistines to burn up his wife and her father (apparently marooned in their home), so that—ironically—the threat at the wedding party (14:15) came to pass (15:6). The Philistines fought fire with fire. That obviously enraged Samson to take vengeance (15:7–8).[4] Yet there is a still deeper tragedy, the writer seems to say, within Israel, for he gives us a stark portrayal of the lethargy of Yahweh's people (15:9–13).

In retaliation for Samson's vendetta, the Philistines threaten Lehi (v. 9).[5] The men of Judah complain: Why this attack? They have come up to bind Samson to pay him back for what he did to them (v. 10). A small army of Judah's men go down to confront Samson at Etam.[6] They feel their opening question should answer the whole matter: "Don't you know that the Philistines are rulers over us?" (v. 11). Sad, sad words. Here is a people who have acquiesced to bondage, who can no longer imagine anything beyond the status quo, who see deliv-

2. See William L. Shirer, *The Rise and Fall of the Third Reich* (Greenwich, Conn.: Fawcett, 1960), 1078–88.

3. See Leland Ryken, *The Literature of the Bible* (Grand Rapids: Zondervan, 1974), 100–102, for the tragic dimension in the Samson materials.

4. The Hebrew of 15:8 reads, "He smote them leg upon thigh, a great slaughter/smiting." Apparently, "a great slaughter" explains what smiting "leg upon thigh" means. Cf. Robert G. Boling, *Judges,* The Anchor Bible (Garden City, N.Y.: Doubleday, 1975), 235, who suggests: "he left them a tangle of legs and thighs."

5. The location of Lehi (Jawbone) is uncertain but must have been in western Judah. The place received its name from the event of verses 14–17, but the writer is writing after that event and so uses that common name here in verse 9, though to a reader it appears to "anticipate" what actually takes place later (v. 17).

6. Location uncertain, but, again, likely in western Judah in the low hill country.

erance as a threat to peace, who look upon Yahweh's enemies as their rightful lords. Israel is a people who can forsake Yahweh instantly but who would not think of being faithless to the Philistines! What a pitiful question.

So Judah fumes at Samson. What does Samson think he's doing? They see Samson as fighting against them rather than against the Philistines ("What is this you have done *to us*?" [v. 11]). Doesn't Samson realize his intemperate outbursts are endangering Judah's safety? Perhaps a Judahite spokesman appeared on Philistine television to read a statement about how "outraged" Judeans were over the "irresponsible and inexcusable behavior" of Samson the Danite.

Samson is nonchalant, even philosophical, about the whole affair. Borrowing a line from the Philistines (see v. 10), he simply retorts that he had paid them back for what they had done to him (v. 11b). After his vengeance it should have been even-Steven; he can't help it if the Philistines overreact.

The men of Judah blurt out their mission; they have come to bind Samson and turn him over to the Philistines (v. 12a). Oddly enough, Samson offers no resistance, which apparently Judah expected or they wouldn't have sent so many men (v. 11a). He only extracts an oath from them that they will not kill him themselves (v. 12b). They willingly assent to this (we may be chicken, Samson, but you can trust us). No reader can miss the irony of their reply (v. 13): Oh, no, Samson, we don't want to kill you; we only want to bind you and give you to the Philistines so they can kill you. The tribe that had formerly waded into battle after battle (1:1–20) has become a collection of spineless wimps (15:13). They regard the Philistines as their rulers and Samson as their enemy. They don't even want to be Yahweh's free people; they don't even see that as a possibility.

It is always a dark day in the history of Yahweh's people when they are content to allow his enemies to hold sway. Something is wrong with us when we no longer despise our true enemies. Such enmity is the gift of God. In the wake of our initial faithlessness Yahweh declared he was imposing *enmity* between the Serpent's seed and the woman's seed (Gen. 3:15). This divisiveness, this hostility came from Yahweh. He was not going to allow even his fallen creature to cuddle up in the bosom of evil. The Maker of heaven and earth refused to walk away from Eden, shrugging his shoulders and muttering, "You win some and you lose some." No, he is the stubborn God who will set all creation ablaze with holy war in order to have a seed and a people for himself. That's why redemption is an act of violence; that's why Jesus came on a mission of violent destruction (1 John 3:8). That's why "lovers of Yahweh" are commanded to "hate evil" (Ps. 97:10, in the Hebrew) and why the compilers of the Psalms did not edit out verses 19–22 of Psalm 139 (unlike editors of responsive readings in modern hymnbooks, who, seemingly, judge the verses too brutal for refined Christian worship). Whether it is the evil and sin within us or some form of it outside us God does not call us to negotiate with sin and evil but to wage war on them, to nurse a holy hatred toward them in all their multicolored forms. We are near hopeless when we begin to adopt Judah's slogan: it has always been this way—how can we expect to change anything?

The Sustenance of Yahweh's Servant

The climax of chapter 15 comes in verses 14–20, where we see the sustenance of Yahweh's servant. The Philistines let out a war whoop as they see their helpless prey (v. 14a), but they could have saved their breath. They did not consider the Spirit of Yahweh. Philistines never do. The Spirit rushed on Samson, who snapped his ropes as if they were flax on fire, grabbed a nearby jawbone of an ass (a fresh one, the text says, so having its teeth intact—a mean weapon),[7] and began making piles of Philistines. By the end of it all Samson was ready with an appropriate pun (v. 16). The Hebrew words for "ass" and "heap" are spelled the same, but it is difficult to reproduce the word-play in English translation. Moffatt's rendering, however, has caught the flavor of it:

7. H. L. Ellison, *Scripture Union Bible Study Books: Joshua-2 Samuel* (Grand Rapids: Eerdmans, 1966), 37. A jawbone of an ass with its "tooth cavities supplied with razor-sharp metal inserts" has been unearthed at ancient Jaffa (see Claus Schedl, *History of the Old Testament,* 5 vols. [Staten Island, N.Y.: Alba, 1972], 3:73). The present narrative does not seem to describe such a doctored jawbone.

With the jawbone of an ass
I have piled them in a mass!

What better name for the place than Jawbone Hill (Ramath-Lehi, v. 17)?

Yet now the punster is desperate; he fears the victor may become victim. Samson is so weakened by thirst that he calls to Yahweh for help. This is the first time we read of Samson explicitly seeking Yahweh: "You [emphatic] have given this great salvation by the hand of your servant, and now I am going to die because of thirst and fall into uncircumcised hands" (v. 18). Here is Samson dependent on Yahweh; here is the savior confessing that he needs saved. We have repeatedly heard that Samson's power comes from Yahweh's Spirit (14:6, 19; 15:14), but, in case these failed to register, we surely cannot miss this picture. Samson is anything but self-sufficient.

In response to Samson's cry God split open the *maktēsh* at Lehi (a hollowed-out depression in the rock formation perhaps) and made water flow out of it, an act that calls to mind Yahweh's provisions for Israel on the wilderness journey (Exod. 17:6; Num. 20:8, 11).[8] The God who brings his people out of Egypt will surely fill every lesser need (Ps. 81:10). Samson had to rename the place: Jawbone Hill became Caller's Spring (v. 19b). God's servants often do that, whenever they realize their endurance does not come from their own adrenaline but from Yahweh's refreshing grace.

8. So C. F. Keil, *Joshua, Judges, Ruth,* Biblical Commentary on the Old Testament (1868; reprint ed., Grand Rapids: Eerdmans, 1950), 416.

19

Let's Play "The Philistines Are Here!"
(16)

Chapter 16 poses both a parallel and a contrast to chapters 14–15. The parallels are not rigid but the two sections do follow a similar pattern (see table 19.1). Samson's calling on Yahweh occurs after the slaughter of the Philistines in the first narrative (15:18–19), whereas it comes before the slaughter in the second (16:28); however, his pleas stand at the climax of each section.[1]

Yet chapter 16—here I refer especially to 16:1–21—also forms a contrast to chapters 14–15. In chapters 14–15 there are three references to "the Spirit of Yahweh" empowering Samson (14:6, 19; 15:14). True, the Spirit of Yahweh is also mentioned in connection with other judges but only once in each case (Othniel, 3:10; Gideon, 6:34; Jephthah, 11:29). Hence Samson's association with Yahweh's Spirit receives special emphasis. There is no mention of "the Spirit of Yahweh" in chapter 16. Again, chapters 14–15 close with Samson dependent upon and sustained by Yahweh (15:18–19), whereas 16:1–21 ends with Samson self-sufficient and deserted by Yahweh

---

1. On these parallels see Barry G. Webb, *The Book of the Judges: An Integrated Reading*, JSOT Supplement Series 46 (Sheffield: JSOT, 1987), 163–64, and J. Cheryl Exum, "The Theological Dimension of the Samson Saga," *Vetus Testamentum* 33 (1983): 34, 45; see also her "Aspects of Symmetry and Balance in the Samson Saga," *JSOT* 19 (1981), 7–8.

Table 19.1   The Structure of Judges 14–15 and 16

Event	Chaps. 14–15	Chap. 16
Samson sees a woman	v. 1 (Timnite)	v. 1 (harlot)
Woman obtains and betrays Samson's secret	vv. 5–18	vv. 4–20
Samson bound	vv. 9–13	v. 21
Great slaughter of Philistines and calling upon Yahweh	vv. 14–17/18–19	vv. 25–30
Judge formula	v. 20	v. 31b

(16:20–21).[2] One can say then that there is a deliberate contrast between the former and the latter Samson. Chapter 16 is eloquent in its silence about the Spirit of Yahweh, so depicting "Samson without the Spirit" in stark contrast to the previous section (chaps. 14–15). The climaxes of both sections are likewise opposed: Yahweh sustains a seeking Samson versus Yahweh abandons a self-sufficient Samson.[3]

The Tragedy of Yahweh's Servant

These comments prepare us for the teaching of chapter 16, for they help us see clearly the tragedy of Yahweh's servant (vv. 1–21).

The first woman of the chapter is a prostitute in Gaza. Samson is spending the night with her. The citizens are tipped off about Samson's presence, assemble an ambush party at the

2. Chapter 16:1–21 begins in Gaza in the harlot's bed (v. 1) and ends in Gaza at the prison mill (v. 21).

3. This drawing of a line between the two sections is reinforced by the concluding formula of 15:20. The writer, knowing the other side of the story yet to be told, concludes (as it were) his story after the "Samson with the Spirit" section, as if to say, "In any real sense of the word, Samson's career as judge of Israel ended here." He will append the formula in a formal way at the end of the whole complex (16:31), but he purposely inserts it at 15:20 to drive a wedge between the two sections to serve his before-and-after design.

city gate, apparently relax during the night,[4] thinking that at daylight they would kill him (v. 2). But Samson is not above leaving a woman in bed to save his skin. While the Gaza Civil Defense Unit is waiting for light Samson uses the night. Probably with a bit of a smile he grabs the doors and the side-posts of the town gate, pulls them out—bar included, and, with a slight "hup," shoulders them and trudges off to deposit them on a hill near Hebron,[5] leaving an opening in the city gate and a dent in the municipal budget.

Then there was Delilah (v. 4), the only woman mentioned by name in the Samson stories. Whether she was Philistine or Israelite does not matter—it didn't even matter to Delilah; all that mattered was Philistine money (v. 5).

Samson always loved a good time and, apparently, so did Delilah. She started Samson on a new game called "The Philistines Are Here!" Actually, Delilah was playing her own game but she needn't tell Samson that. Samson seemed to enjoy himself, snapping both fresh bowstrings (vv. 6–9) and new ropes (vv. 10–12), though Delilah probably seethed when he wrecked her loom (vv. 13–14).

Delilah pretended to tire of the game. She had a right to

4. Cf. Robert G. Boling, *Judges,* The Anchor Bible (Garden City, N.Y.: Doubleday, 1975), 248: "The city gate, where it has been discovered in early Iron Age sites, was an elaborate complex, at least two stories high, with guardrooms flanking the tunnel-like opening. . . . Any Iron Age Palestinian would easily comprehend how Samson might slip past the Gazites at the gate because the latter had assumed that they could wait 'in the city gate,' that is, indoors, until morning." Cf. also G. G. Garner, "Fortification," *IBD,* 1:525.

5. Some hold that verse 3 only requires Samson to have carried the gate apparatus to a hill "toward" or "in the direction of" Hebron. In that case, Samson may have deposited his load somewhere near Gaza rather than lugging it about forty miles to the east around Hebron itself. The Hebrew preposition (*'al-penê*) can be used in the sense of "direction toward" (see C. F. Keil, *Joshua, Judges, Ruth,* Biblical Commentary on the Old Testament [1868; reprint ed., Grand Rapids: Eerdmans, 1950], 418, who cited Gen. 18:16; see also Gen. 19:28). If, however, Samson merely dumped his burden in the vicinity of Gaza why would the writer even mention Hebron? For this reason C. J. Goslinga (*Joshua, Judges, Ruth,* Bible Student's Commentary [Grand Rapids: Zondervan, 1986], 440) holds that the "author included the name Hebron to show that he deposited them in the center of Judah so that Israel would have tangible proof of his victory." In that case, Samson's journey would have taken several days.

know the secret of Samson's strength and he was "playing games" with her. Cool and calculating, Delilah pressed[6] the matter upon Samson over a period of time and kept urging him on till at last he cracked. And no wonder! One can imagine the scenes behind verses 15–16. Delilah likely turned on the relational arguments about trust and intimacy, and about how we must all be vulnerable, and that women really do crave men who are willing to be the latter. And Delilah suspected her psychology would be all the more convincing while she spread her long, soft hair against Samson's mighty chest and stroked his biceps with her soft hand.

One day it all came out. Samson said "razor" and Delilah saw silver. Maybe Samson convinced himself he could trust Delilah with his real secret. Or maybe he thought he had matters under control. Actually, it doesn't matter. Delilah was sharp enough to have the razor used (v. 19), and this time the game was over. The Philistines grab Samson,[7] scoop out his eyes, bring him to Gaza Prison, and make him grind grain with a hand mill (v. 21).[8]

We hear the heaviest thud of Samson's tragedy in verse 20b. Samson awakes with his customary optimism: "but *he* did not know that *Yahweh* had departed from him."[9]

Why tell Israel this story? Why did Israel need to hear this? Why did Israel need to remember both the entertainment and the tragedy of Samson (the tragedy being all the more tragic because of the entertainment that had preceded it)? Because Samson was intended as a mirror for Israel. In Samson Israel

6. The verb in verse 16a (*ṣūq* in the Hiphil, to press upon) was also used in 14:17, when Samson's wife wheedled the riddle out of him.

7. In verse 3 Samson grabs hold of (*'aḥaz*) the doors of Gaza's gate; in verse 21 the Philistines grab (same verb) Samson. Also, ironically, Gaza is the scene both of Samson's great escape (vv. 1–3) and of his tragic confinement (v. 21).

8. Samson's grinding was a calculated humiliation; the celebrated hero now does the work of slaves and women. See further, K. van der Toorn, "Judges xvi 21 in the Light of the Akkadian Sources," *Vetus Testamentum* 36 (1986): 248–51.

9. The emphasis reflects the Hebrew text. Here is a third "did-not-know" statement. Manoah did not know the identity of God's messenger (13:16); Manoah and his wife did not know the intention of God's providence (14:4); Samson did not know the absence of God's strength (16:20).

was to see herself (just as in Luke 15 Jesus wanted the Pharisees and scribes of v. 2 to see themselves in the older son of vv. 25–32). Samson is a paradigm of Israel: one raised up out of nothing, richly gifted, who panders around with other loves and yet, apparently, always expects to "have" Yahweh.[10] So Israel has received grace on top of grace yet persistently carries on her affairs with Baal (see 2:11ff.), utterly ignorant of her true condition (cf. Hos. 7:9), blithely assuming that all is well (Jer. 2:34b–35a) and that Yahweh is always at her disposal (Jer. 2:27b). She is a people who does not know that Yahweh may depart from her—just as a church may believe that God would never write "Ichabod" over its denominational headquarters (cf. 1 Sam. 4:21). How tragic when God's professing people cannot see that they are "wretched, pitiable, poor, blind, and naked" (Rev. 3:17). Whether to ancient Israel or contemporary church, Samson's tragedy still speaks: watch out, lest you abandon the divine call, leave your first love, and forfeit the divine presence.

The Vindication of Yahweh's Honor

But Samson is not to remain a hairless trophy at the prison mill. The rest of the story details the vindication of Yahweh's honor (vv. 22–31). We will explain this in a moment, but first let's have some fun with the Philistines.

I referred earlier to the "stupidity of the Philistines" as a literary theme of the Samson materials. This theme reaches a kind of crescendo in verses 22–30; that is, Philistine stupidity seems to pile up in this section. How obtuse were they? First, the Philistines were as blind as Samson in supposing that blindness alone would render Samson harmless and in failing to notice (seemingly) that his hair had begun to grow again (v. 22).[11] A second aspect of Philistine stupidity may be intended in verses 23–24, where the faithful raise their pre-

---

10. On Samson as paradigm of Israel see Goslinga, *Joshua, Judges, Ruth,* 409–410; Webb, *The Book of the Judges,* 172; and James L. Crenshaw, *Samson: A Secret Betrayed, A Vow Ignored* (Atlanta: John Knox, 1978), 134, 151.

11. Not that there was any magic in Samson's hair. His strength came only from Yahweh (16:20). However, his hair was the sign of that strength and we must not sever the sign from the reality which it signifies.

mature liturgy of thanksgiving to Dagon, a non-god who, as
the sequel shows, cannot prevent the site of his celebration
from becoming a massive cemetery (populated by his devotees).
Thirdly, they summon Samson into their very midst to provide
entertainment (vv. 25–26), never dreaming they were simply
furnishing him the props for his next act. Finally, the shrine
was packed with participants, including all the Philistine
bureaucrats (v. 27; hence they will lose their national leadership). One grunt from the entertainer of the day buries the
whole witnessing crowd under one heap of holy rubble. I should
think any red-blooded Israelite would find it all—to put it in
British idiom—more than a little amusing.

In the Bible, however, hilarity is the servant of solemnity.
Scripture usually tells us something funny in order to sober
us up. Naturally we enjoy this story about how Samson
brought the house down. But the Bible is not merely trying to
get us to laugh but to make us angry, for this humorous literary theme is only the wrapping for the serious theological
concern.

Doesn't anger mix with your laughter when you hear the
Philistine brass belch out their Dagonian confession of faith
(v. 23): "Our god has given into our hand Samson, our enemy."
Don't you seethe when the people sing Dagon's praise (v. 24)?

> Our god has given into our hand our enemy,
> the one who wasted our land,
> who multiplied our slain.

After all, we know that is theological and liturgical baloney;
we know it was the absence of Yahweh, not the power of
Dagon, that accounts for Samson's shame. But Samson's
shame has become Yahweh's shame, for praise that belongs to
Yahweh alone is being heaped at the lifeless feet of a helpless
image, and because Yahweh's servant has been humiliated
Yahweh also suffers humiliation.

It is crucial then that such bastard praises be stifled. That
is the heart of this last section of Samson's story. Of course it's
interesting; God's ways always are. But we must not allow the
details of Samson's movements (vv. 26, 29–30), the archaeology of Dagon's temple, or the panic of his dying worshipers to

obscure what is most essential—that a false god is shown to be the cipher he/it really is.[12] Yet we must confess that this frequently does not interest us much. We are caught up in the humor, the drama, and the tragedy of the story, but somehow, in spite of the religious ballyhoo we sometimes place at the end of our prayers, the honor, praise, and glory of Yahweh move us very little. We don't usually bristle that much when he doesn't receive proper praise. Perhaps repentance should begin before we leave Dagon's temple.

The Nearness of Yahweh's Help

Before leaving verses 22–31, I want to discuss briefly Samson's prayer, for Samson's calling to Yahweh (v. 28) is no minor element of the narrative; in fact, it underscores the nearness of Yahweh's help.

Let us go back for a moment to matters of structure (see the introductory comments to this chapter), to note how both narratives (chaps. 14–15 and chap. 16) reach their climaxes when Samson "called to Yahweh" (15:18; 16:28). J. Cheryl Exum has nicely caught the importance of this structure:

> At the point where Samson appears defeated, both accounts reach their climax. Resolution comes when Samson calls (*qr'*) on Yhwh and Yhwh answers Samson's petition (xv 18–19, xvi 28–30). The structure provides a significant guide to meaning. The theological message toward which each of the cycles moves centers on prayer and divine response, and the position of answered prayer at the end of each cycle is emphatic. In xv 18–19 Samson asks for life. . . . In xvi 28–30 he prays first for vindication, then for death. In both cases he is dependent wholly upon Yhwh, who alone holds the power to grant life and death and who acts in response to human supplication.[13]

In both sections Yahweh is the God who hears the cry of his servant in desperate circumstances. Yet there is a difference in 16:28–30. Here Yahweh's answer comes not only in the

---

12. I am indebted to David Gunn's comments (cited in Webb, *The Book of the Judges,* 165–66) for stimulating my thinking here.
13. Exum, "Theological Dimension," 34.

midst of desperate need but in the wake of miserable failure. This is the Samson who would rather play around with Delilah than protect Yahweh's gift. This is the Samson who faithlessly bartered away Yahweh's strength in order to court a treacherous lover. It is this Samson—this faithless, foolish, fallen Samson—whom Yahweh hears in 16:28–30.

A few pages ago I suggested that Samson was a sort of Israel in concentrated form, that Israel was meant to recognize in Samson the pattern of her own faithlessness. If that is so, how was Israel to hear this latter part of the Samson story? Were they not meant to hear it in hope? Were they not to understand that though Yahweh's hand may justly cast down his unfaithful servants, his ears are nevertheless open to their cries and his arm still ready to act on their behalf?[14] Should Israel not see that even in her sinfulness God was still encouraging her to "call upon [him] in the day of trouble" (cf. Ps. 50:15)?

Of course, there will be objections. Someone will argue that Israel—like Samson—does not deserve Yahweh's help. So what else is new? Those who marshal such objections are frequently those who have little if any sense of their own depravity. And what of the Christian who has stupidly and miserably failed his Lord? Should he not find hope in seeing that being cast down does not mean being cast off? Should he not rejoice that he can call on Yahweh even from Dagon's temple?

The Strangeness of Yahweh's Choice

Finally, as we look back over the whole rollicking and tragic story we must mention the strangeness of Yahweh's choice. That is, why would Yahweh use a character like Samson as his servant? Here is a fellow who shatters all our molds, conventions, and expectations about what a servant of God is to be. Worse yet, Samson is not only unconventional but also unfaithful. He seems to think his God-given strength was his

14. Obviously, if Israel applied this text to her own case it would have to be according to the general pattern (Yahweh still hears and answers his erring servants), not the precise petition ("Let me die with the Philistines!"). We must not imagine that this text would speak to Israel only in or after the exile; there were many other instances of faithlessness before that time.

plaything (at least in 16:1–21); he didn't seem to realize that our gifts are not given so we can toy with them as we please but to serve and care for the good of God's people. But here is this Samson, a sort of wild ass of a man, entertaining yet unpredictable, so promising and so tragic. He seems so unlike an evangelical Christian!

During the War between the States, the story spread that General Grant had been drunk at the Battle of Shiloh. About eleven o'clock one night President Lincoln received his friend A. K. McClure. McClure was on a mission. As spokesman for a number of Republicans he pressed his argument for almost two hours on how popular opinion was against Grant and therefore Grant should be dismissed so that Lincoln himself could retain the country's confidence. Lincoln rarely interrupted. Then, as McClure himself reported it: "Lincoln remained silent for what seemed a very long time. He then gathered himself up in his chair and said, in a tone of earnestness that I shall never forget, *'I can't spare this man; he fights.'*"[15] He may look seedy; he may have trouble with booze; popular opinion may stand against him—but he fights.

We cannot explain Yahweh's choices, though we might vindicate his choice of Samson by a variation of Lincoln's argument. Say what you will about Samson, at least he knew who the enemy was; at least he knew Philistines were for fighting; at least he didn't roll over and play dead in the warmth of the status quo as the mighty men of Judah did (15:11). Perhaps we will eventually get over our surprise at the kind of servants Yahweh delights to use. "There has almost certainly never been another Samson among the people of God, but there have been many other strange characters. We are very unwilling to learn that God wants to use all the gifts He has given, while we should like to confine Him to our respectabilities."[16]

---

15. Bruce Catton, *Mr. Lincoln's Army* (Garden City, N.Y.: Doubleday, 1951), 155.

16. H. L. Ellison, *Scripture Union Bible Study Books: Joshua-2 Samuel* (Grand Rapids: Eerdmans, 1966), 36.

PART 3

The Confusion of a Depraved People
(Judges 17–21)

20

Divine Sarcasm
(17–18)

You have now entered the third major section of the Book of Judges. You may have lost sight of such matters since we have had to spend such a long time in 3:7–16:31, the second and longest of the sections.[1] Immediately you sense the difference. It's like walking on pavement and then suddenly realizing you are crunching along on gravel. Even if you didn't see where the pavement stopped and the gravel began, your feet tell you. So you simply know these last five chapters are different. There is no refrain of Israel's apostasy, no announcing of a new oppression, no central judge-figure. The writer changes his style in order to portray the confusion of a depraved people. He will do this by displaying both Israel's confusion and her depravity. In two narratives he will hold the mirror in front of Israel, as if to say, "Here you are, Israel—making your own gods [chapters 17–18, Micah and the Danites] and destroying your own people [chapters 19–21, Gibeah and Israel]." Here is Israel wallowing in her own religious and moral mess. Here the problem is not the enemy without but the cancer within. Here, so the writer says, Israel has hit bottom. Hard. Yet not without hope.

"In all my life so far (and that's most of it) I have never heard a single reference from pulpit or song writer or study leader

1. See the Non-Introduction and the opening comments on 3:7–11 for these major divisions.

or anybody else at all—never one single tiny whispered sound—that related to the Micah of the Book of Judges."

So writes John Hercus as he begins his discussion of Judges 17–18 in his racy book *God Is God*. According to Hercus, one need not wonder why there is this strange silence about Judges 17–18 in the church:

> The reason is that the story is so crazy, so mixed-up that obviously the parsons and clerics are too embarrassed by it to let out a single peep. And don't think I am being hard on them—not a bit. Even the writer of the Book of Judges is embarrassed by it. As we will see, even he finds it almost impossible now and again to go on with the account. . . .[2]

Indeed one can almost see those concerned creases wrinkling evangelical brows as they read Judges 17–18 and as their hearts whisper softly and tenderly that there is no need to wrestle with such Scripture when they can be meditating on Philippians. How, we may wonder, could that biblical theologian ever have written that "all scripture is . . . profitable" (2 Tim. 3:16)? But if he's right, a study of Judges 17–18 must be worthwhile!

That all Scripture is profitable does not mean its interpretation is simple. In fact, biblical narrative can prove deceptively difficult to interpret. The present story is a case in point. Read it through. (This chapter will make more sense to you if you do it now.) It is all descriptive. Where does the writer clearly interject his own—or God's—evaluation of things? He doesn't. The story concludes but is provided with no moral application or religious judgment.[3] He never turns aside to say, "Now what Micah [or the Danites] had done displeased the Lord" (cf. 2 Sam. 11:27). Nothing like that. The story has been told, but how do we know the standpoint of the storyteller? How then can we know his purpose in relating the story to us? How can we see past this apparently noncommittal element of the narrative?

I propose that careful observation of the way in which the biblical writer tells his story provides us with clear clues about

2. John Hercus, *God Is God* (London: Hodder and Stoughton, 1971), 186.
3. Karl Gutbrod, *Das Buch vom Lande Gottes,* Die Botschaft des Alten Testaments, 3d ed. (Stuttgart: Calwer, 1965), 266.

his intention; hence the manner of his storytelling is as important as the matter of his story. For this reason I want to depart from my usual procedure of concentrating almost immediately on the teaching of the passage. Instead I want to focus first on the techniques the writer uses before outlining the teaching he provides.

The Expressed Viewpoint of the Writer

First of all, let us briefly notice the expressed viewpoint of the writer. Hear how he begins his story (17:1–6):

1. There was a man from the hill country of Ephraim; his name was Micah.
2. And he said to his mother, "The eleven hundred weight of silver which was taken from you, and you uttered a curse—in fact, you said it in my hearing—well, the silver is with me; I took it." Then his mother said, "May you be blessed by Yahweh, my son!"
3. So he returned the eleven hundred weight of silver to his mother, and his mother said, "I have definitely set apart this silver to Yahweh from me for my son, to make a carved idol and a molten image; and now, let me return it to you."
4. So Micah returned the silver to his mother, and his mother took two hundred weight of silver, gave it to the silversmith, and he made it into a carved idol and a molten image. It was in the house of Micah.
5. This man Micah had a house of gods. He made an ephod and teraphim [household idols] and consecrated one of his sons, who became his priest.
6. In those days there was no king in Israel—each man was doing whatever was right in his own eyes.[4]

4. The text of 17:1–6 is a bit rough and difficult at some points but not enough to justify the radical rearrangement in the Jerusalem Bible. I also think that Goslinga is correct about verse 5; the Hebrew most naturally means that Micah already had "a house of gods," so that his mother's contribution(s) did not originate his worship center but decisively enhanced it. She provided the icing on the cultic cake. (See C. J. Goslinga, *Joshua, Judges, Ruth,* Bible Student's Commentary [Grand Rapids: Zondervan, 1986], 458).

There is one point at which our writer clearly declares him-self; it is in his use of the no-king formula in verse 6 (see it in abbreviated form in 18:1; see also 19:1; 21:25). By placing this statement immediately after his report of the genesis of Micah's illicit shrine he quietly indicates his negative esti-mation of Micah's "house of gods" (17:5). "In those days there was no king in Israel—each man was doing whatever was right in his own eyes." That is the explanation for the flour-ishing of all this liturgical junk in the hill country of Ephraim. The writer so much as says, "Had there been a king back then, he would have obviously put a stop to Micah's godless non-sense."[5] Our writer clearly has in mind a particular kind of

5. The simple argumentation in the no-king formula supports an early date for the writing of Judges 17–18 (and of 19–21). When the writer implies the lack of a king explains Micah's mess, one could understand such an unqualified statement if the writer were living during David's reign or, at the latest, the early part of Solomon's reign. But he could never have given such a naive explanation if he had lived in Solomon's later years or during the years of the divided kingdom when a godly king was a rare bird (occasionally found in Judah) and kingship generally had proven almost a consistent disappoint-ment, the king himself often being the source of corruption. Our writer's no-king argument makes sense only if the writer lived at a time when Israel had had little historical experience with kingship and at a time when what Israel had experienced to that point had been—on the whole—positive. I have argued this position in more detail and over against other options in "A Proposed Life-Setting for the Book of Judges" (Ann Arbor: University Microfilms, 1978), 78–84. There I contend that David is the king in mind and that the material dates from early in his reign—possibly from his rule in Hebron. See further, Kenneth A. Kitchen, "The Old Testament in its Context 3: From Joshua to Solomon," *TSF Bulletin* 61 (Autumn 1971): 8; Arthur E. Cundall, "Judges—An Apology for the Monarchy?" *The Expository Times* 81 (1970): 180–81; and Willem A. VanGemeren, *The Progress of Redemption* (Grand Rapids: Zonder-van, 1988), 195–99. I find the argument for an exilic date very unconvincing; cf. William J. Dumbrell, "In those days there was no King in Israel; every man did what was right in his own eyes. The Purpose of the Book of Judges Reconsidered," *JSOT* 25 (1983): 23–33. Note that the terminus of 18:30 ("until the day of the captivity of the land") does not overthrow the case for an early date for chapters 17–18. If it does refer to an Assyrian captivity (as Moore, Hertzberg, and Gray would have it), it need only indicate the latest edition of these chapters; see Goslinga, *Joshua, Judges, Ruth,* 470–74. However, the parallel clause in verse 31 ("all the days that the house of God was in Shiloh") suggests a Philistine captivity or domination like that following Aphek (see 1 Sam. 4) or Gilboa (see 1 Sam. 31). Cf. Arthur E. Cundall, *Judges,* Tyndale Old Testament Commentaries (London: Tyndale, 1968), 192, and Paulus Cas-

king, a king who would uphold Yahweh's covenant standards. That kind of king, so the argument goes, would have put a stop to such bastard worship. It is not simply monarchy as such that the writer says is needed, but a monarchy that is faithful to Yahweh's covenant requirements. Those times of the judges were hardly the "good old days." Rather, they were the days when Israel was out of control, the days when the dictates of every man's own glands formed the standard for life, the days when they needed a godly king.

That is the writer's position. We can touch on it later; for now let us move on to how he says what he says.

The Subtle Manner of the Story

Apart from the no-king formula our writer may appear nearly neutral as he relates his story to us; but if we look carefully, listen carefully, I think we will plainly conclude that his neutrality is only apparent. Notice the subtle manner of the story.

First of all, it is interesting to observe a possible contrast that the writer seems to draw at the beginning and at the end of his narrative, between Micah's "house of gods" (17:5, literal trans.)[6] and the "house of God" at Shiloh (18:31). I suggest the writer places these two sanctuaries, the false and the true, over against one another. There is the true house of God at Shiloh and then there is Micah's collection of cultic Tinkertoys.

Secondly, a close look at the writer's depiction of the characters can scarcely fail to detect an undercurrent of mild contempt directed toward each of the main actors; their incongruities seem especially to attract his disdain. Look at the cast! Here is Micah's mother, who seeks to reverse a solemn curse with a fresh blessing (17:2), who consecrates the returned wealth to Yahweh for illegitimate worship of the same (17:3). Micah, contrary to his name (which in its full form

sel, *The Book of Judges*, Lange's Commentary on the Holy Scriptures, in vol. 2, *Numbers-Ruth* (1865; reprint ed., Grand Rapids: Zondervan, 1960), 238–39.

6. The Revised Standard Version and the New International Version have "shrine," which is not wrong but hides the contrast between Micah's "house of elohim [gods]" here and the legitimate "house of Elohim [God]" in 18:31.

means "Who is like Yahweh?"),[7] manages to reduce Yahweh's incomparability to a few mundane pieces of hardware (17:4–5). The Levite, whom Micah hires (17:10), trustingly accepts (17:11b), and regards as a guarantee of Yahweh's blessing (17:13), nevertheless happily sells his fidelity to the higher bidder (18:19–20). Evidently, the Danites offered a greater potential for ministry, a field of labor where his gifts could be maximized. And the Danites, who are repeatedly described in terms of military bravado (18:11, 16, 17), display their gallantry by slaughtering a peaceful, helpless, undefended people (18:7, 10, 27–28).[8] Yes, sir, aren't those Danites tough customers? How about one stanza of "Onward Danite Soldiers"? Our writer may appear to be dispassionate but there are traces of acid in his ink.

Third, our narrator appears to keep a certain distance from the events he is describing. For example, note that the name *Yahweh* (or, "the LORD" in many English versions) is found only on the lips of the cast (17:2, 3, 13; 18:6). The narrator himself never uses it. It is as if he wants no part of such syncretism, as if he loathes to touch this mishmash of smorgasbord theology.

Similarly, his reference in 18:27 to the Danites taking "what Micah had made" may be deliberate. Micah, of course, had referred to these things as "my gods which I made" (18:24). Our writer, however, refuses to dignify such relics by calling them "gods." Note the same disparagement and distance in 18:31 where he mentions "the image of Micah which he had made."

Next observe the use of irony in the story. The Hebrew verb *laqah* (to take) is a very common one, but it is interesting to note how its usage in the present narrative provides an ironic tone to the whole. It occurs twice in 17:2 in reference to Micah's confession of his theft; then it appears five times in chapter 18

---

7. Though English versions generally render all references as Micah, the full form of the name, *Mikayehu*, is used in 17:1, 4 and may be intended to emphasize the irony of Micah's action; so Robert G. Boling, *Judges*, The Anchor Bible (Garden City, N.Y.: Doubleday, 1975), 255, 258. Elsewhere in the narrative the name is *Mikah* (Micah).

8. There are some difficulties in the Hebrew text of 18:7, 16–17, but they do not materially affect the point here.

(vv. 17, 18, 20, 24, 27) in describing the Danites' purloining of Micah's holy paraphernalia. Micah stole; and Dan stole from Micah. Most fitting! The sanctuary of Dan had its origins in a double theft. What else can come out of it except curse and ruin?[9]

There also seems to be an ironic tone to the evident success in the fortunes of both Micah and the Danites. If the reader places himself in the sandals of Micah and/or the Danites he can see how they might perceive their circumstances as evidence of the course of providence. There are clear hints of this point of view in both Micah (17:13) and the Danites (18:10). Micah, for example, could look back upon his act of theft and curse-laden situation (17:2a) and see how confession had opened the way to blessing and the enhancement (or origin) of his Chapel in the Hills (17:2–5). Then a certain Levite just happened to come his way (17:7–8) and thus providence had provided him with a (nearly) legitimate priest and the assurance of further blessing from above (17:13). Nor should we fail to mention the open, affirming relationship Micah enjoyed with his new priest (17:11b). Not only so, but Micah's cult even becomes a "channel of blessing" to others (18:5–6).

But of course providence was even more favorable to the Danites. They too just happened to bump into the Levite whom they had previously known (small world!) in some way (18:3; perhaps the Lord's sway even involves southern accents!), experienced brilliant success in their spying efforts (18:7), and brought back a "good report" (contrast Num. 13:32 in context) fairly bubbling with divine assurance (18:8–10). On their journey they easily requisitioned the contents of Micah's worship center (18:14–18, 22–26) and won over the priest by presenting him with a lucrative call to a new field of mini$try (18:19–20). And what a priest! None other than the grandson (or descendant) of Moses (18:30)![10] Truly, "God is so good."

---

9. Gutbrod, *Das Buch vom Lande Gottes*, 265.

10. "Moses" is certainly correct in verse 30. Some translations (e.g., KJV, NASB) have "Manasseh." That is because a number of Hebrew manuscripts read "Manasseh" but often with a suspended *n*, that is, a little above the normal writing line. The scribes wrote the *n* (Hebrew letter *nun*) that way to show that it was inserted. The insertion then changed "Moses" into "Manasseh." Rashi (Jewish exegete, 1040–96) explained that the *n* was inserted to

Such is the apparent flow of the story. But the narrative undertow tells us that the writer does not share this view of providence. It is clear that he regards the whole affair as a mess, and he allows that mess to pile up at 18:27, where he informs us that the Danites took (a) what Micah had made (not "gods"), (b) a priest who could be bought, and (c) a city that could not be defended.[11] Such is the writer's tribute to Danite success.

However, the writer does not rest content with a subtle irony but engages in overt sarcasm. This occurs in his report of Micah's complaint in 18:24: "My god(s) which I have made you have taken."[12] Here the theological broadside strikes with full power. Any faithful Yahweh-worshiper would find Micah's cry both tragic and ludicrous. A god who can be made is surely a contradiction in terms; and a god who cannot avoid being pilfered must be a non-god indeed (cf. 6:31)! Thus the narrator artlessly permits Micah himself to emphasize the insanity of the whole affair.[13]

Our writer, then, is no impartial observer but a hostile critic. He hints at this by the way he uses contrast, depicts characters, and maintains distance. He makes his stance even more obvious (if subtly so) by his sustained irony on providence

---

protect the honor of Moses (what shame for Moses' memory to have a descendant officiating in this perverted worship), but it was suspended to show that "Manasseh" was not the real reading. The Manasseh intended is the wicked king of 2 Kings 21. Such worship, the scribes suggested, would have been very compatible with Manasseh but not, alas, with Moses. See C. F. Burney, *The Book of Judges* (London: Rivingtons, 1918), 434–35, and C. D. Ginsburg, *Introduction to the Massoretico-Critical Edition of the Hebrew Bible* (1897; reprint ed., New York: KTAV, 1966), 334ff. By holding back the priest's identity till the very end of the narrative and then disclosing his relation to Moses the writer essentially crushes the reader under a literary load of bricks. Shock, dismay, disbelief, a helpless feeling of tragedy—these are the reactions. "Moses" wreaks literary destruction on the faithful Israelite reader/hearer. John the Baptist was right (see Matt. 3:9).

11. H. W. Hertzberg, *Die Bücher Josua, Richter, Ruth,* Das Alte Testament Deutsch, 2d ed. (Göttingen: Vandenhoeck und Ruprecht, 1959), 243.

12. The direct object, "my god(s)," is emphatic in the Hebrew construction.

13. Micah's complaining "and what do I have left" (also in v. 24) also serves the bitter humor of the episode. It is as if he has lost everything now that his images have been stripped from him. This suggestion was offered me by Kenneth Kok, a former student and now a colleague in ministry.

and vicious sarcasm against images. Literary manner really does feed didactic intent; how he speaks leads us into what he wants to say.

The Vital Teaching of the Text

We have discussed both the overt standpoint and the covert manner of our writer, items necessary for understanding and appreciating this text. Now we may summarize the vital teaching of the text.

We must stay on the right course at this point. One can pick up technical commentaries that reconstruct the tradition history of these chapters, explain geographical movements and locations, provide archaeological background, discuss textual problems, and clarify Hebrew idioms, but make little, if any, attempt to hear the teaching of the text—still less to aid a reader in discovering that teaching. On the other hand, some practical expositions seize upon snips of the text in order to make inane applications (e.g., Micah "had a shrine," 17:5, and you should have a place of prayer in your home; the Danites show a worthy religious impulse in their desire to erect a place of worship in their new home—a church is often one of the first buildings erected in a new community).[14] Since I have found so little assistance in this task perhaps I can be beaten with fewer stripes for the present attempt.

The general theme pervading the whole narrative is its concern over false religion; we shouldn't go far wrong if we outline its theology under this theme.

The Judgment on False Religion

First of all, we can say that the text speaks of the judgment on false religion. This judgment theme is also expressed subtly. It is not expressed with a searing salvo at the end of the narrative, for 18:30–31 is rather matter-of-fact in its description.

14. I do not object to personal places of prayer nor to new church buildings but to violating a text by drawing applications from it which trample upon the text's primary concern. If the text had said, "In a fit of petulant rage Junior spat his peas all over the supper table," would we apply it by observing, "Supper is a meal a family should enjoy together"?

Rather the divine judgment resting upon Micah's cult appears to be announced from the very start by the introduction of his "carved idol" and "molten image" (*pesel* and *massēkah*; 17:3, 4). I agree with Paulus Cassel:

> These words [*pesel, massēkah*] at the same time pronounce judgment against the sin that had been committed, for they are the technical expressions under which the law forbids the making of every kind of image-work for idolatrous purposes. The narrator has his eyes doubtless on Deut. xxvii.15.[15]

That text (Deut. 27:15) stands first in a series of twelve curses and pronounces "cursed the man who makes a *pesel* or *massēkah*—an abomination to Yahweh." Hence even though his mother's curse can be evaded or countered, Micah and the Danites rest under a divine curse which cannot be retracted and under a threat that will in no way be neutralized. If we evade the curse of men, the curse of Yahweh is greater. Micah is living proof that it is possible to be set on a course of religious faith and/or ministry which exudes success in every respect and yet to rest under the curse of God's judgment.

The Antidote for False Religion

Secondly, the writer has suggested an antidote for false religion (17:6 and 18:1). His argument is: if Israel had only had a king back then—the right kind of king—he would have put a stop to such syncretistic nonsense.[16] In short, proper covenantal control ought to stifle false religion. But how do we go about applying the proposed solution for the church of Jesus Christ in our own time, particularly since the church in our culture does not have the same theocratic-national form as did Israel? After all, we don't have a king, do we? Of course we do! Who is Jesus Christ if not our King who rules us? Do we not see Christ ruling as king in Revelation 2–3 in his role of judge over and among his churches? And has not the Shepherd-King entrusted to undershepherds the task of ruling and

15. Cassel, *The Book of Judges*, 229.
16. Syncretism is melting-pot religion, a little bit of this, a little bit of that. Specifically, here it refers to Israel's tendency to combine or blend various elements of pagan (Canaanite) religion with the worship of Yahweh.

defending his flock (cf. Acts 20:28–31; Heb. 13:17; 1 Pet. 5:1–4)?[17] Is it going beyond the text to hold that it teaches the necessity for vigilant discipline among the people of God in order to maintain the purity of worship and life?

The Stupidity of False Religion

The writer is also at pains to stress the stupidity of false religion (see esp. 18:24). As I have tried to show, his narrative abounds with theological broadsides and innuendos meant to hold up Mican liturgy and Danite divinity to ridicule.

We face a problem, however, at this point. How can we bring home this thrust of the text to the modern hearer (sometimes he is us!) in our current western church culture? Our hearer will surely respond, "This story surely does lambast Micah's cult, but I don't make gods like a *pesel*; this doesn't fit me." And of course he is telling the truth. How can we get him to feel the punch of this text, assuming he should?

I think our problem may be that we don't see the stupidity of false religion because we don't see our false religion. Only after we see the forms our false religion takes can we see how stupid it is.

We must first identify the kind of false religion we are dealing with. In this passage what is primarily condemned is not idolatry in the raw but syncretism in particular, not the worship of other gods but the worship of Yahweh in a wrong way (see, e.g., 17:3). And this occurs among the alleged people of God. This too will likely leave our hearer cold. Hence we must ask: What are the particular forms which this kind of false religion takes? How does such syncretism appear? Can we identify these forms of false religion in our own worship and thinking? And, if so, are they not stupid?

17. See the Westminster Larger Catechism, question 45: How doth Christ execute the office of a king? Answer: Christ executeth the office of a king, in calling out of the world a people to himself, *and giving them officers, laws, and censures, by which he visibly governs them*; in bestowing saving grace upon his elect, rewarding their obedience, and correcting them for their sins, preserving and supporting them under all temptations and sufferings, restraining and overcoming all their enemies, and powerfully ordering all things for his own glory, and their good; and also in taking vengeance on the rest, who know not God, and obey not the gospel [italics added].

One form such syncretism takes is that of sacramentalism, believing that some degree of conformity in religious externals will surely draw down the divine approval. Micah thinks this way in 17:13; he is confident he has Yahweh's favor because now he has an actual Levite as his priest (rather than merely his own son). We have our own forms of such magic, of thinking we can switch God's grace on automatic. With some it is a superstitious regard for infant baptism, thinking that if the child is "done," then he/she is covered and protected. Others think that walking down the aisle on the fifth stanza of an invitation hymn is the same thing as entering the kingdom of God. It is still false religion and it's still stupid. It doesn't differ from Micah's in principle but only in form; yet for that reason it may remain invisible to us.

This false religion also appears in the form of what I shall call subjectivism. The Danites' sanctuary stands over against the legitimate house of God at Shiloh (18:30–31). No need to bother going to Shiloh now; Dan is its own little "Israel." The Danites now have their own little convenience-store shrine near by—where they can control it. They can worship as they please. Does this not parallel the contemporary mood (even in the church) that worship is actually a very individual affair, a matter of sheer personal preference, and—like your tooth-brush—a very personal thing? To declare that faith, worship, and religion are rather regulated by royal revelation and subject to sovereign prescriptions sounds like a novel idea. Surely, contemporary Danites tell us, God is not so picky. Such folks really believe that the most appropriate symbol for what we believe and how we worship should be a big blob of fat—which every one can flop, squeeze, and shape the way he or she wants it. And that too is stupid.

The Tragedy of False Religion

Finally, our writer describes the tragedy of false religion (18:27–31). The Danites reenact Micah's folly. It grows from an idea in Micah's mother's perverted brain (17:3–4) to a reality in Micah's used-god lot and spreads, like cancer, to a tribal group. Sadly, the lie can make progress even without evangelists. Indeed, the Danite sanctuary may not be the end of the tragedy, for, whatever the historical and critical questions involved, the existence of the Danites' cult may have provided some of the stimulus for Jeroboam I to inject his own lethal infection into Israel's life (1 Kings 12, especially v. 29). If so, the tragedy continues into 2 Kings 17 and damns a nation.

We would do well, however, not to laugh too heartily at Micah and the Danites. Even we who worship the Image of the Invisible God (Col. 1:15) have our own struggles in worshiping him in wholeheartedness and fidelity.

21

New Sodom
(19–21)

Here is the second major narrative documenting the confusion of a depraved people. Though these chapters constitute a rather long narrative, I believe it is better to treat them together, for they form one connected story. I urge the reader to read through all three chapters at one sitting in order to fix the flow of the whole story in mind. There are a few textual difficulties (sometimes reflected in English translations), but unless these are vital for interpretation I am going to ignore them.

The divisions of our exposition will generally coincide with the biblical chapter divisions. Each chapter expresses a literary theme:

1. The guilt of Benjamin, chapter 19
2. The destruction of Benjamin (and Israel), chapter 20
3. The sorrow for Benjamin, chapter 21

These themes conveniently summarize the whole story.[1] Now to our exposition.

---

1. We should note that the events of Judges 19–21 occurred quite early in the judges' period, for, according to 20:27b–28a, Phinehas, grandson of Aaron, was (high) priest at the time (see also Num. 25:1–15; 31:6; Josh. 22:10–34). Because an event is narrated at the end of a book does not mean it occurred later than the other events in that book; biblical writers sometimes arrange their materials topically rather than chronologically.

The Depravity of Yahweh's People

First, chapter 19 portrays for us the depravity of Yahweh's people. It will help to set down the story in outline form before discussing its literary features. After that, we can summarize the teaching of the chapter:

The beginning of the story, 1–2
The hospitality of Bethlehem, 3–9
The bypassing of Jebus, 10–13
The callousness of Gibeah, 14–15
The compassion of the sojourner, 16–21
The resurrection of Sodom, 22–26
   Attack of the homosexuals, 22
   Appeal of the host, 23–24
   Action of the Levite, 25a
   Abuse of the concubine, 25b–26
The indifference of the Levite, 27–28
The uniqueness of the offense, 29–30

It's a quiet evening in Gibeah, three miles north of Jebus (Jerusalem). The Levite, his concubine, and his servant are enjoying a delightful supper in the home of their generous host (19:22). One of those cozy times that warm memories are made of. Then comes the hollering and the racket, the thumps of bodies throwing themselves against the door,[2] and at last the cries become discernible: "The man . . . have sex with him." Now the reader realizes how very dark it is in Gibeah.

A little reflection, however, reminds us that the writer has skillfully prepared us for this lurid scene. Glancing back we see that we are yet in the wake of a series of contrasts. There is the warm, gregarious father-in-law in Bethlehem-judah (vv. 3–9); no one is his peer in hospitality! He makes the men of Gibeah appear as the calloused tightwads they are (vv. 14–15). The Levite's servant suggested they stay in Jebus (Jerusalem), but the Levite was unwilling to lodge among foreigners who weren't Israelites (vv. 11–12). Did he perhaps say, "You never know what might happen in a pagan town"? Had he

2. The Hebrew participle suggests more than mere knocking or pounding on the door; see the New English Bible: "hurling themselves against the door."

known he was heading for Sodom-in-the-land-of-Israel he might have revised his opinion about Jebus. The one man who did extend hospitality in Gibeah was not actually from Gibeah. He was an import from the hill country of Ephraim (v. 16). The Gibeans were a bunch of social louts. Nor could any Gibean have said hospitality would have been too much expense; they could see that the Levite carried ample provisions for his needs (v. 19). The mob (v. 22) still shocks us, but as we look back on the writer's subtle contrasts of the Gibeans with the father-in-law, the Jebusites, and the sojourner, we almost wonder if we should not have expected the worst.

Our writer, however, uses similarity as well as contrast. This is especially clear in verses 22–26. Specifically, one cannot read Judges 19 without remembering Genesis 19. In that passage Lot offered hospitality to two visitors (angels); a mob eager for homosexual relations with the visitors surrounds his house; Lot counters by offering his two virgin daughters to the crowd; his visitors rescue him and strike the mob with a baffling blindness (Gen. 19:1–11). Unfortunately for the concubine, there were no delivering angels that night in Gibeah. Different outcomes to be sure, but the similarity between Genesis 19:1–11 and Judges 19:22–26 is unmistakable. And deliberate. The writer wants you to view Judges 19 this way. "Yes, that's right," he says, "it sounds exactly like Genesis 19. It's the Sodom Connection. Only here you have Sodom-in-the-land-of-Benjamin. Gibeah is 'New Sodom.'" This is the writer's way of accusing the people of God. He shows us that even in Israel some have plunged into the moral abyss of Sodom and eagerly wallow in its twisted depravity.

Speaking of twisted, we should note that there is a kind of twistedness about the characters in the story. Whose heart would not go out to the concubine as she is brutally assaulted and used throughout a night of unspeakable terror? Yet it all began when she was unfaithful to ("played the harlot against") the Levite (v. 2).[3]

3. So reads the Hebrew text. One recension of the Septuagint reads "she was angry with him," which is followed by some English versions (RSV, NEB, TEV). Some may object that if she was unfaithful the Levite would not seek to win her back but to have her punished. Such objections forget the writer's contention: things did *not* follow a regular course in those days; every man did his own thing.

The Levite, however, is the great anomaly. He is cowardly (v. 25; not that most of us would be very courageous!), calloused (vv. 27, 28), and, if we look ahead, less than candid (20:5). Bad enough to toss his concubine to the perverts of Gibeah, but to open the doors of the house, see her in a heap, with her hands on the threshold (19:27; what a graphic touch!), and to bark "Get up! Let's go!" (v. 28)—well, the fellow is "all heart," as we say.[4] Add to this the way he stacks (and hides) the facts to help his case (20:5), and one loses whatever respect one may have had for the Levite.

Some readers may be upset now. Why drag us through all this literary material again? Because—as we saw in the preceding chapter—how a writer tells a story is a clue to what he wants to say. A writer's literary techniques can tell you his standpoint, which is of immense help in knowing how he intends for us to regard his story.

Let us then set forth the teaching of chapter 19. As noted at the first, the writer depicts the depravity of Yahweh's people, and here he gives us a sample of it, a most extreme sample. That is the point of verses 29–30. When the Levite carves up his concubine's corpse and sends a gory token to each of the twelve tribes, people are appalled: "Nothing like this has happened or been seen from the day the sons of Israel went up from the land of Egypt to this very day!" (v. 30).[5] By "nothing like this" they may mean the ghastly parcel post they had just received; or, conceivably, the Levite could have had his messengers also announce the nature of the crime, in which case

---

4. Our writer may hint at the callousness of the Levite in verses 26–27 when he refers to him as the concubine's *'adōn* (master) rather than her husband (as, e.g., in v. 3). Is he saying she is to the Levite more property than person?

5. The text problem in 19:30 does not affect our point. It may be that the Septuagint/A has preserved something that dropped out of the Hebrew text; if so, verse 30 would read: "So it turned out that anyone seeing it said, 'Such a thing has not happened nor been seen from the day the sons of Israel came up out of the land of Egypt to this day.' Now he had commanded the men whom he had sent: 'Here's what you are to say to all the men of Israel: Has anything like this happened from the day the sons of Israel came up out of the land of Egypt to this day? Consider it, take counsel, and speak!' " Some versions (e.g., JB and NEB) use the Septuagint/A but do not follow it, since they rearrange the sequences of verse 30 to suit their preferences.

Israel's "this" would include shock over the crime itself.[6] Even if their horror is restricted to the pieces of flesh they would surely infer that only an unparalleled guilt would call forth such an extreme reaction. Years later Hosea could simply allude to the "days of Gibeah" to express the abyss of moral rot (Hos. 9:9; 10:9). Even though this event occurred early in the period of the Judges (see n. 1), our writer places it last as the climax of the book. Perhaps he wants to say: "You think that what you've heard to this point has been bad—get a load of this! And you're asking me why we need a (godly) king?"

We must remember the writer's theological geography. Gibeah has put on "Sodom—Act II." He depicts Gibeah's depravity (vv. 22–26) as though it were Sodom's (Gen. 19:1–11)—that is the shame of it.

Our writer also touches on the scope of Israel's wickedness. It certainly is not confined to Gibeah's city limits. Most every actor on the stage displays this twistedness, whether the concubine who was unfaithful (v. 2), or the Levite who looks out for number one (v. 25) and selectively manipulates his facts (20:4–6), or—again to transgress chapter 20—a tribe that would rather defend Sodom than practice justice (20:13). Perversity is pervasive.[7]

But does our writer analyze? Does he go deeply enough to show us the source of this depravity, to get at the root of it all? He hints at it as he breezes into chapter 19, for his quick reminder in 19:1 ("In those days when there was no king in Israel . . .") is meant to call up the fuller form of the formula with which he will conclude the book (21:25; see too 17:6). "In those days there was no king in Israel; each man was doing whatever was right in his own eyes." What does this reflect

6. The inquiry in 20:3b–7 is the formal—one might say legal—announcement of the wrong committed; but the news of Gibeah's sin could well have been disseminated long before these formalities.

7. The situation is akin to Genesis 27 in which the writer of Genesis wants to show that all four main characters were in the wrong in relation to Yahweh's promise: not only Rebekah (scheming over sovereignty, vv. 5–10) and Jacob (pragmatism over righteousness, vv. 11–12), but also Esau (indifference in spite of emotion, Gen. 25:34 with 27:34–38) and, probably, Isaac (palate over promise, Gen. 25:23 with 27:1–4). All four of the principal characters were in the wrong but Yahweh's promise came to pass in spite of what everyone was doing to sabotage or help it.

but each man's departure from Yahweh's covenant law? The problem is not so much with what "each man was doing" but with the standard that governed him ("in his own eyes"). Hence 21:25b expresses the ultimate perversity of every man, demanding the right to be his own lord, insisting on following the dictates of his own glands. The problem is not sins but sin, that declaration of independence—whether stated viciously or politely—which says, "Yes, I do want to be like God, calling my own shots" (see Gen. 3:5–6).

In late 1944 some three thousand English-speaking German soldiers disguised as American GIs were causing havoc behind American lines. They smoked American brands of cigarettes, used American swear words, carried American identification cards, money, and even letters and snapshots. They sped around in captured American jeeps, cutting communications, mixing up road signs, scouting movements of American reinforcements, and removing warnings from minefields. Finally, American troops began the spy hunt. Road checks had to go beyond passwords, papers, and superficial questions. Instead GIs would ask, "Where's the Windy City?" or order the "Americans" to say "wreath" (Germans almost always would say it with a hard *t* rather than the soft *th* sound). Once counterintelligence agents spotted two "American" second lieutenants in a jeep watching American reinforcements rush by. Upon questioning, they offered dogtags, inoculation papers, and detailed stories of their Army experiences. They claimed they had trained at Camp Hood (in Texas). Convincing. Then one agent asked: "Ever been in Texas?" "No, never." The agent had his Germans![8]

Sometimes matters can appear quite proper on the surface; sometimes one must dig deeply to find the enemy. The fact that the writer selected the flamboyant crime of Gibeah for his documentation of Israel's depravity should not blind us to the more basic point he is making. The root of it all is each man doing "whatever was right in his own eyes." That root may show itself in the grossest raunchiness (Judg. 19) or in appar-

---

8. Thomas M. Johnson, "The Most Dangerous Man in Europe," *Secrets and Spies: Behind-the-Scenes Stories of World War II* (Pleasantville, N.Y.: Reader's Digest Association, 1964), 469–72.

ent righteousness (e.g., Mark 10:17–22); but it's all from the same source.

"Each man was doing whatever was right in his own eyes." Who, in this context, is "each man"? He is Israelite man, covenant man. It is precisely those who have been called to be a people for Yahweh's own possession who are refusing to be subject to his covenant law! *They* will not have this God to rule over them. Is this not a word for the church? Are there not many in our pews who would voice outrage over the scandal of Gibeah, people who find religion congenial, morality proper, charity commendable, and God—if he is not sovereign—unobjectionable, and yet share a stubborn and wicked heart with the sexual perverts of Gibeah?

The Manifestation of Yahweh's Judgment

Secondly, chapter 20 focuses on the destruction of Benjamin and exhibits the manifestation of Yahweh's judgment. Because the chapter is so lengthy it will help us to see it in summary form:

The unity of Israel, 1–11
  Assembly, 1–2
  Report, 3–7
  Decision, 8–11
The intransigence of Benjamin, 12–17
  Refusal of extradition, 12–13
  Preparation for battle, 14–17
The narrative of battle, 18–48
  Victories for Benjamin, 18–28
    Direction from Yahweh, 18
    Defeat in battle, 19–22
    Weeping before Yahweh, 23a
    Direction from Yahweh, 23b
    Defeat in battle, 24–25
    Weeping before Yahweh, 26
    Direction and assurance from Yahweh, 27–28
  Victory for Israel, 29–48
    General report, 29–36a
    Detailed report, 36b–48

All Israel from Maine to Florida (or, as the Israelites pre-
ferred to say, from Dan to Beersheba) gathered at Mizpah
(v. 1).[9] Israel's unity is impressive. At least it impressed the
writer. Three times he uses the phrase *as one man* (vv. 1, 8,
11) to describe the total unity of Israel in their assembly and
decision. Even the tribes east of the Jordan showed up ("the
land of Gilead," v. 1). That is far better than Deborah could do
(5:15b–17). It's a far different picture from what we've seen so
far, with Ephraim bellyaching to Gideon (8:1–3) and eating
their words with Jephthah (12:1–6), or with Judah leaving
Samson holding the bag while they went off muttering something about the powers that be having been ordained of God
(15:11).

Israel's unity is both impressive and tragic—and tragic
because it is impressive. An exceptional unity indeed, for an
exceptional crime, to be sure. Yet it is a unity of Israel against
Israel. The story itself breathes an air of tragedy, for three
times it remembers that all Israel and Benjamin are "brothers"
(vv. 13, 23, 28). No, Benjamin's wrong cannot be ignored, but
there is a sadness about it nevertheless. And it becomes a
sadder sadness when one begins to ask: Now why couldn't
Israel ever get that united against the Canaanites or the Midianites or the Ammonites or the Philistines? Why is it that
when Israel can really get itself together it is against—Israel?

Benjamin also had its own brand of unity. When Israel
demanded that the tribe yield the guilty Gibeans up for justice
the Benjaminites "were not willing" (v. 13). Had Gibeah not
committed a gross crime? Of course. But the Gibeans were
Benjaminites. And blood was thicker than covenant.

Yet it is unlikely that bullheaded Benjamin will be a push-
over. They may be far outnumbered (cf. vv. 2, 17 with v. 15)
but their crack Seven Hundred Unit (v. 16) will have to be
reckoned with.[10] This number formed an elite corps of left-
handed super-slingers, renowned for their deadly accuracy.
They may have been the reason Benjamin had initial success

9. Benjaminite Mizpah is probably Tell en-Nasbeh, located eight miles
north of Jerusalem along the north-south road through the hill country of
Ephraim (approximately five miles north of Gibeah).

10. The (minor) textual problem in verses 15–16 does not alter the main
facts.

against the other tribes. Most soldiers were probably right-handed and carried their shields on their left arms. That would provide normal defense against right-handed slingers, but lefty slingers would be hurling at a different angle toward the unguarded side,[11] and, if these left-handers could hit a hair (v. 16), they could surely smash a right ear.

The narrative of battle begins on a tragic note. Israel asks Yahweh, "Who should be the first to go up for battle with the sons of Benjamin?" and receives the reply, "Judah first" (v. 18). This inquiry and answer cannot fail to remind us of the opening scene of the book when Israel asked Yahweh who should lead the attack on the Canaanites and received the same answer (1:1–2). Sadly, Israel must now battle their own brothers, who, by their solidarity with the Gibeans, had become neo-Canaanites.

Benjamin seemed unbeatable; the underdog won substantial victories in the first two engagements (vv. 18–23, 24–28). Before the third encounter, however, Israel dispatched some ambushers. Shades of Ai (Josh. 8)! We have two reports of the third battle, the one a general overview (vv. 29–36a), the other a detailed close-up (vv. 36b–48).[12]

The general flow of this third engagement is clear in spite of some textual uncertainties. Israel faked another retreat and flight in order to draw Benjamin away from Gibeah (vv. 31–32), leaving the town relatively defenseless. Benjamin's cockiness takes the bait, the ambush breaks out from hiding near Geba (about three miles northeast of Gibeah), assaults and cleans out Gibeah's remnant, and hastens to put it to the torch (vv. 33–34, 37–38). The plan was that when Gibeah went up in smoke Israel would counterattack (vv. 38–39), Benjamin would be trapped (vv. 41–42) and soon destroyed. The Benjaminites fled out of Israel's vise to the east and then north, but before their six hundred survivors reached the Rock Rimmon, Israel had cut down twenty-five thousand Benjaminites in

11. John Gray, *Joshua, Judges and Ruth*, The Century Bible—New Edition (Greenwood, S.C.: Attic, 1967), 384.

12. This general-plus-detailed pattern is a common feature of Hebrew narrative and indicates nothing about different sources for the story. I call it the summary-expansion pattern of narrative writing. See *No Falling Words: Expositions of the Book of Joshua* (Grand Rapids: Baker, 1988), 86–87, n. 9.

three substantial installments (vv. 42–47).[13] The major activity seems to have developed as illustrated in map 21.1.

Back to our main concern: In all these setbacks and in all this smoke and slaughter what is *Yahweh* doing? It all seems so chaotic; one might wonder if Yahweh is present at all, and, if so, what could he possibly be doing in such a mess? Happily, we are not left to conjecture. The writer has told us what Yahweh was doing here: "So Yahweh struck down Benjamin before Israel" (v. 35a). That is the theological interpretation of this wild, bloody episode. Benjamin's defeat was the manifestation of Yahweh's judgment. Yahweh used Israel to bring

Map 21.1   The Battle of Israel and Benjamin

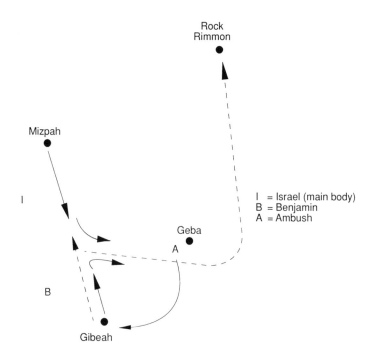

13. The writer describes Benjamin's flight methodically; three times he indicates "they turned" (*wayyiphnû*; vv. 42, 45, 47).

his judgment upon Gibeah and Benjamin. That is what was going on here.

Yet we still have our questions. If Yahweh was acting in judgment on Benjamin, why did Israel suffer those two laming defeats (vv. 18–23, 24–28), especially when they had received direction from Yahweh both times (vv. 18, 23)? They only received clear assurance, however, the third time ("Go up, for tomorrow I will give him into your hand," v. 28). Yet their intent, it seems, was always to seek direction from Yahweh (vv. 1, 18, 23, 26ff.). Was Yahweh also acting in judgment on Israel in their two initial defeats? I don't know.

Certainly after the second defeat Israel does far more than weep and seek more guidance (as in v. 23, after the first defeat); now they weep, "sit before Yahweh," fast, and offer sacrifices (v. 26). The response here is far more intense. Perhaps the writer means to depict Israel as repentant and therefore to imply that the first two episodes brought Yahweh's judgment on Israel as well. He judges both those more in the right and those who are utterly in the wrong. If so, the text functions as a warning to our pride which grows most obese when it gazes on the (more blatant) sins of others.[14]

There is another possibility: Israel's initial defeats may not point to the suffering of Yahweh's judgment but to the mystery of his ways. Yahweh directs Israel, mysteriously, to their own destruction—until the last episode.[15] Israel receives the favor of divine guidance (vv. 18, 23) and yet sees no evidence of divine help. Does this not constitute one of the enigmas of Christian experience—being certain of the divine will (because a matter is clearly taught in Scripture) and yet finding that path marked more by trouble than by success? Does that mean

14. For advocates of the "repentance" view, see George Bush, *Notes, Critical and Practical, on the Book of Judges* (Chicago: Henry A. Sumner, 1881), 243–47; and C. F. Keil, *Joshua, Judges, Ruth,* Biblical Commentary on the Old Testament (1868; reprint ed., Grand Rapids: Eerdmans, 1950), 452–53. Keil is more restrained on the matter; Bush, in my opinion, has seen more in the text than is there.

15. Yet even Israel's two defeats form part of Benjamin's judgment, for by these very Israelite failures the Benjaminites acquire that self-sufficiency (vv. 32, 39) which will bring them to ruin.

we are out of the divine will or simply that Yahweh is dealing
with us in one of his hidden ways?

However we assess the possibility of Yahweh's judgment on
Israel there can be no question about his favor toward them—
and not merely because they were eventually victorious.
Rather, at every point they receive divine guidance (vv. 18,
23, 27–28). The parenthesis in verses 27–28 is very significant:

> And the sons of Israel asked direction from Yahweh (now the
> ark of the covenant of God was there [Bethel, v. 26] in those
> days, and Phinehas, son of Eleazar, son of Aaron, was standing
> before it in those days): "Should I go out to battle again with
> the sons of Benjamin, my brother, or should I quit?" Then
> Yahweh said, "Go up, for tomorrow I will give him into your
> hand."

That parenthetical remark is far more than a tidbit of geo-
graphical/historical data. Rather it is a theological clue. In
spite of her problems, in spite of her setbacks, Israel has access
to divine guidance through the high priest. Theologically
speaking, Israel has the means of grace. Yahweh directs them
through his appointed servant, the high priest. Benjamin—
and we must view Benjamin in light of this contrast—has none
of this. No ark, no priest, no direction from Yahweh, no word
from heaven, no light in turmoil. In this Benjamin already
stands under judgment, for what judgment can be worse than
having no counsel from God, no access to his presence, no way
through divine silence? Is this not divine judgment—that he
leaves us alone? A later Benjaminite will understand this perfectly—and miserably (1 Sam. 28:15). Long before Benjamin's
troops were being hacked down in their panic to reach Rock
Rimmon, Yahweh had already judged them; he left them to
themselves, to the grand isolation of their own wits.

Some Christians will delude themselves by thinking this
sort of judgment could fall on Old Testament Israelites but
never on God's people in this age. They only show they have
never understood their Savior (see, e.g., Matt. 11:25–26; Mark
4:24–25; cf. Rom. 1:24, 26, 28 in context). On the other hand,
we may be veritably crushed and yet have hope, because, in

the middle of all our scourges, we simply have access to the
Father (Heb. 10:19–22).

The Tenacity of Yahweh's Grace

Finally, in chapter 21 the literary theme changes dramati-
cally from the destruction of Benjamin (chap. 20) to sorrow
for Benjamin, and the theological burden is to proclaim the
tenacity of Yahweh's grace.

Israel weeps even after they win. After they nearly anni-
hilate Benjamin, they grieve for Benjamin. Israel's sorrow over
Benjamin pervades the chapter (vv. 2–3, 6–7, 15–17); they are
devastated that one tribe is now missing in Israel (v. 3), hewn
off from Israel (v. 6), wiped out of Israel (v. 17).

Israel, apparently, had intended to eradicate Benjamin.
After they had pinned down Benjamin's six hundred survivors
at Rimmon (20:47), the men of Israel turned back and combed
Benjamin's territory, wiping out human life and livestock,
leaving scorched earth where once there were towns (20:48).
This was completely in line with Israel's policy, for already in
the Mizpah assembly the men of Israel had sworn that none
of them would give their daughters as wives to any Benjaminite survivors (21:1).[16] They were not about to re-seed Benjamin;
they would place Benjamin in the same category as the pagans
(see Deut. 7:1–3).[17] Should any Benjaminites survive, the tribe
would no longer exist within a generation.

Now that war fever has peaked, however, Israel laments the
situation that Yahweh has brought about (v. 3); all of which
is a bit baffling but psychologically possible. Now they long to
preserve Benjamin but their wife-oath will not allow them.
Israel's grief is intensified because they have painted themselves into an ethical corner. Israel now has pity for Benjamin,
"his brother" (v. 6), but no power to revive him.

The whole chapter revolves around this dilemma between

16. The perfect verb form in 21:1 (*nishba'*) should be translated as a
pluperfect.
17. C. J. Goslinga, *Joshua, Judges, Ruth*, Bible Student's Commentary
(Grand Rapids: Zondervan, 1986), 502.

Israel's fresh sorrow and Israel's previous oath. Its structural development is thus:

Dilemma from oath, 1–7
  Possibility for solution, 8–9
    Command to assailants, 10–11
      Provision of women (insufficient), 12–14
        Response of people, 15
Dilemma from oath, 16–18
  Possibility for solution, 19
    Command to assailants, 20–22
      Provision of women (sufficient), 23
        Response of people, 15

Israel's first thought is that their war-oath (vv. 4–5) might be the solution to the wife-oath. Sure enough, Jabesh-gilead,[18] even under threat of death, had refused to send troops to fight Benjamin. Here, Israel thought, was a justifiable loophole. Israel sent an army to requite Jabesh-gilead; they were to spare only virgins (vv. 10–11). Net catch: four hundred girls.

But a two-thirds solution is no solution (v. 14b). "Ah, yes, but there is the annual festival of Yahweh at Shiloh! Those Shiloh girls always come out dancing in the vineyards—what an easy grab. And if their fathers or brothers gripe about the kidnapping, we can say, 'Look, it's legal! You didn't *give* your girls to Benjamin—or you'd be guilty of breaking your oath; but you can't help it if they were *stolen*. Now, c'mon, go along with this, because we didn't get enough girls when we attacked Jabesh-gilead.'" Such is the drift of verses 19–22. That was the final solution. Now everybody—even irate fathers and brothers—could go home (vv. 23b–24).

We now must face the question: What perspective are we to take toward this part of the story? Here again narrative teases us. The writer describes what happens but gives us little or no indication of his position on the matter. He expects us to pick that up (without his actually telling us). Interpreting biblical narrative can be like trying to figure out someone who has a

---

18. Located a little to the east of the Jordan River and approximately twenty miles south of the Sea of Galilee.

dry sense of humor. The person may give no visible indication that he intends humor, so that you have to divine it as best you can. Judges 21 is noncommittal like that. The writer reports but hardly critiques, so that we are left asking how we are to take the story.

This matter of perspective is doubly important in Judges 21 precisely because many readers are confident they already know how to look at it. Why, they say, Israel acts like a bunch of stooges—only altogether too vicious (20:48; 21:10–12), tying themselves in moral knots with stupid oaths and shedding unnecessary blood without even flinching. That view may well have truth in it, but it needs to be chastened, for, whether we realize it or not, we are too apt to judge Israel by a subtle twentieth-century sentimentality that gets upset whenever niceness is in short supply or that is little concerned when solemn promises are broken. I am not suggesting that all Israel's actions in this chapter are right,[19] but that we not wrongly impute wrong amount of wrong to them!

I would enter a few qualifiers then. First, Israel's retribution on Benjamin (20:48) was certainly severe, but remember that Benjamin chose solidarity with New Sodom; hence they could expect to be treated like the enemies of Yahweh (cf. Josh. 6:15–21).[20] Secondly, Israel's wife-oath (v. 1) may have been foolish, but it was taken and so would have to be reckoned with in some way. Finally, Israel could claim justice in taking retribution on Jabesh-gilead. Failure to send troops could be con-

19. As does James B. Jordan, *Judges: God's War Against Humanism,* Trinity Biblical Commentary Series (Tyler, Tex.: Geneva Ministries, 1985), 315-26.

20. This view allows one to take verse 15b ("because Yahweh had caused a gap among the tribes of Israel"), if need be, as the writer's own estimate of Israel's harshness and Benjamin's demise. If so, he implies that Benjamin's desolation rested under Yahweh's authorization. Yet I think it more likely that in verse 15b the writer is simply reflecting Israel's own view of the matter as previously expressed in verse 3. Barry G. Webb's comment on verse 3 is worth pondering: "The inquiry is less a request for information than an oblique form of protest and an attempt by the inquirers to absolve themselves of responsibility. But Yahweh will not be drawn. In the previous episode he chastised them by speaking [20:18, 23]; in this one he chastised them by remaining silent. He will not be used by them" (*The Book of the Judges: An Integrated Reading,* JSOT Supplement Series 46 [Sheffield: JSOT, 1987], 195).

strued as implicitly supporting the enemy, that is, the if-not-for-me-then-against-me argument. However, though the war-oath might justify action against Jabesh-gilead's able-bodied troops (v. 5b), it hardly requires wiping out her women and children (v. 10). Moreover, one wonders why Israel could not have placed no-shows under a curse (as with Meroz, 5:23) and have allowed Yahweh to deal with them.

I think, therefore, that the writer wants us to see Judges 21 as the ambiguous situation it is. There is a certain rightness and a certain wrongness about what Israel does. They justifiably requite Jabesh-gilead with unjustifiable severity (vv. 5, 10). They stand consistently upon their wife-oath (vv. 7, 16–18) but trample happily upon the rights of the Shiloh girls and their families (vv. 19–22). It is a mix of consistency and confusion. It is all correct and yet very mistaken.

The ambivalence pervading chapter 21 simply fits the pattern of incongruities throughout the story from the beginning of chapter 19. We watch a Levite sacrifice his concubine to the mob yet use truth selectively to hide his cowardice. We hear a host offer the protection of his house and also his own daughter and his guest's concubine to the lusts of the crowd. We see a tribe defiantly refuse to cooperate with covenant justice and willfully align itself with the darkest guilt of its kin. We observe Israel seeking divine guidance and yet meeting destruction—until victory at the last. We marvel at an Israel as urgent to preserve Benjamin as they were rabid to destroy him, resorting to injustice to maintain their own consistency. The writer, therefore, surely intends to include the fiasco of chapter 21 as another exhibit of how "each man was doing whatever was right in his own eyes" (v. 25).

What then does chapter 21 declare to Israel and to us? I have already proposed that it proclaims the tenacity of Yahweh's grace. How so?

Consider this. Sodom was wholly destroyed (see, again, Gen. 19). At least a remnant of Benjamin survives, and pains are taken for its restoration. Does our narrator intend for us to see not merely Israel's solicitude for Benjamin but Yahweh's as well, in spite of the bungled way by which Israel tried to restore Benjamin? Does the near-annihilation of Benjamin suggest that Yahweh's grace is reluctantly slow to allow the stroke of judgment to fall in all its severity? It is not strictly true that "one tribe is missing in Israel" (v. 3). It is of Yahweh's mercies that we are not consumed! Even in wrath Yahweh remembered mercy!

But surely "righteous" Israel stands in as much need of Yahweh's grace as does sinful Benjamin. S. G. DeGraaf has put it well:

> By these [Israel's] actions the tribe of Benjamin was preserved. But the Israelites had tackled the problem in a cocky, conceited, highhanded way. How estranged from the Lord's service Israel had become! How little did it live by His light! It is a miracle that anything came of that people, that justice was practiced, that the fellowship of the tribes was preserved. There is no other explanation for this miracle than that God, in His grace in the Christ, wished to dwell in the midst of that people in spite of its sin.[21]

And the sign of that grace that refused to let go of his people is that in the writer's own time a fresh act of Yahweh's grace had occurred—he had given Israel a godly king (v. 25), so that Israel might do whatever was right in *Yahweh's* eyes (cf. Ps. 78:70–72).

So the Book of Judges ends with a miracle. How after chapters 19–21, indeed, after chapters 1–21, can you account for the fact that there is still an Israel? It can only be because Yahweh wished to dwell in the midst of his people in spite of its sin. It can only be because Yahweh's grace is far more tenacious than his people's depravity and insists on still holding them fast even in their sinfulness and their stupidity. Nor is he finished raising up saviors for them (Acts 13:23)! All this sort of wrecks the title of this book, doesn't it? Biblical as it is, true as it is. "Such a Great *Savior*" would be far more accurate.

---

21. S. G. DeGraaf, *Promise and Deliverance*, 4 vols. (St. Catharines, Ontario: Paideia, 1978), 2:56.